Advance Praise for *Camouflage*

"*Camouflage* is a tender journey of real talk of life in the shadows as a military spouse and a quest to forge a self-identity in a culture of blending in. Stripped of the romanticism often ascribed to Navy wife life, Heather Sweeney's journey to herself is one readers will find relatable and inspiring."

— Tia Levings, author of the *New York Times* bestseller *A Well-Trained Wife* and Navy mom

"When Heather's husband joined the military, she assumed her new life wouldn't be easy but welcomed the challenge. What she didn't expect was how easy it would be to lose herself in the all-consuming role of military spouse. Or that the demands of the military on her family would force her to confront cracks in her marriage that she'd long been ignoring.

This deeply personal memoir follows one woman's journey through the hidden challenges of military life: the loneliness, the uncertainty, the slow unraveling of a marriage shaped by constant, daily sacrifice. With unwavering honesty, she writes about what it means to love someone in uniform—and the strength it takes to walk away."

— Karie Fugett, author of *Alive Day*

"A story about endings and beginnings and all that happens in between, *Camouflage* is a powerful reminder that everything in our lives—the good, the bad, and the ugly—was worth it, simply because it made us. Sweeney has drawn a bold portrait of self-discovery filled with warmth, wisdom and heart."

— Simone Gorrindo, author of *The Wives*

"There are few life paths that can subsume a woman's identity like "marrying into the military." Heather Sweeney's clear-eyed and heartfelt memoir deftly underscores the ways that military spousedom can both define and erase you. And when her marriage came crashing down around her, Heather stood up and reclaimed her destiny, fashioning a way forward that introduced her to who she truly was—apart from any role, duty, or expectation. Vulnerable and inspirational, Heather shows us that the true heroine's quest is taking the long road home to yourself."

— Lily Burana, author of *I Love a Man in Uniform*

"In *Camouflage,* Heather Sweeney writes with honesty, clarity, and passion about navigating the demands of being a military spouse, while in a marriage that gradually erased the woman she once was. But, this isn't just a story of loss—it's a powerful tale of reclaiming self-amidst the equally compelling pull of motherhood and the need to feel of service to a greater ideal. With running as her lifeline and writing as her compass, Sweeney breaks formation to reveal a world few civilians understand. At its heart, this is a memoir about letting go of who you were *told* to be, in order to find who you were *meant* to be."

— Estelle Erasmus, TEDx Speaker,
author of the award-winning, *Writing That Gets Noticed*, NYU Writing Professor,
Host of Freelance Writing Direct

"In this unflinching memoir, *Camouflage* reveals the quiet ache of loneliness that comes with being trapped in a military marriage that is slowly unraveling. With a deeply relatable voice, Sweeney offers a rare and honest look at the emotional cost of loving someone in uniform and the courage it takes to walk away. This is an intimate story of a brave and resilient woman forging her own path to freedom."

— Aileen Weintraub, author of *Knocked Down: A High Risk Memoir*

"*Camouflage* is the intimate and gripping story of how Heather Sweeney became someone utterly unrecognizable to herself: a military wife who loses her identity to her spouse, his job, and a lifestyle she never chose. It's also a story of resilience and reclamation. Of how she held onto the belief she deserved more and, bit by bit, built herself back from broken to whole."

— Ronit Plank, author of *When She Comes Back* and Host of *Let's Talk Memoir*

"Entering into a world unknown to me, at once I was taken in. In the aftermath of divorce as a military wife, stripped of the familiar, Sweeney embarks on a path of self-discovery, resilience, and reinvention. A deeply compelling memoir of one woman's journey learning that she was never meant to disappear, but to rise."

— Hannah Sward, author of *Strip: A Memoir*

How I Emerged from the Shadows of a Military Marriage

camouflage

Heather Sweeney

KNOX PRESS

A KNOX PRESS BOOK
An Imprint of Permuted Press
ISBN: 979-8-89565-308-1
ISBN (eBook): 979-8-89565-309-8

Camouflage:
How I Emerged from the Shadows of a Military Marriage

Cover art by Cody Corcoran

All people, locations, events, and situations are portrayed to the best of the author's memory. While all of the events described are true, many names and identifying details have been changed to protect the privacy of the people involved.

Permuted Press
New York • Nashville
permutedpress.com

Published in the United States of America
1 2 3 4 5 6 7 8 9 10

For my family

"Above all, be the heroine of your life, not the victim."

— Nora Ephron

TABLE OF CONTENTS

AUTHOR'S NOTE

Memory is a tricky thing, and people's recollections of the same events might not always align perfectly. This is a true story based on my memory of the events as they happened for me with the help of journals, photographs, interviews, and social media. In some cases, I compressed the sequence of events and omitted events and people for readability purposes, but doing so didn't affect the accuracy of the narrative. To protect the privacy of individuals, names and some identifying details have been changed. Except for the dogs. They would want you to know they're very good boys.

PROLOGUE

Virginia, 2013

By the time I reached the landing where the stairs changed directions, sweat dotted my forehead, and my arms shook. The mattress was winning but I wouldn't let it defeat me. Not this time.

Halfway up the stairs, I paused to catch my breath and give my tingling arms an overdue break. I had to summon up the strength to finish the job. Leaning the mattress against the wall like a shield, I hid behind it and let go. I let go of the tears I hadn't allowed to fall all day. I let go of the tension that had been collecting beneath my shoulder blades. I let go of the uncertainty that had my stomach tied in knots. I couldn't hold it all in anymore. I let it all go, crumpled to the floor, and sobbed behind that mattress as quietly as sobs can be, so my children wouldn't hear me.

"What have I done?" I thought. "How could I have just blown up our lives?"

"Mom?"

At the sound of Grady's sweet voice, I froze. "What's up, buddy?" I tried to temper my shaking voice, but I knew he could hear the tears.

"I can help get the mattress up the stairs," he said. "I'm really strong."

He was standing at the top of the stairs looking down, unable to see me behind the mattress. But he sensed his mother was struggling. I hated that. I hated that I allowed myself to fall apart within his earshot. I was supposed to be the strong one. My lack of strength shouldn't require a nine-year-old child to be strong, to be someone I leaned on. Grady never signed up to listen to his mother crying behind a mattress. He had enough to wrap his mind and heart around—his parents' divorce, a new apartment, starting again at a different school, along with everything else I had turned upside down in his world with my decisions. No, he was supposed to be the kid. I was supposed to be the strong one.

"I know you're strong," I said, with more conviction in my voice. "And so am I. After I take this little rest, how about we do this together? Teamwork."

I wiped the tears from my face and peeked out from behind the protection of the mattress. Grady stood outside his new room looking down at me. When I smiled, he smiled. I reminded myself that my reactions spilled onto the kids. Moms cry in hiding for a reason.

But maybe that had to change. Challenging days happen. Sadness happens. Tears happen.

Grady squatted low and reached out. He pulled the mattress from the top while I pushed it up the stairs from the bottom. He was eager to be able to help, to claim his role in our teamwork. I was proud to accept his help without making him feel a sense of duty that he was now the "man of the house." Because that wasn't his role to claim. Nor should he feel the unreasonable responsibility thrust upon him. I wanted him to just be a kid, with his five-year-old sister. To play tag and hide-and-seek and eat macaroni and cheese while watching cartoons.

Together, we could get mattresses upstairs.

Together, we would provide support and be each other's shields.

Together, we would write our own rules for our new life after divorce.

PART 1

The Beginning of the End

CHAPTER 1

I Do It for You

Alabama, 2000

The vast number of choices in steak knives and bath towels in the department store made it impossible for me to choose alone. I sighed, suppressing my disappointment, as well as my concern, that this was a preview of things to come.

As children, we're led to believe that getting married is one of the most exciting times in our lives. But I had yet to feel like a blushing bride-to-be. Instead, I stood under the bright fluorescent lights as a tired woman contemplating an unpredictable future she didn't fully understand.

"I want to join the military," my fiancé Tristan had said as casually as if he were suggesting we order pizza for dinner.

With two months to go before we said "I do," Tristan's words reverberated in my head. As a young couple, still figuring out adulthood in our early twenties, this wasn't an announcement I had expected.

"I have it all worked out," he said.

And he did. He could barely contain his excitement as he ticked off all the requirements he needed to become a service member. A medical exam, a physical fitness test, an extensive application, then one series of training after another in locations along the East Coast. My head spun with timelines and acronyms and military jargon Tristan suddenly knew.

Though both my father and my grandfather were Army veterans, I knew nothing about the military. My father left for Korea a month after he married my mother, and a year later he was honorably discharged and my parents carried on with their civilian lives.

But despite my lack of knowledge, if Tristan was passionate about this path, I would support him, follow him anywhere, just as I followed him from where we met in South Carolina to the University of Alabama.

So I put my hopes of earning a master's degree and embarking on a teaching career temporarily on hold. I loved Tristan for his charm, his contagious energy, his drive, and I admired his ability to map out options for us and our future together. More than anything, I wanted him to find himself. I wanted him to feel fulfilled and complete. I wished those things for him as I sought them for myself, too.

Over the next two months, as I watched Tristan get in shape for the military physical fitness test, I avoided talking about the implications of what his service would mean for me or our relationship or our future children. Whether out of fear of the unknown or the complete naivete in my belief that his military career wouldn't affect me any differently than any other job would, those discussions never happened.

However, as Tristan's free time was seized by the application and preparation for the fitness test, I couldn't help but sense a shift between us. While I built our wedding registry without him, the military stole his attention away from me. I didn't want to share the spotlight with anyone or anything, including his possible employer, and the seed of resentment took root.

It was the first time I resented the military. It would be far from the last.

* * *

Tristan and I exchanged vows two weeks after my twenty-fourth birthday on a summer day filled with joy, laughter, and a sense of invincibility.

Ours was a whirlwind romance. Tristan had an electricity that instantly pulled me in. As the adage goes, I found love when I least expected it. I had just ended a long, serious relationship with my college sweetheart and wasn't looking for another serious relationship to jump into.

I had a history of making poor choices in men. I even got a broken heart tattoo when I was fourteen. Like most hormonal teenage girls facing their first heartbreak, I thought I was dying when my boyfriend broke up with me. I wanted a reminder not to let my heart get trampled on. I wanted a way to remember that hurt so I could protect myself from feeling it again. A few days later I was in a tattoo shop, and a stranger inked that reminder in the form of a broken red heart onto my left buttock. As much as I thought I knew everything there was to know about love at fourteen, I had a long road of relationships and love lessons ahead of me that the tattoo neglected to shield me from.

But Tristan was different.

He was a natural leader, and even early on, I couldn't help but feel like I wanted to follow him everywhere, like I wanted to give myself to him and I could trust him to protect me, lift me up, and show me the time of my life, whether we were sneaking into a hotel pool in the middle of the night and skinny-dipping or he was reading my bad high school poetry that he had bound into a book as a gift. After three months we moved in together. We stayed up late talking about anything and everything. We went camping and pulled ticks off each other. We pulled our double-sized mattress into the family room to binge movies on rainy weekends. He held the top side while I carried the bottom. He was my best friend, my true love, my favorite person in the world.

So, when he proposed before we'd even reached our one-year anniversary of dating, I didn't question it. I never wondered if it was too soon. I wanted this man in my life forever, and he offered that to me. I would have married him that day if he had asked.

But we waited a year, planning a small destination wedding, with my mother as the matron of honor, his father the best man. And as we slipped the rings on each other's fingers, the rings we had engraved on the inside for each other with secret messages—his with "Now I am whole" and mine with "Love eternal"—I thought all my dreams were coming true.

It wasn't until days after our return to Alabama flipping through photos that I remembered a moment from my wedding day that I had hoped to forget.

When we booked the all-inclusive resort in the Bahamas, no one warned us our stay was during hurricane season. Fortunately, the rain didn't start until the rings were on our fingers and our reception of only my parents, Tristan's parents, and my brother and his then-girlfriend was winding down.

I didn't think about how the overcast sky might have affected our wedding photos until I picked up our developed film from the drugstore. In the year 2000, before the digital age of instant photo viewing, we had no way of knowing if we had a roll of perfect snapshots or a pile of blurs and bad lighting.

As I flipped through the envelope, I discovered photos from the night we sang karaoke in the lobby with another couple getting married the same day as us.

I found photos of the green hair my stylist had promised was hidden, a gift from the highly chlorinated pools and hot tubs we had soaked in during the days leading up to the wedding.

A few pictures captured random vacationers with beach bags and jet skis buzzing by behind the waterfront gazebo as we recited our vows, a reminder that the number of wedding "guests" I didn't know far outnumbered the guests I did.

These photos sparked a brief twinge of regret that we didn't have a big wedding, but I admitted these minor details were part of the wedding I chose. They weren't bad omens; they were merely unexpected subplots.

Then I saw it. The photo that didn't belong with the rest. The photo that triggered my memory with a thought that would plague me for years. The photo I would flash back to throughout my thirteen-year marriage.

In the picture I'm standing beside my father, who looks sharp and distinguished in his beige suit, as we prepare to walk down the aisle. My left hand holds his as my right clutches the bouquet in front of the thirty-four-dollar white dress I had found at the mall that somehow fit me perfectly with no alterations. Neither of us is smiling, unaware we're being photographed. A woman wearing a beach cover-up is mid-stride behind us, as if it was an everyday occurrence to pass through a wedding to get to an oceanfront lounge chair. The camera captured my anxiety, a fear I knew went deeper than the worry I would be unsteady in the stretch of sand in my heels.

The camera also captured the ominous charcoal-gray sky.

Almost all the photos from my wedding are filled with blue skies and sunshine. Behind Tristan, I only saw turquoise water and an endless horizon as I walked down the aisle. Only that one shot of my father and me told the true story of the weather, the storm that was brewing, the imminent downpour that forced every other wedding after ours indoors. At the time, I bragged about how lucky we were, that the universe was letting us know we were special enough to get the sunny beach wedding we'd traveled there for.

But that photo revealed a different story.

It reminded me that right after it was taken, I started my walk down the aisle, my arm hooked into my father's. With my first tentative steps in the sand, I looked up at the man who would be my husband in mere minutes. My first thoughts weren't how handsome he looked, or how I couldn't wait to look deep into his eyes while reciting our vows. As that man looked back at me, I thought, "We're not meant to grow old together."

The thought nearly stopped me in my tracks, almost pressed pause on the entire wedding. I had no idea where it came from, what sparked it, or why my brain chose that moment to doubt my love or my commitment or my faith or whatever it was that was suddenly in question.

But I didn't stop walking. I didn't put the wedding on pause. In that split second, I chalked it up to nerves and allowed the thought to drift away into the ocean that sparkled behind the gazebo. By the time I arrived at my designated spot and my father released my arm, my only thought was how lucky I was to marry a man who promised me forever.

The next photo in the stack caught me from the opposite angle, smiling amid sunshine. That was the scene I wanted etched in my memory. Not darkness. No looming clouds in the distance. No doubts.

I placed the storm photo in the pile of snapshots I wasn't including in my wedding albums and continued flipping, tossing aside rejects—anything that wasn't smiles and sunshine.

***

A month and a half after the wedding, Tristan did what he set out to do. He joined the military. I couldn't pinpoint why, but I felt an overpowering relief that he committed to me before the military.

We road-tripped three hours to Montgomery, and after a small ceremony with a recruiter, Tristan became a commissioned officer in the Navy. It didn't take long after that for me to discover I had a lot to learn about military life.

Our first step was finding the nearest military installation—Maxwell Air Force Base—to get military ID cards, mine donning my new title of "dependent."

We explored the base, which seemed like a microcosm of the civilian world but with guarded entry gates and starched uniforms. It was like stepping into a foreign country where I didn't speak the language.

I watched in quiet awe when Tristan was saluted for the first time at the main gate in our car that now sported military stickers at the top of the windshield. It was borderline comical. To me, Tristan was a young student whose military experience hadn't logged twenty-four hours yet. But to the man standing guard at the entrance of the base checking IDs, Tristan was an officer to be shown respect, to be saluted, to be called "sir."

We were in a whole new world, and I couldn't help but absorb Tristan's buzz of excitement.

As we drove back home to Tuscaloosa a few days later, neither of us had any idea how drastically our lives were about to change.

***

Tristan bought me a book called *Navy Spouse's Guide*, a handbook of sorts that was equal parts informative and overwhelming. I appreciated the explanations of military procedures and terms I didn't yet have a practiced understanding of, but it made me question if I was capable of being the type of person who accepted these procedures as normal, whose vocabulary revolved around these terms. I might have read too much into the author's words, but that book, the first of many I would read about military life, left a vision in my head of the perfect military wife, a vision I would spend my entire tenure as a Navy spouse attempting to live up to.

The book stated that one of the biggest challenges of this lifestyle was the frequent separations. Though Tristan wouldn't be considered an active-duty service member until he finished his degree, and his graduation was two years away, he still had military training to report to. And as the summer of 2001 approached, nearly a year after Tristan joined the Navy, the countdown to our first separation, a long six-week stretch, began.

Most days leading up to Tristan's departure for Officer Indoctrination School in Newport, Rhode Island, I dreaded being apart, barely sleeping through the anxiety of imagining a month and a half without my husband. I loved being married, being a wife. I loved merging every aspect of my life with his, loved the security of having a partner to share everything with, never questioning the independence I was relinquishing because I believed it was what I was supposed to do. I changed my last name. We opened joint bank accounts and credit cards, closing any financial ties to my single self. I added Tristan to my health insurance I was getting through my teacher's aide job. Even Cody, the chocolate Labrador retriever Tristan adopted before meeting me, finally came around to becoming as much my loyal companion as his.

I truly felt Tristan was the other half of me, and I couldn't imagine being ripped apart for six weeks.

But sometimes I wished his departure would arrive sooner. The anticipation of all the unknowns of this training made us both moody and on edge, and instead of making the most of our last days together, we argued, whether it was about whose turn it was to walk the dog or how we should use the money from his Navy paychecks. Exhausted and drained, a part of me wished the hours would move faster, if only to get a break from fighting.

Regardless of the roller coaster of emotions the days before Tristan left, that first day, departure day, was like a million little paper cuts in my heart.

I sat helplessly on our bed watching him dress in the civilian clothes that would soon be replaced with a uniform. He neatly packed shirts and shorts, toiletries and a book for the flight, zipping up his suitcase and declaring he was ready to go. I drove him to our local airport. We parked and sat in the car for a few minutes, the air conditioner cooling us from the late spring heat. Then, in silence, we walked hand in hand through the airport. I sat with him at the gate surrounded by other passengers checking their watches or whispering to loved ones waiting with them. I promised to write him real letters sent in the mail. He smiled, and I tried to memorize the shape of his lips and how they felt as he kissed me.

"Think how romantic it is that we'll be writing love letters to each other that we'll keep forever," Tristan whispered as we waited by his gate at the airport. "Reading your letters will be the highlight of my days."

I hugged him as if our lives depended on it, my tears forming blotchy wet spots on the back of his shirt. Then they announced the boarding call over the crackling speaker, and he broke our embrace.

He boarded the plane, leaving me behind in Alabama with no family, no military spouse friends to commiserate with, and too many questions about how this time apart would affect not only our marriage, but each of us separately as the young adults we still were.

I tried to consider the bright side. Now that I was done counting down to his departure, I could count down to his return. My grocery bill would be cut in half. I could cook dinners he didn't like, but I did. And even though I missed his first phone call from Newport, he left a message so his voice was on a recording to listen to whenever I needed to hear it.

But staying positive didn't last long. The small apartment appeared too big, and too empty. His side of the bed lay untouched, the pillow stiff. Only one toothbrush in a cup stared back at me in the morning and before bed.

I continued to experience insomnia, loneliness reared its ugly head and lingered, and I questioned how I would get through these six weeks apart. Seeing no other option, I decided to stay so busy that I was too exhausted to overthink everything.

"Stay in motion," I told myself. "If my mind and body are busy, time will fly."

So I forced myself to maintain a full schedule. I went to work. I took long walks with Cody. I journaled. I chatted with friends and my mother and Tristan's mother, who called to check up on me. I watched reruns of *Friends* for comic relief and cooking shows as I experimented with new recipes.

But staying busy did nothing to combat my loneliness and how much I missed my husband.

When I finally talked to Tristan, I heard his own fatigue through the landline as he described the drill sergeants, his assigned guard duty, and the marching, all the marching. After five minutes he told me he had to go to "get some sack time," a phrase I'd never heard come out of his mouth.

He was already changing.

* * *

"Your wife shouldn't come," one of Tristan's Navy friends advised him.

Because we were so new to military life and separations and the role I was supposed to play, Tristan asked around to determine whether or not we should spend money we didn't have for me to fly to Rhode Island for a weekend. Even though the Navy paid Tristan while he was in training, we were already bookmarking that money for bills, including the $1,200 in military uniforms he had charged on our credit card because we didn't have the cash. Was a weekend together worth the added debt?

"You two need to wait it out," the friend said. "These six weeks are nothing compared to what you'll deal with from now on. Use this as practice for what's coming."

Tristan and I had only been apart for two weeks, and I already felt lost and deserted. I knew on an abstract level that as a military spouse, I should expect to frequently watch my husband pack up and leave. But instead of accepting the situation and viewing this six-week stretch as a warm-up for the bigger marathons we would face throughout Tristan's career, I questioned my resolve to support his decision to join the military. If military retirement was his goal, that meant twenty years of a life separated by oceans, mountains, and deserts. How would I be able to do this for twenty years if I was barely functioning after two weeks?

But we took the advice, restraining ourselves from booking plane tickets and telling ourselves the longer we were apart, the sweeter the homecoming would be.

If the first week of the separation was about survival, and the second week's theme was reality checks, then the third week screamed insecurity.

By week three, our conversations became dominated by how much Tristan was enjoying his introduction to military life. He mailed me a Navy sweatshirt and a postcard of the base with a thick arrow he drew pointing to the building where he was staying. He dropped names I didn't know, clearly thrilled to be making connections in this club he joined.

Of course I wanted him to like his profession. Of course I wanted him to make friends. Of course I wanted him to call me in good spirits. But sometimes I wasn't sure how happy I wanted him to be. Because sometimes he sounded so happy I worried he wouldn't come back, that he was realizing he liked life better without me. Maybe he would return to Tuscaloosa and announce he liked being single better than being married.

To add to my rotation of unexpected emotions, I also learned an important military spouse lesson—dates on the calendar were fluid, and the Navy didn't care about special occasions unless they directly involved the Navy. Specifically, Tristan would miss our first wedding anniversary.

Like our wedding, our first anniversary would have been simple but enough. I pictured a fancy dinner. We would order wine and sip slowly, recounting our memories of the joy of our wedding day and making plans to return to the same resort on our tenth anniversary to renew our vows. We'd ooh and ahh over a shared dessert that might have "Happy Anniversary" drizzled in chocolate around the edge of the plate because Tristan would have told them about our special day when he'd called to make the reservation. I didn't need anything extravagant. I just needed him.

But the closest I could get to my husband on our first anniversary was a quick early-morning phone call. I tried to push the significance of the day out of my mind, reminding myself we were simply postponing it. Moping with self-pity wasn't going to bring Tristan home, and in the grand scheme of life, celebrating an anniversary a few weeks late wasn't the end of the world. I should consider myself lucky he was even able to call.

In June the school year ended and work was on pause, and with nothing but rejections from summer job applications, I expected long, empty days alone. So when my parents suggested I visit them in Florida, I didn't hesitate. I welcomed the escape.

With my loyal companion Cody, I packed up Tristan's Toyota 4Runner and drove the 550 miles to my parents' house. Knowing how disappointed I was about Tristan missing our anniversary, my parents took me out for the dinner I was wishing for, where we reminisced about the wedding and the trip to the Bahamas. We clinked glasses of wine to toast another year of wedded bliss to come. There was no chocolate-drizzled dessert plate, but being with my family eased my loneliness.

I reclaimed my teenage bedroom at my parents' house for the entire second half of Tristan's training. I let them spoil me and Cody, sleeping in and eating meals I didn't have to cook. I met up with old high school friends, remembering what it was like to have my own friends that weren't Tristan's classmates.

I drove back to Alabama, the survival mode, reality checks, and insecurity of the first half of Tristan's absence vanished. I wasn't sure what it meant that I was a twenty-five-year-old married woman who suddenly longed to move in with her parents, but those three weeks rejuvenated me. Tristan would return to a calm, relaxed wife, not the frazzled woman of a few weeks earlier. I needed him to see I could handle this. This was the Navy career he had chosen, and to show him my support, I needed to handle the homefront. How could I complain about life at home when he was working hard to serve our country?

Homecoming day wasn't the ceremonious gathering I would one day see regularly on social media, crowded events with military spouses in fancy dresses and children clutching homemade posters, waiting for their service members to sprint into their arms and meet babies born during deployments with photographers weaving through reunited families to capture joyful hugs.

Tristan wasn't attached to a duty station or command. No other service members exited with him on his commercial flight. No other military spouses waited at the airport with posters and balloons. I nervously paced, peering around arriving passengers until I saw him, his hair short and rigid with a high and tight cut, his crisp uniform making my heartbeat race. Unable to wait a second longer, I threw my arms around him, and we kissed like we hadn't seen each other in years, the time apart melting away. I don't even remember the drive home because I couldn't take my eyes off him.

Overall, we handled our first separation well. The only noticeable adjustments were that we'd both gotten used to hogging the covers in bed, and Cody's primary loyalty had shifted from Tristan to me. Maybe six weeks apart wasn't so bad, I thought.

Maybe I could do this military life thing.

***

Two and a half months after Tristan returned from that first military training, an airplane flew into the North Tower of the World Trade Center in New York City at 8:46 a.m., a terror attack that killed 2,977 people. It changed everything about our world, including what it meant to serve in the military and what life would be like for a military spouse.

CHAPTER 2

The Homefront

"My detailer called."

I closed the refrigerator door, forgetting all thoughts of what to cook for dinner, and met Tristan in the family room, where we both plopped down the couch, rays of sunshine beaming through the windows behind us as if shining a spotlight on this life-changing information Tristan was about to share. I couldn't read his facial expression, but even with the little knowledge I had of military procedures, I knew the detailer was the person giving Tristan his assignment.

"This is it, right?" I asked, jittery with anticipation. "Where are we going?"

"Well, we have three duty station choices," he said. "Camp Pendleton in San Diego. Naval Station Norfolk in Virginia. Or Naval Air Station Pensacola in Florida."

I nodded, mentally subtracting South Carolina, Hawaii, and DC from our wish list.

"And we only have twenty-four hours to decide."

In the time it took for Tristan to graduate, jobs had come and gone, other families had accepted their duty stations, and options for us had opened or been removed, more evidence that nothing in the military is set in stone until you have orders in hand.

But despite my surprise at the urgency of the decision we had to make—an early example of what I'd later learn military families refer to as the phenomenon "hurry up and wait"—we already knew our answer.

The next day Tristan called his detailer. And we told family and friends we were moving to Pensacola.

"Florida," I thought. "Seven hours away from my parents in the Tampa Bay area. Somewhere familiar."

A good sign, I hoped.

***

In the early days, I didn't know much about military life, but one thing was constant—I should get used to moving.

The process of packing up and moving in the military is known as a "PCS," or Permanent Change of Station. It's a term military spouses accept with a mix of familiarity and dread, not only because PCS moves happen so frequently, but also because spouses have to uproot and replant their entire lives again and again for the duration of their service members' careers, quitting jobs and hoping to have enough time to get new ones, learning new geographic areas, registering kids for new schools, consoling those kids when they have to say goodbye to old friends and make new ones. And all this typically happens without the partnership of their service members, who must immediately report for duty and get accustomed to their new jobs.

After some back-and-forth with the detailer, Tristan had orders for our first PCS move. But before we could call Florida home, he had to report to Rhode Island again for more training, this time for ten weeks. Meanwhile, I would stay in Tuscaloosa again, counting down my remaining days at the teacher's aide job I'd long outgrown.

Because Tristan was getting regular paychecks from the Navy and we had more money in our checking account than we'd ever seen, we splurged on plane tickets for me to spend a weekend in Newport. We felt like newlyweds as Tristan showed me around Newport, a city the Navy had helped him get to know. We visited the Tennis Hall of Fame, then drove up and down unfamiliar roads to the Cliff Walk. We held hands, snapped pictures of waves crashing on the breakers to our left, and Tristan retold the stories he had heard about the famous mansions to our right. We ate at recommended restaurants, savoring mouthwatering seafood and daydreams about our future.

But after an amazing weekend, I wondered if his friend's advice was valid, that even if I *could* visit him during separations, it didn't mean I *should.*

As Tristan dropped me off at the airport in Providence, I strained to hold it together in front of the strangers gawking at the cute couple who couldn't tear themselves away from each other. He didn't escort me to the gate or wait with me until I boarded the plane. September 11 had changed so much. Only ticketed passengers were permitted to pass through airport security and kisses had to be exchanged earlier than our previous airport drop-off, reminding me again that I had to be independent and alone for the next month.

As I stood in the security line, I watched him walk away. It was a gut punch, as nauseating as our last goodbye. I thought it would get easier the more we said it, but the opposite was true.

There was no way to know how many more times I would fight tears while watching my husband leave me behind or how many more times I would wonder if a brief reunion was worth the painful farewell. I treasured my Rhode Island time with Tristan, but saying goodbye again almost eclipsed the joy of being together.

***

Again, I struggled to acclimate to solitude and the side effects of a long-distance relationship. A quiet apartment. An empty bed. Meals for one. A list of things to discuss during our next five-minute call. And even more pronounced than the first time, there was a nagging insecurity about my marriage.

Our phone calls became more business-like than intimate, our brief conversations revolving around logistics like bills that needed paying and the military's TRICARE health insurance. An unfamiliar complacency normalized between us. At the tip of my tongue sat the words I wasn't brave enough to say. We were drifting apart.

I felt separated from Tristan, both geographically and emotionally.

Most days I missed him. But some days I didn't think about him at all, and that worried me. I feared we'd each change so much while apart that we wouldn't know how to live together anymore, that we'd transform into two different people who are no longer compatible.

Coping, I did my best to sidestep boredom. I'd already been accepted into my graduate program at the University of West

Florida, and applied for grants, scholarships, and loans, as well as communicated with my advisor and signed up for classes for the spring semester. My program, which included both a master's degree and a state teaching certificate, would require my full-time attendance and a disciplined focus if I expected to finish before we moved again.

I also stayed busy painting our apartment and organizing everything we owned into piles and boxes, unaware that the military would be paying for movers who wouldn't load any boxes into their truck that they didn't seal themselves. I even started running again, training Cody to jog alongside me on a short leash. To my surprise, by the end of the ten weeks, I was an expert on filling time and enjoying my own company.

When Tristan returned, we picked up right where we left off, falling seamlessly into step with each other. Any worries about our relationship seemed like a figment of my overactive imagination. Maybe absence really did make the heart grow fonder.

So I buried my doubts. Tristan didn't seem concerned about us and never asked if I thought things were rocky. He appeared happy with his job and our marriage, and excited about the next move. His energy was infectious.

Shortly after Tristan returned from Rhode Island, we said a different kind of farewell. Once the movers had hauled off most of our possessions and left us with an echoing apartment, I completed a walk-through to make sure we hadn't left anything behind but memories. When we drove away from our apartment in Alabama heading toward Florida, I didn't look back. I was ready to move on and officially begin our Navy life.

* * *

Tristan and I checked into the Navy Lodge in Pensacola on Christmas Eve with a couple of suitcases. I scanned the hotel room, deflated. No holiday decorations, no Christmas tree. No family or friends nearby. No presents for each other. We didn't know anyone from Tristan's command. We had no parties to attend. We didn't even have Cody, who was staying with my parents until we found a house.

This wasn't the welcome to military life I had been hoping for.

I'd read books written by military spouses. I'd seen movies depicting military families and large, close-knit military communities. Maybe my expectations were unrealistic, but I'd envisioned, at the very least, an invitation to a holiday gathering to welcome us to the command or a gift basket left in our Navy Lodge room. Where was this instant military community I'd heard about?

Our PCS to Pensacola may have been my first, but I sensed I would develop a love-hate relationship with moving every two to three years. I loved the idea of a fresh start, but the process of moving was brutal.

I spent a large portion of that Christmas Day hoping our situation wasn't an accurate portrayal of what military life would be. But as Tristan had already learned during his training in Rhode Island, part of being a military family meant figuring out how to make the best of any situation, good or not so good.

"Put on a pair of jeans," Tristan said as he burst into our room. He'd been exploring Pensacola, while I curled up in bed wishing I was somewhere else. "I'm taking you out for Christmas dinner."

Hoping dinner would inspire some Christmas spirit, I climbed into the passenger seat of our red Acura Integra, the first car we bought together in Tuscaloosa after my 1988 Honda Accord had stalled in the middle of an intersection one too many times. But as Tristan held the door open for me at the Flora-Bama Lounge, the only place he could find that was open, I found no holiday cheer amidst a dive bar with bras hanging from the ceiling.

Each employee of the bar had brought in a dish, and a buffet was spread out for all to dig into. Tristan piled his plate with spinach artichoke dip that was supposed to be hot but wasn't. He ordered himself a beer, a Diet Coke for me, and we found a table in the smoky bar, a live band screeching through the speaker by our heads.

As I ate chicken fingers and nachos, I longed for my mother's feast in front of her perfectly decorated Christmas tree, my grandmother's handmade stockings for each member of the family hanging off my parents' mantle, light music playing in the background before we all cleaned up and watched a movie. This wasn't Christmas.

Eventually, I would learn to at least attempt to embrace the suck, to see the humor in situations like this that were out of my control thanks to the Navy. But only two days into the next phase of military life, I wasn't there yet.

We didn't stay long at the dive bar, but before we left, Tristan asked a bartender for a marker, and as others had done before us, we marked our presence permanently on a wall.

"Tristan and Heather Christmas 2002."

He smiled, and I smiled back, even though this wasn't a cute tradition I wanted to remember. The military forced us to be creative, and Tristan accepted the challenge well.

There that night, I thought it was the absolute worst place to spend Christmas. Little did I know this was a preview of sorts, that the Flora-Bama was actually an iconic bar that would become one of our most treasured landmarks during our time in Pensacola, a bar on the Florida-Alabama border that we would return to often for a fun night out and for annual events like the legendary Mullet Toss, a bar we would bring family to when they visited, a bar we would be devastated to learn was heavily damaged in a hurricane years later, our Christmas writing on the wall possibly gone forever.

But most of all, I would never forget how much effort Tristan put into trying to make me happy.

***

The day after Christmas we stumbled upon another lucky find, this time at the NAS Pensacola housing office. Despite the four-month waiting list for on-base housing, we were offered a house that was open because no one on the waiting list was able to move in immediately. Ecstatic to be out of the hotel, we moved in that afternoon.

The house was beautiful. Two bedrooms, one bathroom, a huge dining room, two gas fireplaces, all hardwood floors, fourteen-foot ceilings, and a screened-in back porch as big as the living room. There was an eight-mile trail we could access across the street, a mini mart close by to do laundry. And it was pet-friendly.

With Christmas money from our parents, we bought a king-sized bed, a television, and other necessities at the Navy Exchange. Living on base meant no security deposit, no pet fees, no rent, no lease agreement, and free utilities. I felt like we had won the lottery.

We wanted to eventually buy a house off base, but the Navy would only pay for one move, so we chose to keep our belongings in storage until we became homeowners. With nothing but the basics, we adjusted to watching TV on camping chairs and eating meals on the floor. On New Year's Eve, my parents drove up to relinquish their dog-sitting duties and gift us pots and pans, kitchen gadgets, and card tables. Tristan settled in at his new job that was already keeping him busy with long hours and a massive learning curve, while I familiarized myself with the base and the surrounding city. After a bumpy start, things had smoothed out.

Or so I thought. A week and a half later I got a slap-in-the-face reminder that our lives were in the hands of the military's timeline. At 8:00 a.m., my phone rang. It was Tristan calling from his office.

"Heather!" he yelled as I wiped Cody's soiled paws with a towel after a walk. "Heather, I got a phone call!"

"Oh my gosh, are you okay?" I dropped the towel and waited for Tristan to share the frantic news.

"I have to report to Norfolk," he said. "Today."

"Wait. That's two days early," I said. Though we knew he had to fly to Virginia to spend two weeks on a ship, he hadn't started packing, and we hadn't tackled an extensive predeparture to-do list.

"Yeah," Tristan said. "I have to be at the airport in three and a half hours."

When the Navy said "go," it was time to go, no matter what we were in the middle of doing, no matter where we were, no matter how underprepared we were.

Shortly after we hung up, he rushed through the front door, and an instinct that would soon become familiar kicked in. I tossed his toiletries on the bed while he shoved folded shirts and underwear into his seabag. I ironed his khaki uniforms while he got a haircut. I rearranged our housing check-in meeting while he changed his plane ticket. It was three hours of heart-pounding chaos.

I maintained composure, focusing on the goal of getting Tristan out the door without forgetting anything. I had no tears because there was no time for tears.

After a rushed goodbye at the airport, I drove back to base on roads I still wasn't acquainted with to face the to-do list that now fell entirely on my shoulders.

I found the Personnel Support Detachment office for the updated dependent military ID I needed since Tristan was on active duty instead of reserve status. I located the housing office to complete our check-in. I registered Cody at the base veterinarian. I sat on hold with the phone company because our landline wasn't working. Finally, at the end of the day, exhausted and already lonely, I broke down in tears, wishing once again I had someone to help me.

That day was also my first lesson in OPSEC, or Operations Security. As a spouse, I learned I was prohibited from publicly sharing certain information about what Tristan or members of his command were doing, including the departure dates of ships. Unprepared, I fielded phone calls from our parents asking for details of the change in plans, and bit my tongue when Tristan's mother guessed his ship was going out to sea Monday when I knew it was heading out Saturday. When asked how long the ship would be out to sea or when Tristan would return to Pensacola, OPSEC was a no-brainer. Because I had no idea.

***

Three days after Tristan left, I started my next professional journey: graduate school. After being out of college for nearly five years, I was unsure of myself and my ability to be a student again, but I welcomed the transition to pursue my own goals.

The drive from base to campus was thirty minutes long. I got lost on the UWF campus. I couldn't figure out where to get my parking tag. I didn't know what a PowerPoint presentation was. One minute I was scared I couldn't handle the workload or the technology I had to teach myself, the next I felt an urgency to learn as much as possible and be the star student in each class.

After an emotional first week, all I wanted was to go home and share my experience with my husband. I wanted to confide in my favorite person about my apprehension and angst, my confidence and exhilaration. I wanted him to tell me change and transition are hard, but he knew I'd achieve every goal I set my mind to. I needed his reassurance. But none of that occurred. He was on a ship somewhere in the middle of the ocean with limited access to phone and email. His sole focus was a job that required him to abide by a strict set of rules that included uniforms, chains of command, military vocabulary, and acronyms.

And I was alone. Again.

I wondered what this next phase in our marriage would look like. But so far Tristan hadn't been home long enough for us to find out.

***

Less than three months after moving on base, Tristan and I bought our first house.

While we enjoyed the convenience of living on base, we both wanted a house with our names on the mortgage, a home we could make our own. I also wanted more privacy, a neighborhood that was a bit more removed from Tristan's job. I quickly learned that living on base gave me the sense that there was no escape from the Navy world.

The three-bedroom ranch in Bayou Place was perfect in every way. We moved everything out of our temporary home on base while what had been packed away since Alabama was delivered from storage. Besides our large master bedroom, we dedicated one bedroom as an office and the third a guest room. Tristan landscaped and planted bell peppers. I flipped through textbooks, immersed in my first semester, and sipped wine on our patio overlooking a pond.

After a rocky few years, everything was falling into place. Maybe everyone had been right all along. Adjusting to military life required patience and agility, and faith in the unknown and unpredictable.

I couldn't remember feeling more content, more comfortable in my skin, despite having to pencil in quality time with my husband. While Tristan socialized with coworkers after hours, I made friends at school, some nights moving on to dinner after class dismissed.

In addition to courses, my first semester included a practicum that had me teaching at a local elementary school. Most of my days revolved around class, practicum, term papers, my professional portfolio, sleep, and maybe a full hour with Tristan when he wasn't away on short trips. Despite it all, we balanced the combination of military and student life, and I was exactly where I wanted to be.

It almost felt too good to be true. Tristan loved his Navy job working for a commanding officer who was easy-going yet an effective leader and mentor. I thrived on the intellectual stimulation of graduate school and the friendships I'd formed. We had a house with our names on the mortgage, making it into a home with upgraded furniture we could finally afford and weekend Home Depot trips.

I was almost twenty-seven years old, and the next step seemed obvious. I got off birth control, made an appointment with my first Navy doctor, and bought prenatal vitamins.

We officially started trying to have a baby.

CHAPTER 3

Storm Clouds

While I embraced this fresh start, a war had begun with the 2003 invasion of Iraq. As worried as I was about my husband's military involvement in the weeks following 9/11, as aware as I was that we already had troops in Afghanistan, those fears became magnified now that Tristan was active duty and we lived a few miles from a military base.

The word "deployment" was a regular topic of conversations. My primary care physician got deployed. A family friend who was a reservist got called up and was on his way to Kuwait. Television reporters came to us live from Iraq, transmitting war scenes into our living rooms.

I understood that September 11 had changed everything, that service members were deploying left and right. But for some reason, my brain refused to make the connection between the troops in combat in the Middle East and my husband, who was so new to the military I don't think even he fully understood what his role could be in the wars.

I never imagined that one day Tristan would come home with news of his own deployment.

Or maybe I just didn't want to imagine it.

I also never imagined I'd be one of those women to obsess over ovulation cycles or put my legs up a wall after sex, but after getting my period at the end of our first month of trying to get pregnant, that's exactly the kind of woman I turned into.

It didn't occur to me that I wouldn't get pregnant the first month we tried. Or the second month. Or the third. I gave myself pep talks about how there was no rush, how I was only twenty-seven and my body had plenty of fertile years ahead.

Sometimes I wondered if it was the wrong time to have a baby. Tristan and I had been together almost four years, we'd both ventured into new career paths, and we'd proven capable of withstanding struggles that would have tested any marriage. At the same time, Tristan and I always seemed to be running in different directions, focusing on different goals, the distance between us too great to even touch fingertips. Was our marriage solid enough to add a family member?

Our third wedding anniversary came and went, and when I still wasn't pregnant, I did the math and decided to stop trying for a few months so I wouldn't deliver a baby in the middle of my upcoming school semester. Military life meant moving again in three years, and I had a finite amount of time to finish my degree. Having a baby at the wrong time could risk my chances of graduating before we moved again.

That's when I found myself staring at a positive pregnancy test.

***

By the end of the second trimester of my pregnancy, I had completed the first half of my thesis, received a graduate merit scholarship, passed two state teacher certification exams, and earned straight As. My efforts at maintaining a rigid academic schedule were motivated not only by my tight timeline to graduate, but also by Tristan's work schedule. His every move affected mine, and sometimes I worked ahead on assignments in anticipation of his impromptu plan changes.

One day in December after I turned in my last semester exam and Tristan returned from a week in Panama City, my cell phone buzzed as I Christmas-shopped.

"Where are you?" Tristan asked, out of breath.

"Downtown and on my way to the mall," I said. He didn't have to say it. I knew what came next.

"Go home. I need to pack my sea bag." I cringed at his tone of voice, his demand rather than a request.

It was another unexpected week on a ship that required me to drop what I was doing and help him pack. He hadn't even unpacked from the last trip.

While Tristan stuffed clothes into his sea bag, I imagined this scene playing out three months from now. Something maternal and instinctual took hold of me. If this happened in three months, I'd be alone, with a newborn. I'd always envisioned having my husband and my family around to help me as a new mom, but I'd have neither. And this thought made me want to barge into the office of anyone with authority in his command and urge them to send Tristan anywhere in the world they wanted for the next three months, because after that, I needed him home with me, with our baby.

When he called me hours later from the ship, I tried to squeeze in all the questions I didn't have time to ask during the packing chaos, knowing we wouldn't be able to talk during the week he'd be gone. Did he pack enough clothes? What would he be doing? Would he have email access? Should I tell his parents what was going on? Where was the ship going? Did I have to do all the Christmas shopping?

But Tristan's cell phone was losing reception as the ship moved farther from land. He had enough time to tell me he loved me and would miss me. Then he was gone.

My first instinct was to aim my rising anger at the Navy. But frustration and resentment toward an entity that was far bigger than simply my husband's employer was pointless. And when I reminded myself of all the troops in Iraq, all the spouses and families left behind while they worried about their service members' safety, I couldn't complain about one week. A safe week on a ship was nothing compared to a year in a combat zone.

So, I finished the Christmas shopping. I washed baby clothes and hung them in the closet of my home office turned nursery. I got our names on waiting lists of two Navy daycares. I played Bunco with other military spouses. I acted the part of the good military wife I was expected to be, sending my husband off on assignments with no complaints. And every night, as I tossed and turned in a bed that was too big for one person, I wondered if I'd ever get used to it all, if I'd ever be a good military wife instead of pretending to be one.

* * *

My pregnancy was still humming along smoothly through January and into February, and my course load was doable. Tristan had one more short trip scheduled to Coronado, California, and then he'd be home for two weeks of leave already approved for after the birth. A few mornings after he left and my parents arrived in town for my father to run the Blue Angel Marathon, a jab in my belly jolted me awake at 5:45 a.m.

The pain came and went, and my impulse was to ignore it until I went to the bathroom and saw a brown discharge. I'd read the books. That was my mucus plug, something I shouldn't see at thirty-six weeks.

Not wanting to worry my parents, who were staying at the Navy Lodge, I didn't call them, instead driving to the Naval hospital myself. I was calm until I saw Dr. G, the young Navy doctor I'd seen, against all odds, for every prenatal appointment. Most pregnant military spouses don't see the same OB throughout their pregnancies, and friends warned me to brace myself to see a different doctor whenever I went in for appointments. But I lucked out with Dr. G. We rode up the elevator to the eighth floor together, giving me a little extra time to describe what was going on. By the time we reached the front desk, I realized how worried I was. And how alone.

The nurse showed me to a triage room and hooked me up to a fetal monitor and a contraction monitor. While I waited for Dr. G, my cell phone rang. It was Tristan calling from the San Diego airport to tell me his flight home was departing soon.

"I can't talk," I whispered as machines beeped around me. "I'm in the hospital."

"What do you mean you're in the hospital?!" Tristan yelled.

He was upset and I'm sure he felt helpless, but the louder his voice got, the more those machines seemed to beep.

"It's probably nothing," I said. "I had a little pain and when I called the Labor and Delivery deck, they told me to come in just in case."

"What is Dr. G saying?" he shrieked. "Put him on the phone!"

Dr. G reassured Tristan I was fine, the baby was fine, and handed the phone back to me as he prepared to examine my cervix.

"Tristan, I'm okay," I said, having no idea whether I was or not. But there was no point in worrying him. He was in California; I was in Florida. He couldn't get home any faster. "I love you and I'll see you in a few hours."

I hung up and looked to Dr. G for answers.

"You're one centimeter dilated and fifty percent effaced," he said.

"No, I'm not," I said, refusing to believe I might be in labor. "That can't be. I have three and a half weeks to go."

"This could mean a lot of things," he explained. "It could mean three more days, it could mean three weeks. But I would plan on sooner rather than later."

"No, no, no," I repeated as I pulled down the paper gown to cover my bottom half.

"Go home and rest," Dr. G said. He knew I had a birthing plan, and this wasn't a part of it.

Almost exactly twenty-four hours after that stabbing pain tried to warn me of what was about to happen, our seven-pound baby boy greeted the world. Grady was three weeks and two days early, but he was healthy and beautiful.

Everything happened so quickly it was a blur in retrospect. Tristan's flight from California arrived in time to attend a carb-loading dinner at the Officers' Club for my father and other marathon participants and their families. At some point after we got home from dinner, my water broke. At some point, Tristan called my parents, and they showed up at the hospital while I was in labor. At some point after meeting his first grandchild, my father left to run the marathon while my mother stayed at the hospital. At some point the next day Dr. G was at my bedside, apologizing for missing the birth but thanking me for refusing to let the nurses call him during my overnight labor because he was running the marathon too. At some point I was overwhelmed with information and engorged breasts and exhaustion and hormones and pain and a level of happiness I didn't know existed. And at some point, Tristan and I left the hospital with a tiny human being and the title of parents.

Tristan almost missed the birth of our child because of the Navy. He didn't miss it, and for that I was incredibly grateful, especially considering the stories I would hear over the years of women delivering babies alone. And even if my parents weren't coincidentally already visiting, I did have other military wives I could have called. I wouldn't have been alone. But the close call bothered me. It was only a matter of time before Tristan missed something big, something so important I didn't think I could do it without him. Maybe this wasn't just a close call but a wakeup call.

Maybe the universe was trying to warn me that I needed to be prepared to handle big things, important things alone. I wasn't prepared to have a baby without my husband, but I should have been. From then on, I vowed to build a tougher military spouse skin. From then on, I would plan to go it alone and be pleasantly surprised when I wasn't.

***

With my laughable plan of immediately resuming life after having a baby shredded to unrecognizable pieces, I was in survival mode. Between middle-of-the-night baby feedings and diaper changes, sleep was a luxury.

Because Grady arrived early, Tristan's approved leave hadn't started so he returned to work the morning we were discharged from the hospital. I contacted my professors, a classmate picked up schoolwork to hand in for me, and my advisor waived the last ten hours of my hundred-hour practicum I hadn't logged yet. I was frantic. Suddenly I had no idea how I was supposed to handle everything, how I ever thought I could excel at both graduate school and the school of motherhood.

But despite my exhaustion, I returned to my Tuesday and Thursday evening classes less than two weeks after giving birth. Most nights I brought Grady with me, thanks to understanding professors and classmates. I slept when I could, did homework while Tristan watched Grady, and somehow, after scrambling for two months and running on fumes, I completed the semester. My reward was the same as my original plan: an entire summer as a full-time stay-at-home mom.

With no homework, no thesis to research, no thirty-minute drives to and from class, the pace of my life slowed to a state that finally allowed me to recover from months of havoc. I got Grady on a schedule, used his nap times to do yoga videos, and almost daily we went for walks with the jogging stroller my parents bought us. I gave Grady the attention he deserved, nurtured my body and mind with exercise, cooked nutritious meals, and caught up on the journaling I once treasured but had to abandon.

As I learned, life with the Navy never stayed still and predictable, but I could pretend we were an ordinary couple adjusting to life with a baby. Even on the tougher nights of Grady's colic, when I paced up and down our long hallway in the middle of the night with him, I welcomed some normalcy and balance.

This glimpse of what it must be like for a family who wasn't military, who wasn't constantly wondering when the next separation would come, made me realize I was still struggling as a military spouse.

Summer is the primary PCS season, a time of incoming and outgoing military families. Personally, that translated to the incoming of new faces and the outgoing of friends I'd probably never see again. It was hard enough that I was no longer seeing my university friends. What was harder was the change in my military friendships.

The atmosphere at Tristan's command shifted with the arrival of a new commanding officer, a phenomenon I would learn was common. COs set the tone of their commands, whether intentionally or not, and for us, what was once a laid-back, fun-loving group of people who enjoyed hanging out together became formal coworkers and their spouses who epitomized the military term for forced interactions known as "mandatory fun."

I rarely communicated with the wives. One couple we once socialized with PCS'd to DC, and it seemed the other wives I knew drifted away until their own PCS moves. I anticipated the challenges of my own moves every three years, but I never thought about the heartbreak of watching others leave. Was military life just a constant revolving door of new faces? Would I have to spend Tristan's entire career saying goodbye? Would anyone stick around long enough to form a lasting friendship, long enough to rely on as a support system?

If military spouses could compile a list of things not to say to a military spouse, one of those taboo sentences would be "You knew what you were getting into."

It's impossible to comprehend and foresee military life until you're in the thick of it. You can read the books. You can watch the news. You can absorb the tales of those who have done it. But knowing the logistics of what you're getting into when your spouse becomes a service member is far different from knowing how you're going to react to it, knowing to what degree those logistics are going to upend your life, his life, your family's life. Even military brats who grow up to marry service members must learn for themselves how to navigate the lifestyle as a spouse, as a parent instead of as a child.

I had no idea what I was getting into when Tristan joined the Navy, and I certainly didn't know that I was about to face far bigger challenges than a lack of meaningful friendships.

Six months after Grady was born, Tristan deployed to Iraq.

CHAPTER 4

I Recognize Those Tears

We had three weeks to prepare for the six-month deployment, a timeframe that was somehow both not long enough and painfully drawn out.

This deployment required legal documents like wills and a power of attorney. It included purchasing gear and creating a staging area in the house to incrementally pack. It included somber discussions about Tristan's possible death and his wish for me to remarry a good man to raise Grady, about where he wanted to be buried, about who should inherit his most valued possessions, conversations meant for an older couple with gray hair and complaints about aching feet and resolutions to wear more sensible shoes. At twenty-eight years old, we were too young for this heaviness.

But the most heartbreaking aspect was planning for what this deployment could mean for Grady, a process that included Tristan filming himself shaving, tying a tie, and reading *Guess How Much I Love You* and *Goodnight Moon*, videos we called "Daddy TV" that Grady could watch to connect with his absent father, to remember his voice, his face, and in the worst-case scenario, to have a piece of Tristan in the event he didn't return.

Watching Tristan film himself talking to Grady, watching the two of them play on the floor with blocks, watching them cuddle in our bed for story time with Cody beside them, all filled me with emotions I didn't know quite how to label. These scenes seemed so natural, so normal for a father and son spending quality time together. But they were far from normal.

I was proud of Tristan for serving his country, but every thought I had between his announcement and his departure was laced with anger. Or anxiety. Or sadness. I was paralyzed with fear not only for his safety, but also for the indelible imprint war would leave on him when he returned, *if he returned.* I needed someone or something to blame for putting me in this spiral of emotions, for giving me only three weeks to prepare to send my husband to war. I could blame President Bush for initiating the war in Iraq. I could blame the Navy for accepting my husband into their club. I could blame Tristan's CO for signing off on the deployment. Or I could blame Tristan because he had volunteered for it.

Tristan's deployment classified him as an individual augmentee, or IA. This meant he wasn't going to Iraq with his command. He wasn't part of a unit that deployed together. He was temporarily leaving his command in Pensacola to join a different one in Iraq.

This also meant I was the spouse of an IA. I didn't have a support system within his command because no other spouses were going through what I was going through. I always imagined that if I ever had to face a deployment, I would have other women to bond with, to commiserate with, to call for help, to chat with while our children played together, to drink wine with as we shared babysitters.

But this deployment wouldn't resemble that daydream at all. Tristan was deploying on his own, and I was being left behind on my own.

Just as I'd been warned about other aspects of military life, I'd heard the preparation for a deployment was almost as tough as the deployment itself. It wasn't a romantic time spent cuddling and gazing lovingly into each other's eyes. And it didn't include promises, because those weren't guaranteed. I fought to ignore the stress, but the stress won. Some days I wished he would leave already and get it over with.

On the outside, I tried to prove to him that I could handle this, that I was the independent military wife he needed me to be, that I could keep the homefront running so he didn't have to worry about his family while he focused 100 percent on his mission.

On the inside, I was crumbling under the facade that I was okay with all of this. I was supporting my husband, but who was going to support me?

***

On a Tuesday night, when we had two weeks to go on the departure countdown, I had to attend an open house at the elementary school I was assigned to for my student teaching. My lack of teaching experience made me jittery with nerves as I swiped mascara on my eyelashes, but after Tristan came home with unexpected news, I verged on shutting down completely.

"They changed my departure date," Tristan said. "I leave this Saturday."

Four days. We no longer had fourteen days. In an instant, ten days were ripped away.

Quiet tears escaped before the pragmatic side of me overpowered the emotional. I grabbed my notepad and frantically scribbled lists of what had already been done, what needed to be done, and what should be done but were secondary concerns. Tristan might have had his own checklists, but organization offered me a sense of control, especially in situations where I had no control. Then I touched up my mascara, transformed back into teacher mode, and left for the open house.

I had no choice but to keep moving forward.

Tristan's departure date changed so many times I just wanted to get my husband on a plane so I could get off the predeployment roller coaster.

When we finally faced our last night together for six months, we barely slept. In the morning, we videotaped the final installment of Daddy TV, with Tristan eating breakfast on the couch and Grady beside him in his bouncy seat, the gravity of the circumstances nowhere to be seen as we all pretended that nothing was unusual about this breakfast, this morning, this day. Then we packed up our 4Runner with Tristan's bags and drove to the airport.

As we pulled up to the curb at the airport to unload Tristan's luggage, we learned his flight was canceled because of bad weather from a hurricane. I felt like a toddler about to throw a tantrum. More chaos. More delays.

Tristan secured a spot on a standby list, and we burned time in an airport restaurant. Our goodbye was choppy and short. A brief hug, minimal tears, and whispered "I love yous." Then he crossed through the security gate, leaving me to wonder whether or not he would get on the flight.

Amidst the morning mayhem, Tristan had accidentally spilled coffee on my cell phone, rendering it useless. We had no way of communicating while he was on one side of security and I was on the other. We agreed that if he didn't make the flight, he would leave the terminal and we'd wait together for his next standby flight.

Tristan was number ten on standby, far enough down the list that I didn't expect his name to be called, far enough down that I didn't take the farewell seriously. There was no way he was getting a seat on that plane. I thought for sure I would wait in a chair by the newspaper stand and see Tristan's gray shirt around noon, when the flight was scheduled to take off. This was our practice goodbye. The real one would come three hours later for his next standby flight.

I watched his gray shirt disappear into the crowd and found a seat with a half-asleep Grady snuggled in his car seat beside me. I attempted to pull together lesson plans for my upcoming week of student teaching, but my brain wasn't processing. I knew that by 12:00 p.m., Tristan would either be heading my way with a defeated shrug or buckling his seat belt. I watched the minutes ticking away on my watch, willing my cell phone to turn on. At noon I stood, craning my neck to watch for the gray shirt.

12:05.

12:15.

12:30.

No gray shirt.

Breathing harder, I grabbed the car seat and half ran to the area where incoming passengers passed to exit the airport.

"Excuse me," I said to two security guards. "Is there any way you can tell me if my husband got on his plane?"

Both guards shook their heads and resumed their private conversation. They didn't notice when silent sobs shook my shoulders, that I continued to helplessly stand there holding a heavy car seat with a sleeping baby.

I ignored the thoughts that plagued me every time I had previously envisioned this moment, that this was the last time I would see Tristan for six months, that if the worst-case scenario became reality, this could be the last time I would ever hug him or kiss him or look into his blue eyes ever again.

"Can I help you?" I looked up at a woman in a flight attendant's uniform. I hiccupped through my explanation.

"How long will he be gone?" the flight attendant asked as she guided me in the opposite direction. I never mentioned my husband was military.

"Six months," I said.

"I recognize those tears," she nodded. "Let's go find out if he's on that plane."

I followed the flight attendant to a line of people I wanted to scream at to move out of my way. Couldn't they sense my urgency?

When I reached the front of the line and asked the airline representative to check the status of a standby passenger, she typed on her keyboard for what seemed like hours.

"Yes, ma'am, he's in seat 9C," she said. I burst into a fresh round of tears, confusing this stranger who thought she was sharing good news. "Is that bad?"

"He's on his way to Iraq for six months," I mumbled. But I doubt she heard me. I was already walking away.

I located my car after getting lost in the parking garage, then clicked the car seat into place in the backseat, Grady still asleep, the blue eyes that matched his father's closed to all that had just happened. I kissed his forehead and smoothed his hair that seemed to get blonder every day, wondering if six months was long enough to erase my baby's memory of his father.

While I was deeply upset at the airport, the real shock of Tristan's absence didn't hit me until the sun descended. After putting Grady down for the night, I curled up on the couch and flipped mindlessly through television channels, glancing obsessively at the loveseat Tristan usually occupied while we negotiated whether we would watch the latest program on the History Channel (his choice) or a rerun of *Everybody Loves Raymond* (my choice). Needing the day to end, I went to bed early, arguably the loneliest part of military separations.

But after tossing and turning for hours, first maintaining my designated space in our king-sized bed, then stretching my entire body across both sides, I gave up. The bed was too boundless without Tristan. I tucked my pillow under one arm and dragged the comforter to Grady's nursery, spreading it on the floor beside his crib. I pulled Cody's dog bed next to my makeshift sleep area and covered myself with a blanket from the guest room. Within minutes I was asleep, comforted by the proximity of the remaining males in my house.

My marital bed remained unslept in for the duration of Tristan's deployment.

* * *

The hurricane that canceled Tristan's original flight to Texas also churned through my parents' part of Florida. Their house in the Tampa Bay area sustained minor damage from Hurricane Francis, but the forecast of a stronger tropical storm brewing in the Atlantic was the real concern. So they packed up their car, evacuating their home with the understanding they might return to a city ravaged by a natural disaster named Ivan. While I told myself I was providing them a place to shelter from the storm, my invitation for them to stay with me for an unspecified period of time was more selfishly motivated. By the time they rang my doorbell, I was so drained from only five days of Tristan's deployment I practically collapsed in their arms.

For the next few days, my parents spoiled Grady and tracked Hurricane Ivan's course, while I got ahead on lesson plans and groceries.

"The hurricane isn't going to our house anymore," my dad said as I packed my teacher tote bag for the next day.

"That's great news!" I said.

"Well, maybe not," he said. "Now it looks like Ivan is coming here to Pensacola."

"That can't be," I said.

"You may need to start thinking about coming home with us," Dad said.

"What? No, I can't leave," I said. "I have student teaching."

"Heather," he said gently. "If this storm goes where they're currently projecting it's going, schools won't be open. It's looking pretty bad. It's time to think about evacuating."

I hadn't heard from Tristan in days, but I knew he was traveling from Fort Bliss for immunizations and equipment, then to Germany and on to Kuwait. The wound from his departure wasn't even scabbed over yet. It was all too overwhelming. There were too many changes.

But more change was about to hit whether I was ready or not.

The following day I went to work, and by the last bell, the superintendent closed all city schools. Teachers shoved furniture to the center of classrooms, unplugged computers, and accumulated materials to take with us. After telling each other to stay safe and saving a phone number to call to find out when schools would open again, we locked up.

I sped home to find that my father had repacked his Honda Accord and my mother had formulated a list of evacuation preparations.

"We're leaving tomorrow morning," my dad explained. "Plan to be gone for a couple weeks and pack accordingly."

Too numb to overthink, I mindlessly tossed necessities into suitcases, my parents hauling large items to the 4Runner. Clothes, toiletries, dog food, diapers. The fireproof strong box with important documents. Photo albums. The storage tub with my journals. Grady's bouncy seat. Toys and dog treats for Cody. With no space for anything else, my mother called her local grandmother friends to borrow a Pack 'n Play, a stroller, a swing, and toys.

I looked around my house, certain I'd packed everything I needed. But what would Tristan want me to save? My heart pounded with indecision that triggered an intense anger toward the military because I didn't know who else to blame. "My husband should be here to choose for himself what he wants to salvage. He should be here with his family in the home we built together, the home we might not see again," I thought.

With those thoughts, something inside me broke, and I dropped to the floor of my walk-in closet, whimpering like an injured animal.

But then a faint sound came from my bed. When I realized it was my phone ringing, the tears stopped. As if the universe was throwing me a lifeline, I answered the unknown number knowing it was Tristan, knowing he was reaching out when I needed him.

"Hey," he said.

I could usually gauge his mood from that one word, but I couldn't waste any time on analyses. I knew we only had a few minutes, so after he told me he was in Kuwait awaiting a flight to Baghdad, I blurted out that a hurricane was coming, that I was evacuating, that I needed to know what he wanted me to pack. I hated dumping this extraneous stress on him while he was dealing with his own, but this call might have been my only chance to tell him what was happening at home, the only chance to assure him we were safe.

He asked me to pack his laptop and his favorite watch, then took a deep breath and said he had to go.

"I love you," he said. "I'll call again when I can."

"I love you too," I replied, unsure whether or not he heard me before we got disconnected.

The call couldn't have been longer than three minutes. I thought I'd feel better hearing his voice, and in a way I did. But in a way, it only intensified the heartache of missing him.

***

The next day started and ended with emergency room visits, the first in Pensacola, the second in Clearwater. Grady's double ear infection with over 102 fever plus odd episodes of eye rolling were ill-timed and left me feeling like a punching bag, but I had my parents to lift me up when I felt like all I was doing was falling.

That night, as I lay in my parents' guest room with an antibiotic and ibuprofen-filled Grady snoring in the Pack 'n Play beside my bed, my thoughts were on overdrive, my mind racing with everything I'd gone through in the last week.

I thought about my husband on his way to Iraq, to a war zone, wondering what was going through his mind. I thought about my house, wondering if it would still be standing when I returned. I thought about hovering over Grady in his hospital bed, holding him still and comforting him as four nurses tried to find a vein for his blood draw, and I wondered if I had the energy to be the only parent for half a year. I thought about my father hovering over me, rubbing my back to keep me calm as he also held Grady's little hand, and I wondered if I could give up on independence and move in with my parents for the duration of the deployment.

Exhaustion eventually turned my brain off, and I cried until sleep found me.

***

I shouldn't have watched the live reports of Ivan pummeling Pensacola as a Category 3 hurricane at 3:00 in the morning. I shouldn't have listened to the histrionics of the Weather Channel reporters. But I had to see it for myself. While I was thankful I had listened to my dad and left town, I was devastated for the city I'd grown to love, drowning in questions that wouldn't be answered for days.

Through neighbors and one of Tristan's coworkers who stayed in our house when his lost power, I learned a tree had fallen on the corner of our roof, causing minor damage to the siding. Otherwise, I was told to consider myself fortunate. My house was virtually undamaged, but Pensacola was a mess. Some residents lost everything. When I heard schools were closed for at least two weeks, I decided my best option was staying with my parents until circumstances improved in Pensacola.

I didn't have to shuttle Grady to daycare, cook, or clean. My parents treasured the quality time with their only grandchild, and I soaked in bubble baths with mindless novels. I finally exhaled after feeling as if I'd been holding my breath for months. Part of me felt relieved to have a reason not to have to be alone.

Three weeks after leaving my beloved home to fend for itself, I returned to Pensacola to find it in better condition than I'd feared. A portion of a window was busted in the family room. The back porch screen had blown away. A handful of shingles on the roof were missing. But the house was structurally sound, our power was on, and Grady, Cody, and I moved back in to resume whatever normalcy we could find. Others weren't so lucky.

The time at my parents' house wasn't exactly a vacation, but it was a reality break I needed, the rejuvenation of the mental strength I needed to return home and figure out deployment life on my own. Not typically one to ask others for help, the hurricane made me realize there was no shame in leaning on family and friends to ease my burdens. Grasping onto my renewed sense of confidence, I felt ready to face whatever was hurled my way next.

Using that strength and motivation, I finally finished school. Despite everything, three months after the deployment began, I completed my student teaching and my thesis, graduating *summa cum laude* with a master's degree and a Florida state teaching certification.

There was no celebration though. For reasons I couldn't explain to anyone who would understand, I chose not to walk in my graduation ceremony. I couldn't imagine commemorating this milestone, expressing this huge sense of relief and excitement, while Tristan was deployed. Not only because he was the only person I wanted to see in the crowd, but also because I felt like, as a military spouse, I had an obligation to deprive myself of happiness to honor the hardships he was going through. In my mind, it wasn't fair to feel such joy while he was so miserable. Reasonable or not, I downplayed my accomplishments and how proud I was of myself. How could I compare my little graduation to his service to our country?

Weeks later, my diploma, that piece of paper I'd worked so hard to earn, arrived in the mail. I smiled as I ran my fingers across my name, then placed it in a drawer of my desk with the hope that one day I would use it, that one day I could have a career too.

***

At any given moment, I had no clue what Tristan was doing, where he was, or what kind of dangerous situations he was facing. He called sporadically, but shared few details. I wasn't sure what to ask or if I wanted to know, even if he was allowed to tell me.

After he had a mailing address, I kicked off a daily letter-writing campaign that continued for the remainder of the deployment. Every day for five months, I jotted down things I would tell him if he were sitting at the dinner table with me, things our baby boy was doing, things that popped into my head that made me think of him. Knowing he would likely receive the letters every few days in batches rather than chronologically, I numbered the bottom right corners of the envelopes so he could read them in order.

With limited email and phone access on his end, those letters were my truest, most consistent connection to Tristan. But I questioned how much I should share with him. Did he really need to know Grady had yet another ear infection? Did he need to know Cody had suddenly developed separation anxiety? Did he need to know I was struggling with his absence, especially during the holidays? There was nothing he could do about a sick baby and canine behavior from halfway across the world, so why worry him? I also didn't want to share too much about what he was missing out on. Homesickness could distract his focus. So I chose not to share too much about my trip to New Jersey to spend Thanksgiving with his parents, or the Christmas Grady and I celebrated at my parents' house. I had the comforts of home when he was surrounded by war. That felt almost cruel to share.

Military spouses often trade stories about their experiences with Murphy's Law, a half joke/half tragedy we all half laugh/half weep about: Anything that can go wrong during a deployment will go wrong during a deployment. The hurricane was my first lesson in Murphy's Law. And while I told Tristan about Hurricane Ivan, I vowed to handle any other lessons Murphy had in store for me—from overflowing toilets to the lack of available contractors to fix our house damage—without burdening him. While frustrating, I tried to view these unfortunate events as stories to tell Tristan once he returned.

In a way, my resolve to shield Tristan from my hardships on the homefront helped me gain confidence in my ability to get through them. If I wrote letters from a place of positivity, regardless of how fabricated it was, maybe that mindset would overtake my negativity and fear and transform me into the military spouse I needed to be. I wished I had another spouse to guide me, another wife dealing with a deployment and single parenting to assure me that my feelings of being completely overwhelmed were normal, but that's not how it worked with IAs. I was on my own.

But not for long.

***

Another struggle I kept to myself was my new job: stay-at-home mom.

Knowing our two-and-a-half-year stay in Pensacola was dwindling, I didn't bother looking for a teaching position that I'd have to quit in a few months. I pulled Grady out of daycare, looking forward to spending my days with him instead of other people's kids.

But transitioning from not enough free time to way too much, from the structure of school and deadlines to no structure whatsoever, I sometimes looked at my nearly one-year-old son and wondered what I was supposed to do with him, what I was supposed to do with myself.

The moral support I expected from Tristan's command was blatantly absent. Not one spouse contacted me during the entire deployment, not even to check my status after the hurricane. I received the monthly group emails from the CO's wife, who organized girls' nights out, but no personal communications. No one offered babysitting services or stopped by with home-cooked meals as they had promised before Tristan left. I wasn't even invited to the command Christmas party.

And then I met Allison.

A nurse and Navy wife with a daughter slightly older than Grady, Allison had recently moved in across the street. One night I spotted her and her husband Mike sitting on their front porch after their daughter's bedtime, sipping cocktails while Mike strummed a guitar.

"Come join us!" Allison yelled across the darkness.

"Me?" I said, wondering if she thought I was someone else.

"Yeah you!" she yelled back.

"I don't know," I said. "My baby is asleep inside."

"Grab the baby monitor," Allison said. "Come have a drink!"

After that first night, I never turned down an invitation. I craved Allison's company, her electric smile, her easy laugh, her open personality, as if no topic was off limits in our conversations. I planned the dog's nighttime outings to coincide with the flickering candles that signaled she was outside. She was the extroversion to my introversion. She told me of Mike's deployments, gave me parenting advice, and listened as I vented about solo parenting. In my loneliness, I gravitated toward Allison even though I wasn't supposed to.

I was well aware of the unwritten rule that officers and their spouses should avoid socializing with enlisted service members and their spouses, that such fraternization could affect the work environment by undermining the chain of command. And I understood my husband was an officer and Allison's was enlisted. But I didn't care. I liked her. Plus, the officer wives I was allowed to be friends with weren't abiding by the unwritten rule to support spouses of deployed service members. Why should I follow the rules if they weren't?

To me, Allison wasn't an enlisted wife. She was my comic relief when my ability to find humor had slipped away. She exemplified the confidence I needed to get through the deployment. She was the embodiment of the strength I so badly wished I had. She was the badass military spouse I aspired to be.

Allison was also a creative, hands-on mom with natural parenting skills I envied. Despite all my training to be a teacher, I sometimes felt like a boring mother who ran out of ideas to entertain my child. But not Allison. She was always outside with her toddler, inspecting plants, drawing on the driveway with chalk, blowing bubbles, and on warmer days, filling up a plastic baby pool with the hose or running through sprinklers.

One day Allison told me she had a routine with her daughter that kicked off with morning outdoor playtime.

"If you see my garage door open, come on over," she said. "The kids can play and we can chitchat."

For the rest of the deployment, every morning after I fed and dressed Grady, I peeked through the blinds of the nursery with a direct view of Allison's house to look for her open garage door. Some mornings I watched the clock obsessively, wondering if her routine had changed. Other mornings the garage door was open early, and I watched Allison set up whatever playtime activity she had planned. I waited long enough so I didn't seem like a stalker before Grady and I joined in on the fun.

Some days Allison was the only reason I got dressed, the only reason I left the house. I'm not sure she ever knew that she got me through the tail end of the deployment. If not for her and her open garage door, I probably would have spent those weeks trapped in my house wondering how to get through my days and worrying my baby wasn't getting enough mental and physical stimulation. She was a gift. She grounded me. She guided me.

Allison's company was more than a friendship, more than the mother of my son's only playmate. She was also a distraction from myself.

One nagging thought that pushed to the front of the rumination line was a repeat of the one I had ignored on my wedding day: We're not meant to grow old together.

I didn't know what it meant on my wedding day, but I couldn't ignore the implications of those words now. I couldn't shake the possibility that this premonition was surfacing again because Tristan wasn't coming home from this deployment. Tristan was going to die in Iraq. I was going to get that knock on my door. Uniformed men were going to notify me that my husband had been killed in action and his body would return on a military flight.

We weren't meant to grow old together because my husband was going to die.

In my loneliness, I envisioned how I would react to the knock on the door. Would I crumble to the floor in convulsing sobs like military spouses in the movies? Would I be paralyzed with acute grief and stare muted at the strangers who changed the course of my life? Would I scream and slam the door in their faces in denial? Would I transfer my anguish to Grady as I held him, clutching him closer to console us both?

I told no one of these irrational introspections. I didn't even tell Allison, despite the experience-based wisdom she could have provided to ease my heightened anxiety. I'm sure her kind spirit and positive nature would have lifted me out of the spiraling hole of sadness I was digging.

But I kept it all trapped inside my head. Because if those words escaped, they might actually come true.

CHAPTER 5

Reinvention or Reintegration?

The knock on the door never came.

In February, two days before Grady's first birthday, Tristan came home.

Homecoming day was as unceremonious as departure day, the opposite of a film-worthy reunion, as casual as the ring of a doorbell, as abrupt as the departure had been.

Tristan attempted to surprise me, but he was never great at keeping secrets.

"When will you be home?" I asked when he called from Texas. "I can't wait to see you!"

"I don't know," Tristan answered a bit too playfully to be truthful. "But I'll find out between five and six tomorrow night." Of course Tristan had just revealed his arrival time.

All day I cleaned the house, stocked the fridge, and prepared to see a man I hadn't lived with in six months. Did he change? Did I change? How would he react to seeing Grady, who was a completely different child than he had been when Tristan had last seen him? How would Grady react to a father he only knew through Daddy TV?

At 5:00 p.m., the house was spotless, Grady was dozing, and I was on the edge of my seat. At 5:15 I heard the taxi pull up to our curb, and I peered out the window as the driver helped Tristan stack his bags on the driveway. I frantically brushed my hair, gargled mouthwash, blotted lipstick, and squinted through the peephole of our front door as Tristan approached the house and rang the doorbell with a smile that weakened my knees.

I flung open the door, and finally, after six long, grueling months, hurled myself into my husband's arms, devouring him with kisses.

His hair was so short I could see his scalp, and what hair remained was darker than when he had left. He was the thinnest I'd ever seen him, a shock even though he had warned me of his twenty-pound weight loss. He looked like he'd aged ten years.

But he was home, alive and physically unharmed, and that was all that mattered.

* * *

We had both heard through the military grapevine to expect an adjustment period when the deployed spouse returned home. We'd each gotten accustomed to living without a partner, not sharing a bed or a schedule. And he was no longer used to sharing space with a child, a little person who was often the priority of my attention.

However, I didn't anticipate how difficult that adjustment would be, and within days my concerns about our struggles to get reacquainted grew. I thought we were supposed to be ecstatic to be reunited. I thought we would fall right back into the old groove of our marriage. The awkwardness between us made me wonder if our marriage was in trouble.

Because I was still so disconnected from Tristan's command, no one warned me what I would learn years later, that the military had a term for those first few weeks after returning from deployment. Reintegration. This meant that not only were our struggles not a sign that something was off between us, but that what we were going through was par for the course and should pass with a healthy combination of communication and patience.

I wish I'd known it was common to forget how to talk to each other face-to-face after a deployment, that we basically had to learn how to be comfortable with each other again. I wish someone had given me a heads-up that it could take four to six weeks for us to feel a sense of normalcy again. The awkwardness was hard enough, but my expectations about the first month after his return made it so much harder than it needed to be. Most of all, I wish I'd been proactive in researching the time period after deployment.

I thought back to the book Tristan had bought me when he first joined the military, the book I could no longer find, adding it to the increasingly long list of random possessions that got lost or destroyed in a move. The *Navy Spouse's Guide* had years earlier planted a vision in my mind of a good military spouse, a spouse with duties and responsibilities surpassing those of a civilian wife. And according to this fictional image in my head, a good military spouse would have known exactly what to expect and would open the lines of communication instead of ignoring the odd range of emotions, quietly questioning if her husband felt the same way.

Without that knowledge at the time though, I overanalyzed every misstep, every abnormality, every minute sign that the deployment had damaged our marriage. Tristan took two weeks of leave to ease back into the transition from Iraq to Pensacola, but the first week of that leave he was sick and the second week his parents came into town to see the son they too hadn't seen in half a year. As he fought jet lag, he also fixed the still unrepaired hurricane damage to our house, since I had never been able to find a contractor who wasn't busy with other homeowners' larger repairs.

I thought we'd use those weeks to get to know each other again, to make up for lost time. We didn't. Instead, I felt like I didn't know this man who was sleeping beside me in the bed I resumed sleeping in the first night he was home. And before I knew it, those precious two weeks vanished, and he was back to his regular work schedule.

Whether he couldn't tell me or he didn't want to, Tristan revealed very little of what he had done and seen and experienced in Iraq. I also didn't know how much of a debriefing he had upon his return or whether he checked in with a counselor to catch signs of post-traumatic stress disorder. Some days I considered suggesting we go to counseling together. Just a few times. Just to make sure this deployment was out of our systems, that there wasn't something else we should do or say to get closure on the strain of the last six months.

But I never expressed any of this to Tristan, in part because he seemed to have already moved on mentally from the deployment, in part because our focus shifted to another priority.

***

During his final month in Iraq, Tristan and his detailer regularly communicated to solidify his next tour.

"We have two choices," he told me on one of our brief calls. "It's Jacksonville or Japan."

I couldn't hide my disappointment. We'd always planned to follow our original wish list, shooting for Norfolk or San Diego after Pensacola, but Tristan wasn't interested in the job openings available in those locations.

I didn't want to stay in Florida, but I also wasn't thrilled about going OCONUS—outside the continental United States. But the Navy didn't care what I wanted.

After much deliberation, I told Tristan to choose the job that would make him happier. I would follow his lead regardless of where that job brought us. I reminded myself that a good military spouse is unwavering in her support, she's flexible, and, most importantly, she can adapt to any duty station even if it terrifies her.

Days later, I announced to family and friends that in June, less than four months after Tristan's return from Iraq, we were moving to Sasebo, Japan.

***

Our remaining time in Pensacola was spent bickering.

We had three months to sell our house, get a passport for Grady and update ours, decide what belongings to bring in our limited household goods shipment, and research how to bring a dog overseas, a process that involved tedious steps and a scare that he wouldn't be able to come with us because of his size and the summertime temperature restrictions. The intense preparations for an overseas move added another layer to the marital strain that lingered from reintegration.

I confided in my childhood friend Charlotte that I was worried about moving all the way to Japan without resolving my marriage problems, but the words had barely escaped my mouth when, in the next breath, I blamed my concerns on the stress of the upcoming move, on my mixed emotions about living in a foreign country so far away from my family. Any couple would be on edge in our situation, I rationalized. Like reintegration after deployment was a real phenomenon, so was PCS anxiety.

I backpedaled, assuring Charlotte I was fine, that Tristan and I were fine, that we'd level out as soon as we got settled in Japan. We got through a deployment, we could get through this PCS. We'd find ourselves and our marriage again once our lives and emotions weren't dictated by relentless Navy timelines and checklists.

We sold our house in a month, and the movers packed up our belongings into three separate categories—Storage, Household Goods that took months to arrive overseas, and a limited-weight Express shipment with only necessities.

I said goodbye to Allison. She would be my role model through military life for years to come, whether I was once again accepting another wife's offer to help or I was finding ways to show kindness to other wives going through a tough time. We weren't supposed to be friends, but Allison was my first proof of the strong bond between military spouses. She wouldn't be my last.

And when we pulled out of our driveway for the last time, I didn't look back. Like our departure from Tuscaloosa, I didn't want to look in the rearview. I only wanted to look ahead.

Military life, as I was learning, was an emotional roller coaster. I thought the ride was bumpy simply because I was inexperienced. Little did I know at the time that I would be on that roller coaster for years to come, even when I thought I'd gotten off. The military roller coaster never stops. Sometimes the ride is too fast; sometimes it's too slow. Other times it goes too high, making the drop back down feel like plunging out of control. While most of the time it chugged along at a steady pace for us, its unpredictability left the residue of uneasiness, an inexplicable sense of constant hypervigilance, of always expecting a sharp change in direction or an upside-down loop of disorientation.

If our first PCS to Pensacola was the slow ascent of the military roller coaster, then the first plunge was the deployment, followed by reintegration, the steady creep back up. Now it was time to tighten the seat belt and get ready for the next plunge.

* * *

When I boarded the Japan-bound airplane with my husband and toddler, I was nervous about living in a foreign country where I didn't know the language and where, as a taller-than-average, blond-haired, blue-eyed woman, I would stand out like the outsider I was. I told myself how fortunate I was to be immersed in a new culture, a new way of viewing the world. I told myself to take full advantage of this once-in-a-lifetime opportunity and embrace the adventure. I told myself to be a yes person, that I had only three years to experience Japan, and the only way to do that was to fight my instinct to stay imprisoned in my comfort zone.

Like my transition from the person I was in Tuscaloosa to the person I became in Pensacola, I could reinvent myself again in Japan. I was no longer a student, and I no longer wanted to be the bored stay-at-home mother who waited for someone else to open their garage door. I could be anyone I wanted to be.

When I stepped off the airplane into the Fukuoka Airport, I looked around at the Japanese signs I couldn't read, the unfamiliar names of bookstores and convenience stores selling unfamiliar products, the restaurants advertising sushi, ramen, and soba noodles. In awe of everything I didn't know about my new home, I reconfigured my fear into excitement, eager to discover what the next three years had in store for me.

Reality hit as soon as the van pulled into the parking lot of the Navy Lodge after a nearly two-hour drive from the airport in Fukuoka to Commander Fleet Activities Sasebo. I was OCONUS and overwhelmed. But I only had a week to overthink the unknowns because the Navy had a timeline for not just service members, but spouses arriving in Sasebo as well. Military spouse was about to become my full-time job.

Tristan reported to work the morning after our arrival, while I fended for myself on the small base. With no license to drive and no transportation, anywhere I wanted to go had to be by foot in the sticky summer heat. We were on waiting lists for both base housing and off-base housing in a Japanese neighborhood, but in the meantime, we made peace with life in a Navy Lodge room.

Cody was quarantining at the on-base kennel, and twice a day, I pushed Grady in his stroller a mile to the other side of the base to spend time with our confused dog. I walked to the commissary every day because I couldn't buy a lot at once, stowing the groceries in the lower basket of the stroller. Most days I walked to the library to check out books and videos for

Grady, and then we put on bathing suits to cool off and give in to our jet lag at the pool.

I'd finally gotten Grady used to that schedule when, during my second week in Sasebo, I was required to attend a four-day indoctrination class at Fleet and Family Support. The Navy paid for Grady to go to the Child Development Center while I studied Japanese road signs and laws for my driver's license.

I aced the written exam, but the road test was a different story. There were no lessons. I wasn't able to practice driving on the left side of the road. And I had to constantly remind myself that everything was the opposite of what I'd grown up learning about cars. The gear shift was on my left, the turn signal on my right.

Somehow, I passed the test and was issued a license, promising the forgiving instructor I would drive more on base before venturing out in town. Getting into the driver's seat with so little training made me feel even more conspicuous in the Japanese community who, I imagined, was irritated with Americans sharing their roads after being in their country for such a short amount of time. But I welcomed the clear protocol, relieved to simply follow the instructions the Navy gave me. As much as the military frustrated me at times, I appreciated whatever agreements they had in place with the city of Sasebo that allowed us to integrate so seamlessly.

Indoc's other purpose was to give a roomful of Americans a crash course on how to behave on foreign soil, teaching us Japanese norms, common words and phrases, and basic information to ensure we all represented the United States well in this country we were guests in. As I collected paperwork and soaked in the deluge of knowledge, I thanked Indoc for another one of its purposes: an opportunity to meet people.

By the end of the week, I no longer worried about making friends or connecting with a support network. I was already part of a community unlike any other.

***

In addition to the Indoc class, I attended an hour-long course at the housing office to learn how to find a place to live. The waiting list for Main Base housing was extensive, so Tristan and I decided to attempt living "out in the *cho*," or off base in a Japanese neighborhood.

I'm not sure how house hunting usually goes in Japan, but the Navy had its own system for service members and their families in Sasebo. After taking the class, we were required to view at least three houses per week to receive the monetary compensation the Navy hands out while families live in the Lodge. This meant walking twenty minutes to the housing office, studying the board for listings, and setting up a meeting with a Japanese realtor through a translator. On the day of each viewing, the realtor, who rarely spoke English, picked me up outside the base, drove me to the house, and then dropped me back off after the walk-through. Then I had twenty-four hours to notify the housing office if we wanted the house.

All of this I did with Grady, but without Tristan, who was swamped at work, the whole process thrusting me into a culture I didn't understand, with no partner to bounce opinions around with. And for three weeks, I viewed three to five houses a week with no success.

We'd been warned of the shortage of Japanese houses that allowed dogs. We were also warned how small Japanese houses were, particularly doorways and stairwells. Tristan and I had a list of requirements for our ideal house, but we quickly modified those unrealistic demands once I saw the options with my own eyes. Tristan wanted a ten-minute commute and a view. I wanted a yard for Cody and a bathroom upstairs near the bedrooms. Apparently, no such house existed.

When I finally stumbled upon a house with no deal-breakers, we didn't hesitate. It was two stories, 1,400 square feet, and had a traditional Japanese bathroom with a shower area and a separate tub, shoji doors and tatami mats in two common areas, storm shutters to pull down when tsunamis blew through, and a small yard surrounded but not fully enclosed by a wall. It was a twenty-minute commute to base and dog-friendly for Cody. It didn't check all the boxes, but the next day we signed the paperwork the Navy gave us to accept the house, and Tristan requested a one-year hold status for the on base housing waitlist in case we changed our minds.

We'd been in the Navy Lodge a month, long enough that both our Express and Household Goods shipments had arrived. The Japanese movers were the quickest, most efficient movers I'd ever seen, abiding by the custom of removing shoes at the entrance of the house even while lifting a bulky American sofa.

Just as we had been warned, the stairways in the house were narrow, and our gigantic dresser didn't make it up the stairs to our bedroom. We decided to keep it in the kitchen, converting the drawers to storage for canned goods, bath towels, and other random items we couldn't find space for. Other than the dresser and several pieces of jewelry I still couldn't find even after we unpacked the last box, the pack-in went smoothly.

With the move complete, we cleared out of the Navy Lodge with our meager possessions, signed Cody out of Paws-N-Claws, where the poor dog had been living because he wasn't allowed in the Lodge, and started settling into our new home at 653-1 Tanagata-cho.

***

Through coworkers, Tristan figured out how to buy a motorcycle for himself and a Daihatsu Naked for me. My car resembled a silver tin can and shimmied going up hills, but I loved it. With practice on my own and with friends, I got the hang of driving on the left side of the road and soon learned four different routes to and from base, although I never quite got used to scooters buzzing by and cars abruptly pulling over so drivers could answer their cell phones.

The twenty-minute commute to base didn't bother me at first. I was close enough to shop at the commissary, but far enough away that I felt like a part of a Japanese community. Despite my concern about the isolation from my fellow Americans, living out in town allowed me to dip a baby toe into Japanese culture. While Tristan was at work, I walked up and down the streets with Grady in the stroller, waving to neighbors, stopping at the convenience store down the block and testing out the phrases I knew how to say.

Once I gained confidence in my driving skills, I visited shopping areas I learned about from other spouses, writing down their directions based more on landmarks than GPS. I frequented hundred-yen stores, the Japanese version of our dollar stores, and "the Bunny Store," as we Americans called it, because we couldn't pronounce the real name of the store with the rabbit logo. My favorite was the Arcade, or "the Ginza." Our Sasebo Ginza, not to be confused with the famous Ginza in Tokyo, was a strip mall within walking distance of the base. It was a fun walk with Grady in his stroller because there was always something to look at, but if I wanted to do any real shopping, I had to do it without him. Most stores were several stories high with no elevators, and even some on the ground level had such narrow aisles that I could barely squeeze my stroller through without Grady kicking items off shelves.

My new friend Laura and I signed our toddler boys up for a local Japanese daycare that accepted drop-ins. While I explained the expense to Tristan as a way for Grady to get an appreciation for Japanese culture, I also selfishly loved exploring Sasebo without him. I wasn't working, but Tristan's salary was padded with a cost-of-living allowance that elevated our checking account enough that I wasn't worried about my lack of employment opportunities. My job was to be a good military wife and a stay-at-home mother teaching our son about the diversity of the world.

The Navy also provided endless ways to get involved and connect with others. Remembering my loneliness in Pensacola, I participated in one activity after another that the Navy made readily available for families.

I competed in triathlons and 5k runs offered by Morale, Welfare and Recreation, or MWR. Tristan and I attended auctions and bazaars, where we purchased Asian furniture and gifts for loved ones back in the States.

Throughout the summer I took Grady to Mommy and Me classes at the base pool, and when the pool closed in autumn, I took him to indoor playgroups. I joined the Officers' Spouses' Club, or OSC, who met once a month for unique outings, from dining at the delicious Chinese restaurant on nearby Mount Yumihari to touring oyster farms and picking mikan, a type of mandarin orange.

Tristan's Hail and Farewell—an informal social event that welcomes new members to the command while saying goodbye to those departing—was at a karaoke bar that eventually became one of our favorite hangouts. We attended potlucks, birthday parties, going-away parties, and the Navy Ball. It was the most social Tristan and I had ever been as a couple. This was the military life I had read about, the close-knit community I had hoped for in Pensacola but never found.

***

As fall temperatures nudged out the sweltering summer, I got my first glimpse of one of the biggest downsides of *cho* life: the lack of heat.

When we first moved to Tanagata-cho, I didn't believe the rumors of shampoo freezing in bathrooms in the winter. But as mild temperature drops cooled our house, I slept in sweatpants and used the warming function on the toilet seat. We had to switch from our four air-conditioning units to kerosene heaters, distributed by the Navy with carbon monoxide detectors. With a toddler and a large dog, I didn't think kerosene heaters would be the best addition to our home decor.

Tristan called the housing office to remove our one-year hold status, and immediately we were offered houses on base. We knew we'd lose the privacy we had in the *cho*, that life would be different when we moved to what everyone referred to as "the fishbowl." But the four months we lived in town gave me a sufficient feel for a Japanese neighborhood, and with winter approaching, I couldn't think of any reasons to stay. Once again, we were moving.

The base assigned us a "T house," the section of older homes for officers, two streets over from the base CO. The T houses were slated to be torn down in 2007, but Navy dates tend to be pushed back, so we figured we would still be living there when Tristan's rotation date rolled around in mid-2008. Even though we felt like moving experts by then, we didn't want to move again before our PCS back to the States.

Once in our new home at T-581B in Dragon Vale, Sasebo's Main Base housing, I once again had access to American amenities I had been trying to forget I was missing in the *cho*. We had a corner lot with a fenced-in yard for Grady and Cody to play. Unlike in the *cho*, where I had to bake with a convection oven that scorched dinners and do laundry with a Japanese washing machine that fit exactly three towels and a dryer that took two hours to complete a cycle, I had a real oven and an American washer and dryer. We could walk to the commissary, our friends' houses, restaurants, and Grady's playgroups, and we had a list of teenage dependents to hire as babysitters.

We were in the fishbowl, surrounded by Americans in Japan. That meant my neighbors couldn't hide their secrets.

It also meant I couldn't hide mine.

* * *

If my time in Pensacola left me bitter about the military spouses who neglected to step up to support me when I needed it, then my time in Japan provided the exact opposite.

Living on base was my truest lesson in the close bonds of military spouses, bonds I wouldn't have formed if we had continued living in the *cho*. We took care of each other while our service members were gone. We celebrated holidays together. We raised our children together. These women became my village; they were the ones I gravitated toward, the ones I leaned on even if they weren't aware of the weight they were helping me carry.

But living on base was a double-edged sword.

Most of the military spouses in Sasebo were women, and most of the women in my immediate circle were stay-at-home moms. While some spouses taught at the Department of Defense school for military kids, had part-time jobs teaching English to Japanese women, or worked on base at the video store or the commissary, job opportunities were scarce. Being in a neighborhood of other women at home with their children meant I had friends within a stone's throw, but it also meant all social boundaries disappeared.

Spouses called needing emergency babysitters. They knocked on the door asking for recipe ingredients they forgot to pick up at the commissary. They looked out their windows and knew whether or not you were home and available. And they picked up on marital troubles.

Tristan and I still didn't seem to be on the same page, despite my hope that leaving the deployment and Pensacola in the past would improve our marriage. We seemed to be growing further apart, and I couldn't figure out why. In fact, the more I analyzed it, the more I realized we'd been having relationship issues for so long that I couldn't remember a time when we were happy together, when I wasn't convincing myself we'd be fine as soon as we got through whatever challenges we were dealing with. Our issues hadn't resolved with age, with financial security, with a change in friends, or with a move to the other side of the world.

Every conversation had the potential to flip a switch into an argument. We fought about the division of household chores, about parenting philosophies, about how much money to spend on Christmas gifts, about what time to go to bed. I looked forward to his TAD trips—Temporary Additional Duty—when I got a break from walking on eggshells. As tiring as solo parenting could be when he was gone, it was less tiring than fighting.

Even when Tristan was home, we weren't often together. In addition to multiple 5k runs, I competed in a 20k relay at the Japanese Army base Camp Ainoura with friends and then a half marathon an hour away in Saga where MWR bused American participants. Training and competing while Tristan stayed home with Grady went beyond my passion for running. It was my excuse not to spend time with my husband.

I always kept our private matters private. But I couldn't ignore one man who showed up at our house more and more for a couple of beers with Tristan because he didn't want to go home to his wife, and another man who yelled at his wife in their driveway when he thought none of his neighbors could hear. I wondered if other spouses noticed the cracks in my marriage.

One night, Tristan planned a romantic date, and since my friend Nicole owed me a night of babysitting, I dropped Grady off at her house before we headed out to town for a night that was a disaster from start to finish.

The fancy restaurant we both wanted to try was unexpectedly closed, and the restaurant next door had no English menus and was too expensive to risk the typical American method of pointing at pictures of food. After driving around for a half hour in the snow in search of another place to eat, we were hungry and cranky.

But the discord went deeper than hunger, and even after eating, we argued about where to go next. I'd barely popped my last bite of shrimp tempura into my mouth when Tristan jumped up to pay the check. We walked to the car wordlessly.

I grasped onto any shred of civility remaining. I didn't want to go home. We had a free babysitter and a clear schedule, and I didn't want to waste this rare night out.

"Where are we going?" I asked, as if I couldn't see Tristan's clenched jaw as he drove.

"Home," he muttered. And just like that, with no justification, date night was over. I was livid, too pissed off to bother with an attempt to convince him otherwise.

Tristan pulled the car into our designated parking spot in front of our house, and while he went inside, I headed to Nicole's house to pick up Grady. It was only 7:30, and I dreaded answering why our date lasted only ninety minutes.

Two other military spouses, Laura and Tracy, sat at Nicole's kitchen table so I had to face the "Why are you back so soon?" inquisition from not one, but three of my friends. I laughed it off and claimed we were old and tired, but they could read all over my face that we had a fight.

As I put Grady to bed, I thought about my marriage, desperately searching for the good. Maybe I wasn't looking hard enough. Maybe it would magically appear when I least expected it. Or maybe, as I sadly suspected, it wasn't there to be found.

That night would be the first of many that I lied to friends about my marriage. It would also be the first night of many that I rolled out our Japanese futon on the living room floor and voluntarily slept alone.

CHAPTER 6

Relics

"Pretend you actually like each other," our friend laughed.

I didn't think it was funny. In fact, I was overcome with embarrassment.

Tristan and I stood beside each other at a New Year's Eve party, a camera pointed at us, the first time all night we weren't on opposite sides of our friends' house. As I faked a smile, I still believed our friction was invisible to the outside observer.

During the countdown to midnight, I noticed one couple cuddling on a sofa, another couple standing in an embrace, and another couple dancing, while I stood alone. Tristan was nowhere to be seen. The countdown hit zero. All the husbands kissed their wives to ring in the new year. Except mine. Embarrassment turned to anger.

The next morning, both tired and distant, we had what I would come to call a state-of-the-marriage talk. The usual trading of blows began with my gripes.

"I don't like how you speak to me. I don't like how you don't prioritize me. I don't like how you don't listen to me. I don't like how you spend money. I don't like that I don't feel like your partner in this marriage."

He blurted his own jabs, which, to my ears, always sounded arbitrary, defensive reactions to mine.

"I don't like how you don't make efforts to book a babysitter for more date nights. I don't like how you nag me about how I spend my own money when you don't have a job. I don't like how you iron my uniform. I didn't like that dessert you brought to the neighbor's potluck so next time you should consult me first."

Not a single issue was new, just the same ones rehashed. The specifics of the issues had evolved, but the overarching themes persisted.

"We need marriage counseling," I said.

"You know we can't do that here," he replied.

He didn't have to explain why. We couldn't go to counseling because Sasebo's Navy community was so small that not only did we know employees at the Fleet and Family Support Center where help was available, but we socialized with them. How could we ask for marriage guidance from the same people we drank sake with at karaoke bars?

With counseling off the table, we compromised to hold weekly meetings to discuss grievances to prevent bottling problems up and exploding. We also agreed that, after getting this far in our marriage, it was worth fighting for, worth making the effort to communicate more effectively.

I couldn't help but wonder if all marriages were this much work, this much of a daily struggle, this weighed down with resentment, embarrassment, and anger. I couldn't help but wonder if our marriage really was worth the fight.

***

A couple days later, while putting away laundry, Grady zoomed Matchbox cars around my bed, his toddler obsession with all things cars and trains occupying his attention while I did chores. I shoved a pair of Tristan's socks into a drawer of our dresser that had mysteriously stopped fully opening after our move from Pensacola. Suddenly overcome with frustration at this drawer that had mocked me for months, I yanked on it until it came off its tracks and crashed onto the floor, spilling socks everywhere.

However, it wasn't the flying socks that caught my attention. Leaving the mess on the floor, I examined the empty space where the drawer had been. Above that drawer was a thin, secret compartment designed to hide jewelry. Weeks after we moved into the *cho*, I realized I'd forgotten to look there for the jewelry I was missing, but when I opened it, I had found only a handful of mismatched earrings, one necklace, and a watch. I was frantic, realizing I'd neglected to empty the compartment before the movers in Pensacola had put the dresser on the truck, and most of my beloved jewelry I'd stored there was gone.

But there, in the tiny space in the front corner of the dresser where the sticky drawer had been, were twenty-two earrings, six necklaces, and another watch. All my lost jewelry had been there all along.

Some of the necklaces were tangled together, some earring posts were bent, but otherwise nothing was beyond repair. The jewelry had hidden in that corner all the way from Florida to a warehouse in Japan to Tanagata-cho in Sasebo to our T-house on base. It didn't seem possible.

In the pile was the sapphire pendant Tristan had given me before we got married as well as a necklace I had bought in the Bahamas during our wedding week. After all they went through, they were undamaged, still whole, still functional, still beautiful.

These relics from before our marriage survived. This had to be a sign, a promise that the old Tristan and Heather would show up again and survive too. And maybe, like the jewelry, we'd appreciate our marriage even more because we retrieved the missing pieces we thought we'd lost inside the dark tiny spaces.

***

Our post-New Year's Eve discussion seemed to put our marriage back on track. Maybe all we needed was to release the pressure valve. Maybe we figured out for ourselves the work a counselor would have assigned us.

Our communication improved, and we spent more time together when Tristan wasn't traveling. We planned adventures, like taking a train to Hotel Lorelei near the popular Huis Ten Bosch Dutch theme park to soak in hot springs. We signed up for an MWR trip to Fukuoka for a professional baseball game and then another one to Kumamoto to tour a samurai house. Other weekends we hopped in our newly purchased car, a minivan-like Toyota Spacio that was much bigger than the Naked, and followed a map to Hirado to explore a castle or visited local hangouts like Saikai Park to snap pictures of the cherry blossoms. And when Tristan could request leave, we took the Shinkansen bullet train to Kyoto.

The revived security in my marriage and my affection for Japan combined to catapult me to a level of happiness almost too good to be true. With that lightness of invincibility, the next stepping stone in the foundation of a solid marriage was clear.

We started trying for baby number two.

After gathering details from women at Grady's playgroup who'd given birth in Japan, I made lists of the complexities of American pregnancies in Sasebo versus waiting to have a baby when we moved back to the States.

Because the base didn't have a hospital, I'd see my Navy doctor until week twenty of my pregnancy, then transfer to the Higashijima Ladies' Clinic. Dr. H, who spoke enough English to hold a conversation, would see me for the remainder of my pregnancy and deliver my baby.

As with most military family endeavors, there were countless what-ifs and unknowns, but I couldn't let that stifle my desire to grow our family. Filled with hope, I visited my Navy doctor, filled the prescription for prenatal vitamins, and began tracking my ovulation.

But in the seven months it took to get pregnant, my marriage gradually fell apart again, all the hard-fought improvements and efforts slipping back into old patterns of vacillating between fighting and avoidance.

***

Japan is known for its *onsens*, or hot springs, where public baths invite users to literally strip down and relax. The Bonshoro *onsen* was an easy fifteen-minute walk from our front door, and about once a week, while Tristan stayed home with Grady, I got naked and soaked in the steaming water, losing myself in this other dimension where I could close my eyes and everything disappeared.

No one spoke English so I didn't have to socialize. Soon, I was such a regular that the front desk employees recognized me, taking my yen entrance fee and holding up their fingers to let me know which floor of the building the women's tubs were on that day. Even Japanese guests started recognizing me, ladies nodding in approval of my knowledge of *onsen* etiquette, like washing myself in the shower before entering the bath and keeping my hair out of the water. My favorite times were the evenings when I was the only person in the outdoor roof spa, where I read books, stood bare and exposed by the ledge overlooking the city lights, and if the weather cooperated, floated on my back as rain sprinkled on my face.

I would walk to the *onsen*, tuck myself in an unoccupied corner of water, and surrender to the heat. When my internal timer declared I was sufficiently cooked, I slipped on a robe, drank a *chu-hi* or two from a vending machine while melting into a massage chair, and blasted sad music on my iPod. I walked home a lighter version of myself, having sweat out whatever toxicity lived inside me, all in under two hours.

This ritual became my refuge and my self-care. I was surrounded by strangers instead of the confusing emptiness I felt around my husband. Arguments didn't happen after *onsen* visits, and I started believing my plan to fix my inner self was working, which in turn led me to believe everything truly was my fault. And if everything was my fault, then it was my responsibility to repair the damage.

CHAPTER 7

New Life, Old Life

"You want to take a test?"

The clock hit midnight, and fireworks boomed outside our bedroom announcing the arrival of 2007.

"Yeah," Tristan said through a childish grin. "I can't wait until morning!"

We both knew what the result was going to be. I was late. My stomach was off. My breasts ached.

I hopped out of bed, where we'd been reading books after skipping out early on our neighbors' New Year's Eve party, and closed myself in the bathroom, ripping open the EPT wrapper. I could see the faint vertical line across the horizontal line already, but rested the stick on the edge of the bathtub to wait out the two-minute processing time in bed with Tristan.

I didn't tell him it was already positive. I wanted to hold that moment to myself. I wanted to savor the before and after, the news I was certain would transform my marriage. During those two minutes, I imagined this baby propelling us closer, bridging the gap between us. I imagined this baby, this human we'd tried for seven months to create, fixing us.

At the two-minute mark, I returned to the bathroom and the unmistakable positive sign in the results window of the test stick. Back in the bedroom, I answered Tristan's curious expression with a smile.

"Congratulations!" I said, as I handed him the pregnancy test, a second round of fireworks popping and horns honking outside, a celebration that felt custom-made for us. It was perfect timing, and I embraced this omen of an amazing new year with new beginnings and a new life to bring into the world.

Our reactions were subdued, far less dramatic than the first pregnancy. We hugged and kissed, but no jumping up and down, no tears of joy. I was relieved more than anything else. Relieved that I could stop tracking my ovulation. Relieved that my envy of other pregnant women who seemed to appear everywhere was now unnecessary.

Relieved that I had a reason for Tristan to give me the attention I was craving.

* * *

My second pregnancy wasn't as straightforward as the first. My blood work was consistently abnormal, and spotting led to the discovery of a polyp in my cervix. And while I remembered the exhaustion from pregnancy number one, this time I didn't have the luxury of resting, thanks to an active three-year-old who decided he was done with naps.

When I was ten weeks along, Tristan went TAD for ten days in Osaka, came home for seven days, then went to the States for three weeks. He missed Grady's third birthday, my prenatal appointments, veterinarian appointments as Cody's health started failing, and housing meetings as our neighborhood prepared for the demolition we were warned about.

Tristan was home when I got word at eighteen weeks along that I needed to be medevacked to the Navy hospital in Yokosuka for advanced tests, and he was able to take leave for my entire eight-day trip. After two days of testing and two days of resting in the Navy Lodge, we turned our remaining four days away from Sasebo into a mini vacation in Tokyo.

Like usual when we escaped, all our troubles disappeared as soon as we checked into the New Sanno Hotel, the swanky US Navy-run hotel in downtown Tokyo. Meeting with the hotel's English-speaking travel and tours expert and plotting adventures with highlighted maps and sightseeing pamphlets took our minds off the strain of my pregnancy.

We took a bus to Shibuya, home of the renowned busiest intersection in the world, and trains to Tokyo DisneySea and Yasukuni Shrine. We dined at Standing Sushi Bar and a delicious noodle shop. We used the hotel's babysitting services to go on a Grady-free date at Alcatraz ER, a restaurant where customers eat inside jail cells. We explored the Imperial Palace East Gardens and the Ginza—the real Ginza, not the mini version of the shopping district we called the Ginza in Sasebo. Tristan and I exhausted ourselves. But we weren't fighting.

***

Shortly after our return from Tokyo, we received the phone call that our baby was healthy and thriving. Our baby girl.

By then I was twenty weeks along, time for my switch to the Japanese OB. The initial appointment with Dr. H worked on a walk-in basis, so on a Friday in early April, I picked up my paperwork from Navy medical, Tristan left work early, and our family of three ventured out in town to the Higashijima Ladies' Clinic.

After figuring out that I was supposed to remove my shoes and put on slippers provided in a glass cabinet by the front door, I studied the waiting room. It was packed. And as quiet as a museum. No Americans, no young children, and only one husband. I'd never felt more conspicuous.

The clinic was nothing like I expected, nothing like an American hospital. The atmosphere was like a hotel lobby, a hotel only for pregnant women. Piano music filtered down a tall winding staircase. The ladies at the front desk spoke broken English, enough to communicate that our wait time would be about an hour and a half. I told Tristan to take Grady somewhere for an hour while I waited at the clinic to avoid a public American toddler meltdown.

When I was finally called back to an exam room, and Dr. H finally made his appearance, he didn't introduce himself, didn't shake my hand, didn't acknowledge Tristan, didn't apologize for the wait. He got right down to the business of the baby.

The exam had barely begun when one nurse wiped the ultrasound gel off my belly, another handed me a VHS tape and a plastic photo album with 3D ultrasound images, and I was shown the door to make my next appointment and return the slippers. I assumed if something was wrong Dr. H would have told me.

My second prenatal appointment once again included a long wait, but I chatted with a Navy wife I recognized from Grady's playgroup and read magazines in the fancy waiting room, chuckling when the piano played "Hotel California." This time, Dr. H spoke after performing the 3D ultrasound.

"Baby is breech," he said matter-of-factly.

"Should I be concerned?" I asked, panicking.

"Not yet," he answered, already walking toward the door. "Still has room to move. Next month we hope she moves."

"If she stays breech, will I need a C-section?"

"Probably." He explained he could do a C-section in his clinic, but if I had other complications, such as the cord wrapped around the baby's neck, I would have to go to the hospital. I had so many questions. But he was gone.

* * *

After the drama of the first half of my pregnancy, I vowed to focus on lowering my stress levels during the second half.

I tried not to stress when the base housing office informed us we had to vacate our house, despite our hopes of a postponement of the plan for the neighborhood to be torn down. Instead of dreading yet another pack-out, I looked at the bright side that my pregnancy qualified us for a more spacious home.

I tried not to stress when the DoD school called with the news that my substitute teacher application was finally processed and I could be placed on the sub list, but since Grady's name never moved to the top of the waiting list at the Child Development Center, I had no full-time childcare. Instead, I told myself my time would come to teach, to use the master's degree I worked so hard for, but now was the time to focus on my children.

And when Tristan suggested an adventure before baby made four, I tried not to stress about the hidden implication that he needed another escape from reality. Instead, I considered the trip a celebration of our seventh wedding anniversary as we brainstormed destinations in Asia that allowed for my restrictions, namely, no airplanes in the third trimester.

A week and a half later, we boarded a cruise ship heading to South Korea.

I always relied on getaways to renew my spirit—and our relationship—but our whirlwind three-day trip to Busan and Seoul did the opposite.

For the first time, our marital squabbles joined us as we traveled. I blamed it on my seven-month-pregnant swollen feet, Tristan's disappointment that we couldn't visit the DMZ with a child under eleven, and my diminishing patience to locate yet another bathroom for our recently potty-trained son. Maybe those were legitimate reasons for a husband and wife to bicker and maybe we should have postponed this poorly timed trip that required too much walking and not enough food options for a pregnant woman and a three-year-old child.

But maybe that was all we were capable of anymore. Maybe there wasn't a getaway where we could get away from ourselves.

***

Exhausted from the trip, exhausted from growing a human being while mothering another one, exhausted from high thyroid levels and low iron levels, exhausted from whatever fill-in-the-blank emotion surfaced at any given moment about my husband, I decided that nothing significant was going to get resolved until after our daughter was born.

Baby girl was breech, then sideways, and finally, when Dr. H was about to schedule a C-section, she showed up in the proper position on the 3D ultrasound. Friends told me he didn't like delivering big American babies, so I wasn't surprised when the topic of induction came up during the appointment when he predicted I was expecting over an eight-pounder. As soon as I stopped worrying about going into preterm labor, as I had with

Grady, I let Dr. H convince me to induce just under a week early, conveniently when Tristan's parents were in Japan to help.

The Japanese birth experience was as unique as I'd imagined, the polar opposite of Grady's birth, in part because it wasn't a surprise, in part because of cultural differences.

Other than my inability to stomach anything but miso soup from the trays of food the nurses urged me to eat to keep up my strength while in labor—lasagna, salad, sushi, fruit, juice, bread, cookies, raspberry tea—I mimicked what Japanese women did. That meant no drugs other than the induction pills, no epidural. At eight centimeters dilated the nurses helped me walk to a birthing chair, a contraption that resembled a rocking horse with a pillow in the front. I faced Tristan and clutched his hands as a nurse rocked me back and forth and rubbed my back. When my contractions were less than a minute apart, I stood and shuffled to the delivery chair to give birth sitting up.

Tristan sat at my right side, a nurse at my left, and in front of me was a television screen of swimming dolphins. Four nurses repeatedly counted to ten in English while I held my breath and pushed with all my might, pulling up on the handles on the sides of the chair with each number counted. After a half hour of pushing, the pain stopped.

As I held Ava for the first time and Tristan kissed me, I believed everything was as it should be. My daughter was perfect. This strange foreign birth process was perfect. My family was perfect. My marriage was perfect.

For two days in a private recovery room, I vacillated between the after-birth pain and sleepless nights and the pleasure of a kind clinic employee washing and styling my hair, as well as the extravagant lobster dinner included in our stay. But when I said goodbye to the Japanese nurses, who had spent two days giving us privacy to bond but were also available to assist with the press of a call button, I was ready. We brought Ava home and started our life as a family of four.

All was right with the world.

***

But as with anything in military life, nothing stays the same for long.

The most glaring reminder that time is getting short at a duty station is securing orders to the next one. While I was excited when Tristan got orders to Virginia Beach, the reality that the calendar had turned to another new year and our last months in Japan were counting down left my priorities spread thin.

The five months since Ava's birth were a whirlwind of activity. Thanks to the upcoming demolition of our house, movers once again packed up everything we owned and unpacked it all down the road from our T house at 547D Pennsylvania Avenue, a two-story, three-bedroom house. It was our third house in Japan in under three years. Grady got his placement at the Child Development Center, so I resumed Officers' Spouses' Club events, strapping Ava to my chest for pottery shopping in Nakaoyama, a sake factory tour in Ureshino, and a stroll through a pearl plantation in Hirado. My parents flew in to meet their granddaughter, and my brother Kurt and his wife visited for our final Christmas in Japan. And after Cody stopped eating and Tristan had to carry him up and down the stairs, we said our devastating goodbyes to our children's first pet that they'd never remember.

Online house hunting for our next duty station also stretched our limits. Buying a house sight unseen was risky, but

Tristan wanted a home waiting for us in Virginia. So during our last weeks in Japan, we obsessively searched the internet, fielded late-night phone calls to accommodate the time difference, and squabbled over neighborhoods until we had a contract. I was skeptical, but I looked forward to breaking free of the fishbowl of military housing and being a homeowner again.

Blatantly missing from that list of priorities was time with my husband.

Tristan and I existed on parallel planes, always in each other's peripheral but never quite intersecting. When Ava arrived, it was easy for me to sweep our problems under the rug, to believe we were fine. With a newborn and an almost four-year-old, I had my hands full. The kids were my priority. Getting dinner on the table was my priority. Getting enough sleep so I could function was my priority.

I figured all couples with young kids encounter this phase. Babies and preschoolers rely on their parents for everything, so we put our full attention on them and their needs. I told myself things would be better when Ava was sleeping through the night. Things would be better when Grady got into preschool. Things would be better when the kids were a little older and more independent. Things would be better if we could get past the present.

In hindsight, I realized we'd never put our marriage first, never made our relationship a priority. Maybe we were too young, too naive, and too optimistic.

But that mindset, that projection that the future would bring happier times, a happier us, seemed to be the mindset I'd latched onto throughout our marriage. Things would be better when Tristan was no longer a student, and we left Alabama. Things would be better when I could go to graduate school and work toward my career. When the deployment was over. When reintegration turned into normalcy. When we got settled in Japan. When we got pregnant again.

But there I was, nearly eight years into my marriage, still wishing time and milestones away for a future that never made good on its promise to restore us.

***

With three months remaining in Japan, Tristan had to unexpectedly fly to the Navy base in Yokosuka. The timing was a surprise, but unplanned travel had become the norm over the years. If Tristan's job taught me nothing else, it was to expect the unexpected.

Weeks passed, and I found myself completely run down. But on those nights when Tristan was gone and I tucked the kids in bed and disappeared to my own room with a glass of wine and whatever mindless television show AFN—the American Forces Network—offered, I realized what was actually at the root of my exhaustion. It wasn't the chaos of getting ready for an overseas move. It wasn't the stomach bug I caught after Easter. It wasn't the single parenting of two kids. Sure, those were contributing factors, but those were all manageable and temporary.

No, something on a deeper level, more lingering, more damaging, more cumulative, was the base of my burnout, my loneliness, my resentment.

I couldn't stop replaying the morning Tristan left. It was last-minute. It was frantic. It was my husband barking orders at me like I was one of his subordinates. Wash my uniform! But first you have to find my uniform! Get my bags in the car! Get the kids in the car! Now! We have to leave now!

I followed his orders silently, letting him rant through his travel anxiety. Once in the car, he weaved in and out of traffic, speeding to the train station, pulling the Spacio into the taxi drop-off lane, and barely putting the car in park before jumping out of the driver's seat and sprinting around to the trunk. With the driver's side door open and the car running, he yanked his bags out of the trunk with such force that the two golf bags that also happened to be in the trunk were sent flying out, scattering clubs all over the ground.

"Bye babe," he panted as he jogged into the train station without so much as a glance behind him.

No kiss goodbye. No "I love you." No "Thanks for the help." No "Sorry for the rush." No "I'll call you when I get there." No "I'll miss you."

That's all he said, leaving me to play pick-up-sticks with a dozen golf clubs, a few of which I had to fetch from the edge of the highway after they were nearly run over by oncoming traffic. *Bye babe.*

I should've been livid. I should've stood up for myself. I should've had some sort of emotional reaction. But I felt nothing but relief. He was gone.

Despite the hardships of parenting alone with a stomach bug and the added responsibility of managing the homeowner's insurance and mortgage documents for the house we had bought in Virginia Beach, I was content in my solitude.

Despite it all, life was easier when he was gone.

CHAPTER 8

Unlocking a Door

On my thirty-second birthday, Tristan handed me divorce papers.

The aftertaste of our unresolved morning argument still lingered when the front door creaked open. I sat on the couch we were borrowing from the Navy, folding the mountain of laundry that never seemed to shrink, waiting for him to come to me, waiting for an apology I knew I wasn't going to get.

Tensions were high in our house. Stress over our upcoming move back to the States bounced off the empty spaces where our belongings used to be a few weeks earlier, before the Japanese movers loaded them into their trucks. It was reasonable to blame some of the bickering on the nerves we both felt about this transition, our mixed emotions toward leaving the home we'd made in Japan the last three years, and while his words weighed like a brick in the pit of my stomach, I wasn't overthinking it. It was one fight amongst countless.

I assumed he was home midday to eat lunch, or maybe to wish me the happy birthday he'd neglected to say before he'd left for work. We often met in the middle after arguments like this, acting as if we hadn't thrown verbal daggers at each other, dancing around hot-button issues to maintain a level of peace until the next one and relying on avoidance to wipe ourselves a clean slate. I always told myself to let it go and move on, all the while doing the opposite, forgiving but not forgetting, adding each argument to my growing list of reasons why I was unhappy.

I folded a pink onesie and placed it in the laundry basket atop the stack of others as Tristan walked into the family room, his lack of eye contact alerting me he didn't carve out time during his busy day to acknowledge my birthday, or to share his latest professional accolade, or even to ask me to make him a sandwich, any of which I would have accepted as a show of remorse.

Without a word, he handed me a sealed, unlabeled manila envelope, his calm silence a dramatic gesture I learned to dread.

"What is this?" I asked, neither of us bothering with greetings.

He continued to stand over me, maybe in an attempt to appear bigger than me even though we were the same height, enjoying the buildup I would later wonder if he rehearsed. I hated myself for hoping it was a birthday gift, for not bracing myself for the contents inside this mystery packet.

While he looked on, I turned the envelope over and over in my hands, wondering if I should open it or if I should make him explain it, wondering which option would give him the least satisfaction. The red flags waved in my mind until my indecision was interrupted by the baby monitor's announcement that our nine-month-old daughter was stirring from her nap.

"Tristan, what is this?" I repeated, finally looking up at him.

"I'm done," he said. "These are divorce papers."

I shouldn't have been as blindsided as I felt. After all, I had my own divorce daydreams, my own images of walking out the door with my two children and never returning. I guess I didn't realize his unhappiness had surpassed mine, reaching the point of taking action.

I looked back down at the envelope, imagining the legal jargon on the pages inside, the words that held the potential to alter the trajectory of my life. It suddenly felt too heavy to hold, and I dropped it on the ugly wicker coffee table that, like the couch, like my entire identity, belonged to the military.

"I have to go back to work," Tristan said.

I knew him well enough to know he wanted a dramatic reaction, that he wanted me to be shocked and devastated, giving him the upper hand, the control.

But I didn't give him the reaction he wanted. I didn't shed a single tear. I didn't promise to do better. I didn't ask why. I didn't even open the envelope. And I didn't stop him when he turned and left the room, slamming the front door as our baby cried upstairs.

I went about the rest of my day as if it held no significance, as if it was neither a day that was supposed to be dedicated to me nor a day that made me question everything. I fed my infant daughter mashed bananas. I gushed over my four-year-old son's drawing of Thomas the Tank Engine that he had made at preschool. I finished folding that mountain of clean laundry before tossing a dirty one into the washing machine. I cooked dinner from my list of Tristan's favorite recipes. I did everything I was supposed to do as a mother and wife.

After Tristan got home from work that evening and we shared a silent family dinner, the two of us fell into our practiced dance, splitting off into our designated routines that didn't involve each other. I got the kids ready for bed and he disappeared to unwind, both of us pretending that a conversation about the state of our marriage wasn't long overdue.

When we couldn't avoid each other any longer, when sleepiness led us both to our bedroom, we almost simultaneously muttered weak apologies for the argument that had kicked off our day, the last phase of our now predictable pattern that allowed us to ignore our problems a little bit longer. I crawled into bed beside him, snuggling into the curve of his body as if we hadn't just hours earlier faced our dissolution. There was no birthday celebration, no birthday cake, no birthday gifts, no mention of the birthday divorce papers.

Our daily lives moved around the untouched, unopened envelope that sat on the ugly wicker coffee table for the next seven days, the packet that was never discussed again but acted as a reminder that words can't be taken back. It was a reminder that an option was presented, a fork in the road created. For a week, the envelope mocked me, forced me to confront buried emotions that surfaced because of its presence.

I spent that week trying to outwardly portray myself as the perfect stay-at-home mom, the perfect wife, the perfect military spouse, a gesture equivalent, in my mind, to begging him not to leave me. But my internal struggle proved more difficult to fake as I attempted to press stop on the mental replays of the day my husband told me he wanted to end our marriage.

In the moment, I wasn't thinking how crushed my heart was, or how I couldn't fathom how I could live without him, or how I had to win him back. Instead, my initial thoughts went straight to logistics.

In the moment, I wasn't wondering how my husband of eight years could decide he didn't love me anymore. Instead, I was worrying about how I would support myself.

In the moment, I wasn't thinking about the fact that my life partner wanted to live his life without me. Instead, I was wondering how quickly I could find a place to live, a job, and childcare.

In the moment, I wasn't feeling any sense of longing to put the pieces of my broken marriage back together. Instead, I was concerned about how I would piece together a life on the other side of the divorce I think I always knew was coming.

In the moment, I wasn't scared of being alone without him. Instead, I feared being alone with myself. Because I didn't know who that was anymore.

When I couldn't stand to look at it anymore, the envelope I never opened and for all I knew housed a stack of blank papers, I folded it in half and in half again before burying it in the trash underneath dirty diapers and mashed bananas. Then I forgave Tristan, and I forgave myself, letting us both off the hook for getting too close to the edge of giving up on almost a decade of marriage.

Despite the veiled sense of security I pretended we still had, I knew we had unlocked a door that could never be fully closed again, a crack that let in a sliver of doubt and distrust.

I may have forgiven. But I never forgot.

***

Shortly after that, we moved into the Navy Lodge, coming full circle to the hotel where our Japanese adventure launched.

After going to my final Bunco, the women's game night I was nominated to organize months earlier, and relishing that uninhibited time with friends who'd become family, laughing, reminiscing, and passing around the bottles of alcohol from my house that couldn't be shipped to the States, I wondered if I'd find another military spouse community in Virginia Beach that was as special as this one. I said countless "see you laters," the mantra of military families because the word "goodbye" is too permanent. And as I fell asleep on my last night in Sasebo, I assured myself I would see these women again somewhere down the Navy road.

In the days after Tristan handed me an envelope and told me he wanted a divorce, I pondered the decisions I had to make. At first, I believed we'd weathered a storm, urging myself not to read too much into what I would come to refer to as our "Divorce Talk." I ignored the fact that, while the Divorce Talk didn't end with a divorce, it also didn't end with a conversation about how to prevent the next one.

But I couldn't stop thinking about what would have happened if I had opened that envelope and pulled out divorce papers, if Tristan really did leave me, if my marriage really was about to end.

As we boarded the plane that ended our tour in Sasebo, Japan, the day before our eighth wedding anniversary, I knew I had to define what this fresh start in Virginia meant to me. I had to devise a plan, but before I could do that, I had to figure out what I wanted, which path in this crossroads I wanted to take.

Because the life waiting at the end of this flight would either change everything or nothing at all. And I didn't know which I feared more.

The flight attendants performed their required safety speech, then buckled into their designated seats to prepare for takeoff. They had no idea that, as our plane gained altitude and the Japanese landscape disappeared beneath the clouds, I was debating whether I wanted to fight for my marriage.

PART 2

The End of the Beginning

CHAPTER 9

Virginia Is for Lovers

Virginia, 2008

"Prosper where you're planted."

That's what military spouses say about PCS'ing, a way of putting a positive spin on the frequent moves, especially to locations that weren't on their wish lists.

As we kicked off our tour in Virginia, that was the philosophy I hoped to cultivate. Every new destination was an opportunity for reinvention. When we moved to Pensacola, I vowed to portray myself as a more confident woman than I was in Tuscaloosa. When we departed for Japan, I wanted to be the adventurous mother I wasn't in Pensacola. Stepping off the airplane in Virginia, without another word about divorce, the one thing I knew for certain about my personal refresh was that I wanted Tristan by my side.

Although I never opened the birthday envelope, never confirmed Tristan's claim that divorce papers were inside, neither of us brought it up again. Maybe he had changed his mind. Maybe it had all been a grand gesture to induce change. Or maybe he was waiting until our move back to the States, where he could hire an attorney. I didn't know what he was thinking. And I was too scared to ask. And as we flew from Japan to Hawaii, and Tristan and Grady dozed alongside the other sleeping passengers, I stayed awake with a nearly ten-month-old Ava who didn't understand time zones. But I couldn't blame my restlessness on her. My brain was busy manifesting.

It was time to toss aside all my expectations about marriage. I was a thirty-two-year-old mother of two who couldn't rely on the romantic notion of eternal love to keep my family intact.

Marriage can't survive on love alone.

"Be patient," I thought as I listened to Tristan snore. We had four days in Hawaii as a mini vacation before getting back on a flight to our final destination, where Virginia would greet us with unknowns. But once we got settled, I could really focus on my marriage. After all, wasn't it a good sign that the state motto is "Virginia is for lovers"?

I decided to give it a month, a grace period to shake the jet lag, move into our house, and let Tristan adjust to his job. By the end of summer we'd be the couple I always thought we could be.

Japan was behind us. Virginia Beach was our blank slate.

***

When we pulled into the driveway of our new house in Virginia Beach, my nervous anticipation quickly transformed into shocked disappointment.

Greeting us wasn't a plush, neatly manicured lawn leading up to a bright, welcoming front door. The yard was an overgrown disaster area. The storm door was rotted and falling off.

The single-car garage door wouldn't stay open and threatened to fall on anyone walking under it.

The inside matched the exterior. The refrigerator sank into the kitchen floor. The banister on the stairs was breaking. The master bedroom looked too small to fit our king-sized bed. The closets were almost non-existent. While the online photos had revealed the dated decor and the premonitions that we'd soon be scraping off wallpaper, painting multiple rooms, and replacing the dilapidated backyard fence, I was wholly unprepared for the extent of the work this house needed.

"You're just tired," I thought. "Be the good Navy wife you're supposed to be. Adaptable. Optimistic. Resourceful. Energetic. And most of all, supportive. Tristan's military career is the priority. The military always comes first. Prosper where it plants you."

I could prosper. I knew I could. But not that day. I gave myself twenty-four hours to be upset. Tomorrow, I'd shrug off the jet lag and reset.

But the more time we spent in the house, the more issues we discovered. The drain in the kitchen leaked. The dishwasher died. The dryer cord didn't match the outlet. The thermostat on the air conditioner was broken. The electricity in Grady's room didn't work. I wrote lists as I unpacked, cleaned, and stored things in a house that had no storage, all while entertaining two young children.

Tristan fixed what he could and hired professionals to fix what he couldn't, but two weeks after our arrival, Tristan had to report to his new command. Alone with the kids, I constantly reminded myself that moves always presented challenges, that it was all part of the process of turning a house into a home.

Our first Fourth of July back in the US opened with promise. A neighbor invited us to a party and a viewing of the annual fireworks at Mount Trashmore, a nearby City of Virginia Beach park with a mountain created from a former landfill, which we could partially see from our backyard. But after the festivities and an early bedtime, a storm front moved in, and in the middle of the night I woke to the sound of hissing.

My eyes opened to see sparks flying out of the electrical outlet across from my bed. Panicked the house was about to go up in flames, I heard more hissing followed by sparks shooting out of an outlet in the bathroom.

Our air conditioner had been struck by lightning.

I was trying so hard to like our house, but all I could see were dollar signs. The following day I wrote a check to the electrician, who informed us that none of the outlets in the house were grounded, and another check to the HVAC company installing a new unit.

It didn't help my stress levels that we had to wait six weeks for our household goods delivery. When the final pack-in day arrived in mid-July, I practically kissed the moving truck. I couldn't wait to see our belongings. I couldn't wait for the nearly empty house to fill up with furniture and framed photographs and Japanese art and the familiar style of our family that had been trapped in a giant box for months. I couldn't wait for the waiting and the improvising and the discomfort to end.

No one enjoys pack-ins, but I'd been spoiled by both efficient Japanese movers and Navy spouses who understood the chaos and offered a wide range of assistance, from free babysitting services to meals. I had many moves under my belt, but our household goods delivery to Virginia Beach tested my limits as a military spouse.

The movers arrived early on a Friday morning, the same day Tristan attended a work-related social event. Because I had no friends yet to ask for help, ten-month-old Ava flopped around in a portable Pack 'n Play on our front lawn all day while four-year-old Grady watched too much television inside. Because I was the only adult monitoring the activity, I was the only person who noticed one of the movers was ill, giving him a lawn chair to rest in and glasses of water. With one mover out of commission, the process slowed.

I entered our guest bedroom seconds after those two remaining movers scratched our hardwood floors with our oversized dresser, the one the Japanese movers had to leave in the kitchen of our *cho* house three years earlier because it wouldn't fit through the stairwell, the dresser these movers decided was too heavy to lift across the room so they pushed.

By the time Tristan came home that evening, buzzing with the excitement of hanging out with his new coworkers, I was nonfunctional. The movers refused to unpack our boxes, a task included in their contract, but I was so tired I told them to leave. I was tired of a crying baby and a bored preschooler and the documentation I had to make of the damaged floor, the one beautiful thing in the house that these movers had managed to ruin. And I couldn't hide the resentment I felt toward my husband, who spent the day drinking beer with the guys while I dealt with to-do lists and parenting and reality.

This wasn't the fresh start I'd hoped for.

***

One of the primary duties of a military spouse is to understand and accept the hardships inherent in military life. Being a military spouse was more than a title; it was an entire identity.

Every Navy event I attended, every military officer I met, I was less myself and more Tristan's wife. Even when meeting other spouses, the introductory questions rarely included interest in who I was as a person. It was, "What does your husband do?" or "What command is your husband in?"

At first, I didn't mind living in the shadows. I wanted to support Tristan and his career, thankful for his steady employment, for his paychecks that provided for our family. But after exiting a community of close friendships and entering one where Tristan's job supported operations of an elite command he wasn't a member of, where not a single spouse welcomed me, I wondered if the shadows were enough for me. More importantly, I wondered if emerging from the shadows after all these years was even possible anymore, if the woman hidden in the darkness had the strength to move toward the light.

As I doled out a steady stream of self-blame for not being a proper military dependent, a title I despised, I also wondered when another deployment was coming.

Tristan warned me he'd likely deploy at least once during this three-year tour, and while the thought of him returning to the Middle East sickened me, I almost wished for the orders to come.

Selfishly, I wanted time to dip a toe outside the shadows. When he was home or preparing to leave, I was a military spouse performing my expected duties. But when he was gone, I could be someone other than Tristan's wife, someone other than a woman whose entire existence revolved around a man and his ambitions, someone other than the shell of a person I'd become.

***

My self-inflicted, month-long grace period came and went. Our dissonance persisted. The gripes we ignored remained unresolved, and the unresolved issues attracted other issues that collected and multiplied in a snowball effect.

Two months after our move to Virginia, Tristan once again told me he wanted a divorce.

What Divorce Talk Number Two lacked in shock value, it made up for in depth. Words wedged under the surface, anchoring in a place where hurt goes to hide. He didn't hold back. Neither did I. All of the thoughts I'd trapped inside in order to keep the peace, to maintain politeness, to avoid this very conversation, came spewing out. Our mutual dislike electrified the walls, our love for each other retreating to the dark corners of the bedroom, out of reach.

This Divorce Talk didn't wrap up with regrets and hugs and a snuggle in bed. We weren't relieved to hash out our unspoken truths. This sting lingered.

This second Divorce Talk ended not because we apologized but because we had to get dressed for a Hail and Farewell celebration. So, we simply stopped talking. One minute we were formulating child custody schedules, the next we were greeting the babysitter and driving to a party.

In the morning, we agreed to work on our marriage. We made general statements about listening more, being more patient. But the promises landed flat, more obligatory than heartfelt. Days passed with no mention of real steps. Tristan's demanding job had him leaving early and coming home late. I had to stock up on groceries at the commissary, take the kids to the clinic at Joint Expeditionary Base Little Creek for physicals, and wait for contractors to fix one piece of our house after another.

Life was too busy to dig deeper into the details of what working on our marriage even meant, let alone do the actual work.

"I have no life," I wrote in my journal. "I have no support, no help. I'm sad, angry. I've lost my identity. I don't even know where Heather is anymore. I am ALONE."

I wasn't prospering where I was planted.

Virginia Beach boasted a large military population, and it seemed every other person I came in contact with had some affiliation with the military. I befriended mothers on the playground of Grady's preschool, many of whom were also Navy spouses, but I still missed Japan, still missed the fishbowl, still couldn't find my footing.

The longer we'd lived on base in Japan, the more claustrophobic I'd felt, and the more I couldn't wait to leave it behind. But as months went by in Virginia, and Tristan's travel schedule sent him to Spain, California, DC, and Rhode Island, and our home repair list grew instead of shortened, I longed for that fishbowl I'd wanted to escape. I longed for someone to ring the doorbell and offer a playdate with my kids. I longed for a calendar filled with social events and a list of teenage military brats in walking distance who babysat. I longed for that readily available companionship. I longed for that tight-knit community. I longed for an invasion of my privacy.

I longed for anything other than this loneliness.

CHAPTER 10

Glimpsing Myself

At home, we largely operated in a state of avoidance. We didn't call it the "silent treatment." We just conveniently found places to be that didn't include each other.

That's how my passion for running reintroduced itself. The local YMCA offered free childcare, and as long as the staff had a phone number to call in case of emergencies and we stayed close enough to return quickly, we could trade treadmills for outdoor runs. I was there almost daily.

My workouts soon transitioned into training for the Turkey Trot, an annual 5k race on Thanksgiving Day. As I built up my mileage, my excitement built as well, knowing Tristan would be home for Thanksgiving, knowing he would be at the finish line with the kids, maybe even holding up a motivating sign like other family members did.

When I completed the 5k, I spotted him, not standing near the finish line cheering me on like the other friends and family of the hundreds of runners, but sitting in the car. Days later, I couldn't shake the image of him reading a book in the driver's seat, not even bothering to watch me finish an event that was special to me. I'd stood by his side for nearly a decade of marriage, following along wherever the Navy sent him, coping with his absences, thrust into the job of military spouse, and he couldn't get out of the car.

After the race, I slid into the passenger seat and Tristan drove us home. There were no congratulations, no questions about my race time or age group finish. It was as if Tristan had simply picked up an acquaintance who needed a ride.

I barely spoke to him the rest of the day, barely tasted the Thanksgiving spread I had spent hours cooking on wobbly, race-sore legs. I had nothing to say, or at least nothing productive. I wasn't sure he even understood why I was upset. What I did know was if I mentioned the race, if I hinted at my disappointment in his lack of support, I risked opening old wounds, risked popping the fragile bubble of rage I hid deep inside because of my fear of the next Divorce Talk.

That night, as I claimed fatigue and crawled into bed alone, my brain was wide awake and plotting. "Do something," it said. "You can't live like this. The reset button you thought you pushed is broken. Nothing has changed. Make change."

I knew then I needed to stop fearing the next Divorce Talk. I needed to expect it.

***

As Christmas approached, I took the kids to Arkansas for a family reunion that included my parents, my brother Kurt and his family, aunts, uncles, cousins, and my aging grandparents. There was talk of TAD—Temporary Additional Duty—travel overlapping with the reunion, but when that got canceled, I assumed Tristan would buy last-minute plane tickets and join us. He didn't.

The kids and I returned home a few days later. Tristan announced he had a surprise for me. He was practically giddy as he led me upstairs to our bedroom, urging me to close my eyes so he could present our unrecognizable bathroom. I'm sure most wives would have been thrilled with a surprise bathroom renovation. I was not one of them.

I stared at our tiny bathroom that he had gutted while I was away. Nearly everything had been replaced, from the decorative mirror to the pedestal sink, eliminating the only storage we'd once had in the cramped space. Everything about the updates screamed Tristan's tastes, which never quite meshed with mine. Not only did I hate it, but his expectation that I would love it made me wonder how a person who'd known me for a decade could know so little about me. I didn't want a renovated bathroom. I wanted him at my family reunion.

I pretended I liked it, but my real feelings were obvious. My reaction sparked his reaction.

"You're ungrateful, Heather."

"I worked really hard on this, Heather."

"I spent all weekend doing nothing but this, Heather."

Maybe I was ungrateful. Maybe I should have praised his do-it-yourself skills. He put a lot of hard work into this project. But as I cleaned up the dust and dirty tools he'd left scattered around the bathroom that no longer had a closing door or a functioning shower, as I made space in the kids' bathroom for my hair dryer, makeup, lotions, and tampons that were rendered homeless, I silently fumed.

I lived with a stranger. This man I called my partner wasn't just on a different page than me, but in a different book in a different genre. How could he not know I didn't want to burn money we didn't have on a new bathroom we didn't need when our electrical wiring still wasn't fixed? How could he not anticipate that I would want to have input in a home renovation? How could he not see that our marriage was anything but a partnership?

A week later, a routine spat about something inconsequential after Tristan's command Christmas party finally exploded my bubble that had been building since Thanksgiving. I couldn't listen to his voice a second longer. Inhaling every ounce of calm energy I could muster, I locked eyes with him and said, "I can't take this anymore."

Tristan told me again he wanted a divorce, and for two hours we argued about the same issues we always argued about. It baffled both of us how no progress had been made, how stale our marriage remained.

One thing had changed though. Unlike the first two Divorce Talks, this time I conceded.

Instead of suggesting counseling, instead of convincing both of us that our marriage was worth fighting for by arranging more quality time together, by trying to be a more active military spouse, by making stronger efforts at communication, I agreed we should split up.

"Let's pull the trigger," I said. "Let's get divorced."

We mutually decided to remain civil through the holidays for the sake of the kids and then make it to his deployment that we learned would be in May. At that point I would take the kids to my parents' house in Florida for a trial separation. We even started a list dividing our possessions. It was happening.

A wave of emotions caught up with me and I let the tears fall freely.

“Why are you so upset?” he asked.

I was too choked up to answer.

“I don’t think you’re crying because you would miss being married to me,” he said. “I think you’re crying because you’re scared of change.”

I didn’t respond because he was right. His life wouldn’t change a whole lot if we got divorced. He’d continue to go to work every day and move every three years with the Navy. My life on the other hand would flip upside down. I’d not only be raising two kids on my own, but I’d have to secure a full-time job. He’d be a bachelor earning a comfortable salary. I’d be a broke single mom living with her parents. Of course I was terrified of that kind of change.

But fear of change wasn’t a good reason to stay in a marriage with a husband who didn’t love me anymore. Or one I didn’t love either.

* * *

We maintained civility for a couple of weeks, polite as college roommates who just needed to get through the school year before going separate ways. In the holiday spirit, we poured some drinks, laughing and reminiscing while wrapping Christmas presents for the kids, the surprising ease offering a glimmer of hope that if we could find our way back to being friends again, then maybe our love would follow. There seemed to be an unspoken agreement that maybe we’d try again. Perhaps reverting back to basics was the solution.

But Divorce Talk Number Four materialized mere days later between the thin walls of Tristan’s family house in the mountains, his parents and our children unfortunate witnesses.

There were no tears. I didn't seem to have any left. Four Divorce Talks in seven months. I was numb.

Repetition had stripped the word "divorce" of all significance.

Back at home, we fell back into our avoidance routine as the year ended and another one introduced itself with question marks. The energy in our house drained me, emotional baggage crushing me into helplessness. I scribbled a list of New Year's resolutions, not out of optimism, but pragmatism. I had to take stock of every facet of my life. I had to prepare.

Because divorce was not a matter of if, but when.

* * *

I needed something in my life that was just for me.

Topping my list of resolutions was a renewed career focus. I listed all the necessary steps to obtain my Virginia teaching certification, and along with my friend Tracey, who'd also moved to Virginia Beach from Sasebo and was in the same teaching boat as I was, purchased a study guide and signed up for my first of three exams.

For two months, Tracey and I studied together, and after the kids went to bed, I studied on my own. I had hustled to earn my master's degree, and it bothered me that I'd never used it. Maybe a job in a classroom would provide the fulfillment I craved.

That process would take at least a year, so in the meantime I searched for other methods of self-improvement. I exercised more, expanding my workouts beyond running and incorporating swimming, weightlifting, and spin classes. I applied for a teaching job at Grady's preschool, and although I didn't get it, I occasionally stepped in as a substitute teacher. I kept a gratitude journal and set a goal to smile more.

I was willing to try anything to find myself again.

But my list of personal improvements seemed endless, leading me to believe, once again, that our marriage troubles were all my fault.

* * *

By the time I took my first Praxis teaching exam in March, Tristan had been back and forth to Indiana, Spain, California, Michigan twice, and the Middle East. The trips were usually a short week or two each, but the cumulative time apart was adding up. And the transitions before and after the trips ate up time that could have been better spent figuring out how to end our vicious cycle of uncertainty in our marriage.

The repeated trips exacerbated our already established communication difficulties. When I heard the garage door open, announcing he was home from work, a dark cloud would envelop me. I never relaxed around him, the Divorce Talks putting me perpetually on the defensive.

Tristan frequently asked me if I was depressed. I frequently said no. One day he asked a follow-up question: "If you're not depressed, then are you happy?"

"Of course I'm happy," I answered.

But was I? I was happy when I socialized with the few friends I had in Virginia Beach. I was happy when I communicated online with friends not in Virginia Beach. I was happy when I exercised. I was happy when Ava giggled, when Grady beamed with pride after learning a new skill in preschool.

But I wasn't happy when I was with Tristan.

There were snippets of happiness. Like one night when we put the kids to bed and lounged on our patio with a couple of beers and talked about our visions for the house that still wasn't a home to me. And another weekend morning when I woke up to discover he'd gotten up early to cook a family breakfast while I slept in. But those moments were rare and short-lived. We didn't follow through on those visions for the house. And after that breakfast, I had to clean up the mess he left in the kitchen.

I thought spouses were supposed to be best friends. But Tristan wasn't my best friend. He wasn't my friend at all.

CHAPTER 11

The D Word on Repeat

When Divorce Talk Number Five rolled around at the end of April, four months after the previous one, I didn't know what else I could do to improve the relationship. It takes two people to get married. It takes two people to get divorced. And it takes two people to put in the effort in between.

The day after number five, Tristan spoke with a divorce attorney, learning that in the state of Virginia, a couple with children was required to be legally separated for an entire year before a divorce could be finalized. However, we could still live together as long as we testified in court that we'd been sleeping in separate rooms.

He started sleeping in the guest room that night. I didn't try to stop him. And when I closed the door of our bedroom to sleep alone, I realized each Divorce Talk had shoved us further along the road to actually going through with it.

***

My thirty-third birthday rolled around while Tristan was on a trip. My new military spouse friends, Colleen and Shannon, surprised me on a McDonald's playdate with cupcakes, saying they empathized with the disappointment of celebrating a big day without my husband and they wanted to cheer me up. What they didn't know was that I wasn't missing my husband. I wasn't blowing out birthday candles wishing he was with me. All I wanted for my birthday was a day free from drama and arguing, questioning and ruminating, stewing and bitterness, a guarantee I could only get if he was gone.

But I didn't tell my friends that. I nodded, agreeing that it sucked how much our husbands traveled, how much of our lives they missed, how I was sure Tristan would come home with an extravagant gift to compensate for his untimely absence.

I didn't tell my friends that I was relieved Tristan had no gift for me, that the last birthday present he had given me was an envelope of divorce papers, that I feared every birthday going forward would leave me riddled with angst as I tried to purge the memories of my thirty-second birthday.

I didn't tell my friends that I would much rather spend my thirty-third birthday with them, chasing after our young children and plucking discarded chicken nuggets off the McDonald's floor, than be with my husband, whose interactions with me were more jarring and unpredictable than our toddler's tantrums.

And I didn't tell my friends that the only reason Tristan moved back into our bedroom when he returned a few days later was because his parents came to visit, that they were staying in the guest room where Tristan had been sleeping, that we were hiding our marital problems from them as well, that

Tristan sleeping anywhere other than our bedroom would raise red flags we weren't ready to explain.

Yet we still had moments when everything temporarily clicked back into place, like the Lego towers Grady built before knocking them over and rebuilding them into a fresh masterpiece. Occasionally, the time we spent apart altered our perspectives, and brought us closer together.

I picked Tristan up from the airport after his latest two-week trip not knowing which version would get into the passenger seat of my car. Would it be the Tristan who slept in the guest room, testing the waters of a separation? Or would it be the Tristan who missed me, who thought the idea of separating was irrational?

Neither of us seemed armed for a fight. In fact, it was a simple smile and a reach for a hand to hold at a red light that melted us both. What was wrong with us? We had a life most would envy. Our love spanned over a decade. We created two beautiful, healthy children. We owned a house and had money in the bank. The only roadblock getting in the way of us was us.

Maybe we'd spent too much time reacting instead of interacting, stuck in a merry-go-round, spinning until we lost sight of each other. We forgot to interlace fingers throughout the journey. We forgot what made us fall in love. We forgot to continue getting to know one another through the changes that life and age infused in us. We forgot to interact. We only knew how to react, and those reactions had grown into bad habits.

During that car ride home, we clasped hands at the stoplight and didn't let go until we pulled into our driveway. We talked and listened to one another. To react differently, we agreed we both needed to act differently. This car ride home from the airport was a breakthrough.

The next day, Robert, one of Tristan's friends from college, mailed him a dollar bill. Confused, Tristan asked what it was for. Robert reminded him that back in 1998, Tristan had bet him a dollar he was going to marry me. For some reason, Robert decided to pay Tristan for the bet he'd lost years ago.

"Don't you think that's symbolic?" I asked Tristan.

"Why?"

"It means we aren't meant to get divorced," I said. "Can you imagine if Robert sent you that dollar because you claimed all those years ago you were going to marry me only for you to have to return it and admit we're splitting up?"

Tristan shrugged and stuffed the cash in his pocket. He didn't believe in signs. And I probably wasn't making sense. But I needed a sign. At that moment, a week before our ninth wedding anniversary, at that precarious juncture in our marriage, I needed that dollar bill as a sign to stay hopeful.

* * *

After the appearance of the dollar, the remnants of the last Divorce Talk seemed to evaporate along with the four previous ones.

Tristan planned date nights, and my old self returned. I put on lipstick, grabbed that cute dress hidden in the back of my closet, and let the babysitter worry about the kids' bedtime routine.

The popular Irish pub Keagan's became our go-to bar in Virginia Beach. Though we were practically a generation older than the evening crowd, it was close to home and local bands played good live music.

On one summer date night at Keagan's, Tristan spotted a group of Navy SEALs he knew drinking beer at a table near the entrance. They waved Tristan over, and the men introduced themselves. I didn't want to socialize with strangers on our date, especially because I was the designated driver and the only person at the table ordering water, but Tristan was already deep in conversation.

While he chatted with the SEAL beside him, the man across the table shifted his attention to me, sharing it was one of his last nights out before a deployment to an undisclosed location. As our conversation continued, he leaned in closer, and I sensed this guy might actually be flirting with me.

"That can't be," I thought. "I'm misreading this." I'm a thirty-something, Volvo station wagon-driving mommy. He was a young, attractive man who knew that every woman in that bar longed to be sitting in my seat.

Navy SEALs are uber fit, mysterious, and exude confidence. The air of secrecy surrounding their missions and movements makes them inherently intriguing, and their qualifications and selections into such an elite club classify them as real-life superheroes. It was laughable to entertain the ridiculous notion that this Superman would waste his time flirting with me.

But he *was* flirting.

And I liked it.

"You should come home with me tonight," he said. He was dead serious. Shocked by his audacity, I giggled like a middle school girl talking to her crush.

"You do know I'm married, right?" I said. "And my husband is sitting next to me?"

"I do know that," he said. "And I think you should come home with me tonight instead of going home with him."

"Oh yeah? Why would I do that?"

"Because I see you," he said, leaning in even closer. "And your husband doesn't."

"What makes you say that?" I wasn't giggling anymore.

"I'm openly flirting with you with your husband sitting right next to you," he said. "And he hasn't looked over at you a single time since we started talking."

I glanced at Tristan, who was so engrossed in his discussion that, while another man was asking me to leave the bar with him, he'd moved his chair farther away from me to be closer to the other SEALs at the table.

Tristan once told me that somewhere in the years that passed, I stopped seeing him.

"You don't even notice when I get a haircut," he'd said.

I had laughed because it was absurd. Of course, I noticed when he got a haircut. How could I miss the high and tights he got at the barber shop on base, the haircuts that once startled me with their severity when he first joined the military?

"You laugh," he'd said. "But tell me, when was the last time I got a haircut?"

I couldn't answer. I had no idea. There was once a time when I could spot a fresh high and tight the instant he walked in the door. But at that moment, I couldn't fathom a guess as to when he last visited the barber shop.

I didn't see his haircuts. But he didn't see me either. He didn't see how chiseled my muscles were from my mornings at the YMCA. I couldn't name the titles of the books he was reading. He couldn't tally the movies I wanted to see. The list went on. Like roommates sharing a space rather than husband and wife sharing a life, we were merely coexisting.

The hot Navy SEAL continued flirting with me until Tristan scooted his chair over and joined our conversation. After asking about the man's impending deployment, Tristan bragged that I assemble great care packages.

"I love care packages," the SEAL said, his eyes locked on mine. "You should send me one."

"Absolutely!" Tristan answered for me. "Give her your email so you can send your mailing address once you have one."

As Tristan finished his beer and flagged the waitress for the check, the SEAL scribbled his email address on a cocktail napkin and slipped it across the table. Our fingertips touched as I took the napkin, his gaze unwavering and burning through my soul, my husband still oblivious.

This is what it felt like to be seen.

"Hey man, we're gonna take off." Tristan stood up and shook the SEAL's hand. I stood too, zipping the napkin inside my purse.

"Nice to meet you," I said as Tristan walked toward the door.

"Email me," the SEAL said. "Maybe I'll see you when I get back."

This man sparked something inside me. It wasn't lust or desire. It was the resurgence of a memory, a glimpse of the woman I once was. I used to be audacious too. I used to have things to say that others found interesting. I used to be a woman worthy of being seen.

I followed Tristan to the exit, but turned around to steal one last look. The SEAL watched me, smirking. I smiled in return, holding eye contact a beat longer than I probably should have. When I turned to leave, Tristan was already outside, the door closing in my face because he hadn't held it open for me, hadn't noticed I was no longer behind him.

That night at home, as Tristan brushed his teeth and got ready for bed, I took the cocktail napkin with the SEAL's email address out of my purse and placed it face down in the corner of the top drawer of my nightstand. I had no intention of emailing him, and I never did. But for months to come, every time I opened that drawer and saw the napkin, I was reminded that one night a man saw me. And being seen as a woman by a man reminded me what it felt like to feel attractive, alive, visible.

* * *

By August, we'd been in Virginia Beach for over a year, and it was beginning to feel like home. But with its sixth sense of knowing when a family is getting too comfortable in its stability, the military stepped in to mix things up.

A deployment to Iraq was happening. And then it wasn't. And then it was. And then it wasn't. I couldn't keep up with the fluctuations, telling Tristan I didn't want to hear about the updates until he had orders in hand.

When the deployment seemed set for April, I planned a trip to Florida to see my parents in June when Grady's preschool ended. But then the deployment was pushed to June, switching my trip to July. I was finalizing my itinerary when the deployment was postponed to August. With Grady starting kindergarten in September, I couldn't wait much longer to travel with a wide-open summer schedule. Finally, after months of pivots, after his bags were packed and I booked my plane tickets, the deployment was canceled altogether.

I wasn't surprised when Tristan chose not to join us for at least part of the two weeks the kids and I would be in Florida, and the trip without him became a miniature version of the separation we'd anticipated. I also hoped my time away with the kids would nudge him to appreciate me a little more, to experience what it felt like to be the one left behind instead of the one leaving.

I didn't miss him while in Florida. He didn't seem to miss me either. He called for Ava's birthday, but otherwise we rarely bothered to communicate, the ability to pick up a phone at will a luxury we had once desperately craved during his first deployment but that now seemed unnecessary and borderline irritating.

I dreaded returning to Virginia Beach, wishing I could walk into an empty house instead of the unpredictable one waiting for me. As it turned out, my feelings of dread were validated.

Two days after my return, right before his promotion ceremony, Tristan and I got into an argument. Our mutual silent treatment was surely evident to all the high-ranking officers at the event, as well as his family at the dinner afterward. Two days after that, I ran a half marathon, a race I'd trained diligently for, causing yet another resentment, yet another race Tristan neglected to attend. Less than a week after that, I told him I wanted a divorce.

***

I blamed Divorce Talk Number Six on a turkey sandwich.

It was a warm Saturday evening in September, and Tristan spontaneously invited multiple neighbors to come over with their children. I wasn't expecting company. I had no food to offer our guests. And I wasn't in the mood to entertain.

Before noticing the growing crowd in our backyard, I made myself a sandwich. I was starving and couldn't wait to eat that sandwich. The end of a hectic day of parenting young kids was approaching, and I deserved a turkey sandwich.

As if in slow motion, as that sandwich sat on the kitchen counter unguarded for the half a minute it took me to walk to the fridge for a drink, Tristan appeared and snatched the plate.

"Oh great, food!" he said. "Our guests are hungry."

He gave my sandwich to guests I didn't know were coming. It was just a sandwich, but really it wasn't.

I avoided interacting with Tristan until our last guest left, and then a pressure valve flew open and released everything trapped inside me.

It had been five months since our last Divorce Talk. This time, I was the one sleeping in the guest room. This time, Tristan called his family to tell them our marriage was over. This time, no tears fell. This time, my anger formulated an escape route. As I mentally packed my suitcases, I fell asleep to the rhythm of my new mantra: I refuse to live like this.

But I did live like that. For three more years.

CHAPTER 12

Riding the Roller Coaster

When I least expected it, the self-fulfillment I had been seeking ended up finding me. And it came in the form of a blog.

It was 2010, and I'd never read a blog before. But when Tristan's mother bought me a cookbook for Christmas, she sparked a vision that grabbed ahold of me and wouldn't let go.

"The author made a resolution to use her slow cooker every day for a year and then wrote about the challenge on a blog," my mother-in-law explained as I flipped through *Make It Fast, Cook It Slow* by Stephanie O'Dea.

"You should start a blog," Tristan's mom said.

"Really?" I said. "I don't know anything about blogging. What would I even write about?"

"What about a blog about being a military spouse during a deployment?" she suggested. We'd just learned that Tristan's previously canceled deployment was back on, and he was leaving on January 11. The timing was right.

As we wrapped up the holidays at the family house in the mountains and road-tripped home to begin preparations for the deployment, I couldn't stop brainstorming about my future blog.

With renewed confidence, I taught myself what to do. I followed the lead of Stephanie O'Dea's slow cooker challenge and focused the blog on trying something new every day, with being a military spouse as my backdrop (beyond the deployment).

Knee-deep in researching military spouse blogs, I found something I wasn't seeking: connection with other women going through exactly what I was.

I compiled a list of activities to try, tasks that were realistic to achieve as a mother with two young kids and a deployed husband. From taking a Zumba class to attending a local writers' group to simply watching a movie with my kids without multitasking, I would focus on one to-do a day and then write about it.

"Military life is a roller coaster ride," I wrote in my introductory post. "It is jolting and unpredictable and breathtaking. And sometimes it makes you want to throw up. Because I won't be getting off this ride anytime soon, I need to find ways to stay grounded. This brings me to the reason for creating this blog. I need distractions. Distractions from those late-night phone calls, unexpected separations, missed holidays and misplaced and unironed uniforms. Therefore, I am going to challenge myself to do something new every day."

On January 11, less than three weeks after the initial spark of an idea, the *Riding the Roller Coaster* blog officially launched.

***

At first no one read the blog but family. Tristan wanted me to write anonymously and avoid sharing personal photos, in part to protect our family's privacy, in part because of the OPSEC rule not to publicly disclose details of service members' jobs and missions. I referred to myself as Roller Coaster, my identity a secret to any reader who stumbled upon my little corner of the internet.

One military spouse blog led me to another and another after that. I was stunned. An entire online community was available at my fingertips. When my daily posts were published, and the kids were in bed, I read those blogs voraciously. I devoured their experiences, their heartaches, their struggles, their advice, their lives they were choosing to share with complete candor. These women were living the military life. This was my village.

And it was true what tutorials advised: The more you comment on other blogs, the more likely those bloggers are to visit yours and comment back. I felt like I was chatting with women all over the world who empathized with me, whether they were cursing Murphy's Law for their car that broke down during a deployment or praying they'd be able to get a job before their next PCS move. I may not have been meeting up with these women for coffee or playdates, but I considered them my friends, nonetheless.

Within two months of blogging, I had a hundred followers. Within three months I was looking into freelance writing beyond my blog. Within four months I attended a military blogging conference in Washington, DC, with Jane, a friend I'd met in Grady's playgroup in Japan. Now that she lived in Virginia Beach as well, she worked with Blue Star Families, an organization that advocates for military families.

By then I'd passed all the requisite exams, received my Virginia state teacher certification, and completed an online application for the City of Virginia Beach public schools. But there were no job openings whatsoever in the local elementary schools. I checked the city website daily, I called individual schools, and I even considered substitute teaching before calculating that I'd never earn enough money subbing to justify the cost of childcare.

I still pursued teaching positions as I composed blog posts, but my priorities switched direction. I created Facebook and Twitter pages as my Roller Coaster persona. I accepted an offer to write a weekly column for Blue Star Families under my blog name, and soon after that I signed a contract for a paid gig to write a five-piece series on a PBS blog about military issues.

I maintained anonymity, as I always had, always in the background of my husband's life and career, often wondering if I'd ever be able to write under my real name. I was itching to reveal my name to the world, but the most important part was the writing.

I had a voice. My own voice that others wanted to hear.

I finally felt heard.

***

The more blogs I discovered, the more I learned about different branches of the military and about the lives of enlisted families. Despite our diverse specifics regarding branches and our spouses' ranks, we all shared so many overlapping thoughts, fears, and disappointments that I was certain I'd never feel alone again.

But every now and then I came across blog posts that made me question how much I really wanted to know.

A week before Tristan left for deployment, a military spouse blogger I followed posted about the details of the recent knock on her door that we all dreaded but rarely talked about: the news of her husband's death in Afghanistan. For the next week, as Tristan and I counted down our time together, I thought about that young wife I'd never met but knew through her words. I imagined her opening her front door in slow motion to see the uniformed service members who were about to change her life forever. I imagined it like a scene in a movie that leaves me in a puddle of tears whenever I watch it, even though I know what's coming. I imagined this woman as I read her post again and again because I couldn't allow myself to imagine that in five, then four, then three, then two, then one more day I would be sending my own husband to the Middle East, that I could be the one falling to my knees on my doorstep with strangers consoling me, that I could be a wife one minute, a widow the next.

I didn't know any military widows. Reading that blog post made death suddenly very real. As I said goodbye to Tristan at the end of March, I couldn't help but think of that post, how that woman had no idea that, when she said goodbye to her husband, it would be the last time she'd ever see him alive. Would my goodbye be permanent? Would this be the last time I saw Tristan alive? Would I be writing a blog post about the knock on my door?

Our deployment goodbye was quiet, too quiet. There was no airport goodbye. No baby in a car seat. No spilled coffee on cell phones. No tears. This time he waved from his rental car and drove away. He called from his brief destination at Fort Bragg in North Carolina, and then the countdown to his return from Iraq began.

***

As my blog shifted from daily challenges to more military life-focused posts, the responses to my applications for teaching positions remained scarce. One day while dropping off a resume at a local preschool that included kindergarten, the director asked if I could interview right there on the spot.

Grady was in school, but I had Ava with me, unaware she'd be playing with train sets in the preschool's lobby while I sold myself as a teacher they should hire.

Like most job-hunting military spouses, I worried about the gap in my employment history on my resume, but I hoped that living in a highly populated military city meant this was a common occurrence and that employers made exceptions.

For that reason, I planned to bring up my husband's career and our overseas tour as an explanation for why I hadn't worked in several years. On the other hand, I wondered if I should avoid the topic altogether. If there were other qualified candidates who weren't military spouses, employers would likely prefer to hire one of them instead of someone like me, who would move in two to three years, quitting the job shortly after starting. It was times like these that I felt like I wasn't just married to someone in the military; I was also married to the military itself.

When the director asked how long my husband's tour was and I answered, I could see her doing the math in her head, mentally calculating if I was worth hiring. Even though I assured her my husband was only putting in for jobs in the Hampton Roads area so we could stay an additional two to three years, I'm sure she knew that was an empty promise.

A month later I was offered the job. Evidently, I was one of three women with teacher certifications and master's degrees vying for the same job that provided no benefits and a salary so low I couldn't have survived on my paycheck alone had I been single. But it was a job in my field where I had little experience after not working for years and after job hunting for six months. It was a gift, and I felt fortunate to call the job mine.

I had the summer to buy supplies and set up my classroom. Between the preparations to become a working mom, my writing, and a weeklong trip to Florida to visit my parents, the summer vanished, and Tristan's four-and-a-half-month deployment was over.

***

By early August when he rang our doorbell—once again a homecoming that involved no one but us—he'd missed my birthday, our tenth wedding anniversary, Grady's last day of kindergarten and entire baseball season, and the Fourth of July. Once again, we shuffled around reintegration issues, as I reacclimated to another adult in the house who no longer understood our schedule, and Tristan adjusted to cohabitating with three other people while fighting jet lag and a return to a job he hadn't done in five months.

Tristan's parents watched the kids so we could privately enjoy a short vacation in Jamaica, and then I joined the workforce after being a stay-at-home mom for nearly six years. Life in our house was changing, and for the first time in years, the change was because of me, not because of Tristan, not because of the Navy.

Between my writing and my teaching job, I was gradually emerging from Tristan's shadow, proving I was my own person and not just his wife. I was still getting to know this woman blossoming inside me, but already I was certain I had to do everything in my power to convince her to stay.

CHAPTER 13

Love Languages

Two weeks after my first day as a teacher, Tristan left for Afghanistan.

It was a short trip, not quite a month. We had no countdowns for his departure or homecoming, the trip so unexpected I didn't have time to freak out. He'd been on longer trips in the past to random, safe locations so I tricked myself into thinking of this as three weeks in Spain or San Diego or any spot on the world map with a US military base, any base other than the one he went to.

I was still embracing my denial about Tristan's whereabouts when a breaking news ticker flashed on the television in the waiting room of the Volvo dealership where my car was getting serviced. A helicopter crash. In Afghanistan.

Panic punched me in the gut. Tristan never told me details about his locations, travel routes, or duties when he was in the Middle East. Not before or during the deployments because of OPSEC, and not after his return because he seemed uncomfortable when I asked, and I felt uncomfortable when he answered.

But at that moment in the Volvo dealership, I knew Tristan was in Afghanistan and I knew he sometimes traveled via helicopter.

Hours passed as news outlets heightened my fears. Nine US service members were killed in the crash in Zabul Province in southern Afghanistan. Some of those service members were Navy. It was the deadliest helicopter crash for coalition forces in four years.

The military wouldn't release the names of the deceased until family members were notified, until loved ones got the knocks on their doors. So as afternoon faded into darkness, I forced myself to attempt to sleep despite listening for a knock. My mind raced. Would the ombudsman who checked in on me once when Tristan was in Iraq call me if our guys were involved in the crash? Would the command give me a heads-up to expect bad news or was the knock on the door the heads-up?

I was in a fuzzy half slumber when my phone rang at 1:50 a.m.

"I thought you were dead," I said when I heard Tristan's tired voice.

"I figured you saw the news," he said. "But I'm okay."

"I love you," I whispered.

"I love you too." I truly believed we both meant it.

Our conversation was over in seconds. I couldn't remember the last time I so desperately wished he was home.

As I tossed and turned the rest of the night, wondering what kind of chaos Tristan was living through in the aftermath of the crash, worrying about his mental state after such a tragedy, I realized I missed him so acutely my body ached. The fear that I'd lost him triggered a need for him that had been dormant a long time.

I also realized a year had passed since our last Divorce Talk. Had we finally figured out our marriage? Had we found the magic marriage formula? Had the positive changes in my life led to positive changes in our marriage?

Was I really the problem all along?

* * *

I got the answers to those questions weeks later when Tristan and I participated in a marriage retreat.

The weekend getaway, held at an indoor water park and resort, was for service members and their spouses in Tristan's command and run by an organization called FOCUS. The purpose of FOCUS—Families OverComing Under Stress—was to help families cope with the demands of deployments, providing resiliency training with a family-centered approach. I'd never heard of FOCUS going into this "Reintegration Retreat," but I entered with an open mind. Tristan and I still hadn't made our way to marriage counseling, and I hoped we could gather some insight in this group setting, find other couples struggling with the same things we struggled with, and get advice from professionals without openly sharing our own vulnerabilities.

With our kids occupied in the free childcare, Tristan and I attended seminars like "Refreshing Your Connection," "Reconnecting Your Communication," "Family Dynamics," and "Problem Solving," workshops that focused on reintegration after deployment. We left with handouts on "Family Reunion and Reintegration Strategies" and "Resources for Military Families," and handbooks called *Strengthening Long Distance Relationships* and *250 Activities to Help Your Children Stay Connected to Their Long Distance Mom or Dad.* I took meticulous notes on the deployment spiral (each deployment affects each subsequent deployment), parenting and reintegration (readjustments may take weeks or months to enjoy being together), and managing expectations (are my expectations of reintegration realistic?).

I tried to take in all the information, relieved to learn I wasn't alone in some of my feelings after Tristan's return from deployments and extended trips. Military spouses tend to have this romantic notion that after hitting pause on our marriages on day one of deployment, we can push the play button when they return as if nothing happened. I always thought everything would fall back into place, that we could pick up where we left off, as if the marriage had simply hibernated.

But that's not how reintegration works. Deployments affect everyone involved, sometimes in minor ways, sometimes in significant ways. It's normal to struggle to get back into routines. It's normal to struggle to reconnect. It's normal to struggle to be patient. It's normal to struggle.

While the reintegration seminars reassured me, another more general exercise opened my eyes wider to hidden cracks in our marriage that weren't so normal.

The exercise was based on Gary Chapman's book, *The 5 Love Languages: The Secret to Love That Lasts.* I was instantly fascinated by the author's theory of five distinct love languages, or ways couples express and accept love, and how, as partners, we help fill our spouse's emotional tank.

The instructor passed out worksheets detailing each love language and after a brief discussion, we crafted two lists, covering our notepads so our spouses couldn't see. One list was the love languages in the order we want to be shown love. The other was a list of the love languages in the order we believe our partner wants to be shown love. When everyone finished, we flipped our lists over to compare them to our partners' lists.

If this was a test, Tristan and I failed. Miserably.

As we studied the lists, I first noticed our list of preferred love languages couldn't have been more different. But as the instructor noted, that in and of itself isn't a problem. Couples don't need to have identical love languages. The problems arise in the second red flag I noticed. His ranking of my love languages was completely wrong, and my ranking of his love languages was completely wrong. We were speaking different languages.

We proved the point of the love languages. Our problem may not have been our individual differences. Our problem was that neither of us was being loved the way we wanted to be loved.

How could he have no idea that my most prevalent love language was acts of service? How could he not know by now that he could fill my emotional tank by relieving some of my burden, by washing the dishes after dinner, by taking the kids to the park when I needed quiet time to input grades on my students' report cards?

How could he have no idea that my least preferred love language was gift giving? How could he not know by now that I didn't want extravagant gifts, that not only was I not impressed but my awareness of our budget caused me to stress out about expensive gifts?

But my inattention to Tristan's love languages was unsettling as well. I suspected his list wouldn't match up with mine, but somehow, I was still falling short on what he needed from me to fill his emotional tank.

We were both missing the target. And we both resented each other for it.

We hadn't figured out our marriage. We hadn't found the magic marriage formula. And while the personal changes I made might have improved our relationship, they didn't fix it.

I wasn't the problem. We both were.

With those questions answered, another one presented itself. Now that we possessed this insight into our behaviors, what were we going to do about it?

***

If my preferred love language was acts of service, then my second was words of affirmation.

On a surface level, this meant I wanted Tristan to communicate that he loved, appreciated, and respected me. On a deeper, more specific level, this meant I wanted him to express his support for me and my endeavors as equally as I supported him and his.

This wasn't an epiphany. This issue went back years, maybe back to the first twinkles of our courtship when we were young and discovering each other, whispering cheap beer-induced secrets and dreams. His dreams always appeared larger than mine, his aspirations manifesting successes that far surpassed my visions. In the grand scheme of how our society defines success, it made sense on paper that I would support him. He wanted to be an officer in the Navy. I wanted to be an elementary school teacher. He would always make more money than I would; he would always have a flashier job title.

While, in the past, I had asked him to encourage me as I focused on my studies in grad school or to cheer me on at races I ran, my unfulfilled need for him to be my loudest cheerleader was never more evident than when my writing started opening doors, big doors I never imagined I'd get close enough to unlock.

I think at this point, Tristan understood something in me had shifted, and in the only way he knew how, he expressed that he was proud of me, that he respected the hard work behind my accomplishments. At first. But when we got into a fight over my name, it sunk in that I had to be my own loudest cheerleader. Because my husband never would be.

***

When a friend from Blue Star Families told me a *New York Times* reporter had requested an interview with a military spouse blogger for a quote in an article he was writing about the DC conference, which I had attended for the second time, and that she had passed along my name, I could barely contain myself. Ignoring my imposter syndrome voice mocking me that no *New York Times* reporter could possibly care what I had to say, I answered his questions with the poise I imagined real writers projected. When he said he was the managing editor of *The New York Times' At War* blog and suggested I write for him, I hid my shock as I promised to send him a pitch. I was invited to write for *The New York* freaking *Times*. This was a big deal.

Two days later, the article in which I was quoted appeared on page A14 of the print edition. It was May 2, 2011, the same day the front-page headline screamed in block letters "Osama bin Laden Killed by US Forces in Pakistan."

Not wanting this high of recognition to fade, not wanting this editor to forget me, I frantically formulated a workable idea for my pitch. In between a round of back and forths with drafts and revisions, he asked me if I wanted to be interviewed on NPR about being a military spouse blogger. I'd never done anything like that before, but I pushed through my nerves and said yes. If I wanted to have a voice, I needed to use it.

I was still psyching myself up for the interview and practicing key points when the NPR contact called me to cancel. They were going with a blogger who wasn't anonymous. I lost the opportunity to speak on NPR because I didn't write under my real name.

As an added setback, when the editing process was complete on what I considered the most important piece I'd ever written and I was a signed contract away from seeing my first *New York Times* byline, my name once again posed a problem.

"By the way," the editor emailed. "I can't run your piece under a pseudonym. We only run real names."

The anonymity I originally viewed as mildly annoying was now a huge hindrance. It killed an opportunity with NPR. But I refused to let it ruin my chances of a byline at one of the most coveted publications in the world.

When I told Tristan I no longer wanted to write anonymously, it, of course, caused an argument.

"I understand the need for OPSEC," I argued. "I understand your desire to keep your coworkers in the military from connecting you to my blog. I understand you want privacy for our family. But this is important to me. There has to be a way to compromise."

Compromise wasn't one of our strengths. I wanted to scream, "This is MY career, not yours. This is MY passion, not yours. This is MY decision, not yours. This is MY make-or-break moment, not yours."

As adamant as he was that I write under an alias, I was just as adamant in my refusal to go back to the editor with my tail between my legs and pull the piece.

"What about using your first and middle name?" Tristan suggested. "Your middle name could pass as a last name, right?"

It was a terrible idea, but I emailed the editor anyway, asking if that would fly. Not surprisingly, the editor said no. It was still considered a pen name.

Back to the drawing board.

"Tell me again why I can't use my maiden name?" I asked Tristan. The ever-patient editor mentioned that lots of female writers go that route. But Tristan shot it down.

"Anyone with access to Google could connect me to you even with your maiden name," he said.

"Then what about using my maiden name and not connecting the essay to my blog?" I said.

It was an option I'd been chewing for weeks, but one I deemed a last resort. If I didn't affiliate the essay with my blog, I couldn't include my blog in my *New York Times* bio and link back to it, losing potential new followers. I couldn't share the essay on my social media. I couldn't tell my blogging friends, who were my most significant support system. Readers wouldn't know I was an established writer and not a random military spouse who generated no Google results. The essay would be my greatest writing accomplishment and my biggest secret.

Tristan agreed. "Do that. Problem solved."

I tried to shake my disappointment as the editor approved that great idea and we moved forward with the publishing of my essay. I tried to celebrate my *New York Times* byline—a feat most writers strive for—even though that byline wasn't my name and I couldn't brag to anybody but my family and close friends. I tried to convince myself I didn't resent Tristan for a compromise where I made the majority of the concessions. And I tried not to add this to the ever-growing list of sacrifices I made for the sake of my husband's career.

The post went live on July 8, 2011. I lurked as commenters debated over my words, scrolling past trolls criticizing me and focusing on the intelligent and empathetic comments. While I could have increased traffic if I'd shared it with my blog readers, the editor was pleased with the essay's performance and invited me to pitch him again with more ideas.

It was a writer's dream come true. So why was I celebrating alone?

CHAPTER 14

A Very Angry Person

"There is no love left between us. I'm done."

Divorce Talk Number Seven ambushed us with a heated argument and a dramatic conclusion that featured my pillow in the guest room and the astonished expression on Tristan's face when I glared into those blue eyes and sputtered the words that had taunted my subconscious for far too many years.

Two years and three months had passed since our last Divorce Talk, but despite the half dozen seemingly real threats of divorce, this was the one that landed us in the unfamiliar territory of marriage counseling.

I begged Tristan for years to go to counseling. I had to give him credit for taking the initiative to find a therapist and book us an appointment the day after the spat, but I was walking into the first session with the mindset that it was too late.

The counselor was employed by the Navy, specifically assigned to Tristan's command, and bright red flags waved in my head when Tristan instructed me to meet them at a local library after he got off work.

"Why aren't we meeting at her office?" I asked Tristan on the phone.

"She doesn't have an office," he said. "She's an off-the-record kind of therapist." I understood what he meant. The stigma attached to therapy prevents many service members from using it. Seeking therapy might be construed as a sign of weakness, an unacceptable perception in a profession that thrives on strength and mental toughness.

While I applauded Tristan's command for instituting an unofficial way to get these service members access to therapy without fear of tarnishing their military records, I wasn't thrilled that my first marriage counseling session was outdoors on a picnic table in the early-December chill after sunset.

Linda was a formidable woman, nothing like the soft-spoken, huggable expectations I had of therapists, with a firmness that made me want to curl inward and protect myself. She was all edges in both appearance and speech, and I instinctively distrusted her. I didn't want to confide anything to her, let alone put my marriage in her hands.

After brief introductions, Linda got right down to it.

"Tristan tells me you're ready to end your marriage," she stated matter-of-factly.

My thoughts froze as Tristan and Linda waited for my response. I looked around, taking in the awkward scenario. The two of them sat across from each other at the picnic table. I stood with my arms crossed at the chest a few feet away, shivering in my jean jacket that I'd grabbed on my hasty way out of the house because I had no idea our counseling session would be outside, that Linda was supposedly unable to book a meeting room inside the library.

Then my brain clicked into motion, and I recounted my side of the story, chronicling all my reasons for ending the marriage.

When I finished, Linda paused theatrically before nodding as if she had the solution for all our problems.

"You're a very angry person, Heather."

With that statement, I knew this woman wasn't impartial. She wasn't going to listen to what I had to say. She'd already made up her mind.

Linda stamped me with a broad personality trait, a generalization instead of a situational assessment. Within ten minutes she judged me, handed out the guilty verdict, and sentenced me to make all the significant changes.

"I'm angry right now," I replied with exaggerated calm. "But I am not an angry person."

She nodded again, then asked Tristan to share his side of the story, a counterbalancing tale she'd clearly heard before. Of course. Tristan had talked to her on the phone when he booked the appointment. Tristan had one-on-one time with her before I got there. Her job was to advocate for service members, to keep them happy, to do what was necessary to build up their mental and emotional states so they could do their jobs.

I would always wonder if that wiped out her ability to be neutral, if, in order to complete her mission, she would invariably have to side with the service member she was hired to safeguard.

Because for the next month, that's exactly what she did.

***

The one advantage to Linda's out-of-office meet-ups was that our sessions didn't end at the fifty-minute hour. I'm not sure how she built her schedule, but she implied we had all the time in the world, that we could talk until we were done talking. That meant our multiple sessions a week ran anywhere from ninety minutes to over two hours.

Maybe that was why, even though our final session with her was only a month after our first, I felt like we'd seen her long enough, not to have put our pieces back together, but to at least posture us in a way that we could put the pieces back together ourselves.

Throughout that month, I maintained my reservations about her and what I considered a lack of professionalism that included her bias against me. She was abrasive, hypercritical, and exhibited substandard listening skills. But Tristan responded to her advice, which was more important than my impression of her and her methods.

In between sessions, Tristan and I both took Linda's homework assignments seriously. I moved back into our bedroom. We talked for ten minutes each evening about the events of our days. We shared a daily reason why we appreciated each other. We opened separate slush fund bank accounts for a new family financial plan. He gave me two nights a week off from cleaning up after dinner and child bath duties. I booked babysitters for more date nights.

I couldn't wait to report back to Linda about our progress when I met her at the library again—this time inside a conference room—for a solo session about a week after our initial appointment. But she didn't care about my progress report. Despite the bullet points I wanted to hash out without Tristan in the room, she had her own agenda. I tried redirecting her back to the list on my notepad, but she wouldn't budge. I left the session bewildered. She talked more about herself than I did.

Whereas our first ninety-minute meetup was disjointed and draining, this two-hour session was frustrating and wasteful. I didn't feel heard. I didn't feel validated. I didn't feel unburdened. I didn't feel like this woman gave a shit about me or my marriage.

Two days later Tristan met with Linda alone. For two and a half hours. We agreed not to discuss our solo sessions, but I quietly questioned what Linda was feeding him, particularly when the very next day he made a large purchase from our joint bank account without discussing it with me, directly opposing me on a hot-button issue Linda had actually allowed me to vent about. Was she giving us different advice behind each other's backs?

My concern led to a confrontation. The confrontation led to an argument. The argument led to Tristan blurting out, "Linda says our marriage can't be fixed, it can only be improved. Because you're not receptive to counseling."

I was floored. I was confused. And yes, I was angry. This confirmed my marriage counselor was gaslighting me.

I promised myself I'd give Linda one more chance before I found another therapist. She may have given up on me already, but I would show her I wasn't giving up on her. Yet.

***

The following week our usual library was the original plan, but Linda called that afternoon to inform me that all the city libraries were closed. She suggested Panera. Her choice of venue baffled me. A restaurant at dinner time. She expected vulnerability in a public place surrounded by people and noise.

When I pushed back that I didn't think libraries were closed and that I wasn't comfortable with a counseling session at Panera, her tone turned aggressive.

"I've exhausted all ideas of meeting places to accommodate your comfort zone," she said. "I'll see you at Panera."

After reluctantly agreeing, I hung up and called two nearby libraries. They were indeed open that day. And they both had availability that evening for conference rooms.

I questioned her about it at the beginning of the thirty minutes I had alone with her because Tristan was late getting off work. As I lowered my voice so the other customers eating their soups and sandwiches couldn't hear me, she answered flippantly that someone told her libraries were closed. I realized she wanted to orchestrate my uneasiness.

But I moved on, accepting that my marriage counselor and I shared a mutual dislike. There was no point in arguing with her. My aim was to prove I was "receptive to counseling." And despite the rough start to the session, despite the total lack of privacy, I ignored the strange glances from customers searching for a table and I opened up. By the time Tristan slid into the booth beside me, I was calm and focused. Yes, I still felt like the two of them were conspiring against me. I still felt defensive about Linda's animosity toward me. I still didn't trust she had my marriage's best interests in mind. But by the end of the ninety minutes, I felt like I had taken a baby step toward progress.

It was the first session I walked out of without anger.

***

Christmas festivities came and went, and we didn't see Linda for two weeks. However, as usual when Tristan and I both had time off from work and could escape day-to-day life, things were going well between us. We mistakenly believed it was a result of therapy.

We cruised into our fourth appointment together with Linda, unable to hide our pride as Tristan and I ticked the checkmarks off on our homework assignments. He stuck to his counseling goals. I stuck to mine.

Therefore, as we looked ahead at Tristan's upcoming loaded travel schedule, we all agreed to take a counseling break. His comings and goings, as well as the high probability of changing dates, made it pointless to book appointments. An inner voice pestered me to book some anyway, because even if Tristan was away, attending alone was beneficial and stopping this abruptly might slow our momentum. But my friction with Linda overpowered that rationalization.

We said our goodbyes with smiles and optimism and promises to leverage those counseling goals while we were apart, and planned to meet up with her when Tristan's schedule slowed down.

We never saw Linda again. But she was only the beginning of our marriage counseling journey.

***

For the next three months, Tristan bounced from airport to airport with brief stops at home. When he finally stayed home for longer than a handful of days at a stretch, I expected everything to fall back into place. Although I'd seen him several times in those three months, quality time together eluded us, his frequent homecomings and departures making it impossible to test if those short-term counseling goals had turned into long-term habits.

By mid-March, we had regressed back to square one, as if we'd never gone to counseling at all, as if our marriage was a child with a fever and Linda had sent us to school with a dose of ibuprofen that wore off and left us symptomatic again. I made excuses for Tristan. I told myself he was jet-lagged, that we hadn't yet surpassed the typical adjustment period after his return. I ignored the needling voice scolding me not to quit counseling.

It was a half marathon that turned that timid inner voice into a shriek urging me to return to therapy immediately or there'd be nothing to salvage.

My running was a persistent source of contention. I hungered for the solitary hours pounding the pavement, the training culminating in the stride across a finish line alongside thousands of fellow runners, while Tristan's inability to understand that drive translated into a lack of support. More specifically, I asked him to help Grady and Ava decorate signs to hold up. At every race, I read spectators' posters and, with a pang of jealousy, longed to see my own family joining the hundreds of others cheering on their favorite runner.

He didn't make the signs.

Ultimately, I got my signs, my support, just not from my husband. My parents were in town, and after watching us bicker, they bought poster boards and sat down with the kids to design the simple signs I'd requested for years.

"Go, Mom! Run fast!"

That was all I'd wanted.

On race day, a renewed energy kicked in as I spotted my children and my parents tucked into the massive crowd of spectators, pumping those signs up and down in the air and shouting, "You can do it!"

I didn't see or hear Tristan. I knew he was there, hidden away somewhere in the crowd, but the damage was done.

And once again, so was I.

***

The strain between us was tangible when Tristan left for Fort Lauderdale and then to New Orleans, and I was thankful for the time apart. The tension released from my shoulder blades the second he walked out the door. I don't think I kissed him goodbye.

A few days later, as I was setting clothes aside to pack for another family reunion in Arkansas, Tristan called to tell me he'd scheduled a trip to DC the same day as our flight. I seethed in disbelief he was missing my second family reunion for a trip that, as it turned out, was voluntary. I hung up the phone, restraining myself from pitching it across the room.

Not knowing what else to do with my fury, I laced up my running shoes and practically sprinted the mile to Mount Trashmore, even as my hamstrings screamed in pain. When I reached the top of the hill, I looked out to Interstate 264 on one side and toward my neighborhood on the other, then plopped down on the grass, hugging my knees to my chest to shrink into a tiny ball. And I cried.

I heard people side-stepping around me, likely wondering why a grown woman was on the ground crying, while I battled with my thoughts. I wondered what a good marriage was supposed to look like. I wondered how my life would have turned out if I'd married my college sweetheart. I wondered how other military marriages lasted through the unrelenting time apart. I wondered if I could blame the military for my unhappiness anymore.

Being married to Tristan was like living from one disappointment to the next. And as I sat alone at the top of Mount Trashmore, with tear-filled eyes facing the direction of my home, my back toward a highway that could transport me somewhere else, I realized it wasn't military life causing the disappointments. It was the man I no longer wanted to be married to.

CHAPTER 15

Fake It Til You Feel It

I found Owen through Military OneSource, a Department of Defense-funded program that offers all sorts of information and support to military families, ranging from tax services to spouse employment assistance, as well as access to local counselors. Not knowing what to expect, I called, told the kind woman on the phone I was searching for a marriage counselor in Virginia Beach, and I had an appointment the following day.

I'd just returned from my family reunion and Tristan was back from DC only to soon depart again for Poland. But I didn't care that he wouldn't be at the session. This was an emergency. I felt like I had one foot out the door, that I was a suitcase away from leaving my husband, and I needed someone to order me to stay.

The only commonality between Owen and Linda was physical stature. But while Linda carried her height and heft with sharpness, Owen was a big teddy bear. His demeanor instantly put me at an ease Linda had never induced. Maybe he could help us. Maybe he would find our magic reset button.

Despite my state of mind, I recalled my discomfort at my first session with Linda, knowing Tristan had the advantage of time with her before I arrived, so I tried to remain as neutral as possible as I told Owen our story, painting a picture of both sides that included my issues with Tristan as well as his issues with me. It wasn't until he asked me the simplest of questions that my emotions spilled out, overcoming neutrality.

"Do you love him?"

A choking sensation gave me pause as I bit my lip to keep from crying.

"I'd like to say yes," I said, gazing down at my fidgeting fingers. "I'd like to say that love is hiding somewhere under all the hurt, anger, and resentment."

Owen nodded as if he could decipher my noncommittal answer. Handing me a box of tissues, he assured me we'd get to the bottom of that pile to see if the love was still there. We booked a second appointment, which my current calendar showed Tristan would be home for, and Owen smiled as if to say, "Hang in there. We'll figure this out."

After Tristan came home, traveled to Florida, and returned again, we met with Owen together. We hadn't been to therapy together in four months, and it was a disaster. We bickered, we interrupted, and we launched condemnations at each other like poison darts, landing with stings and outrage.

When the fifty-minute hour was almost up, Owen stepped in to referee. He stared at us sitting on the couch with the body language of two people who wished the room had more seating options.

"I see absolutely no connection between you two," he said.

I turned to Tristan, and when he didn't respond, I let loose, as if the filter between my brain and my mouth had been disabled.

"I see no connection either," I said, my voice getting louder.

"And I don't miss you when you're gone."

"And I don't enjoy being around you."

"And I don't think I want to be married to you anymore."

I closed my eyes and exhaled.

That felt good.

* * *

Our second appointment with Owen arrived after seven days of searching not for our lost connection, but for ways to avoid one another. This one varied only slightly from the first, the main difference coming in the form of Tristan questioning his own desire to stay married. This time, he declared he wanted a trial separation.

"Tristan, what is your definition of a separation?" Owen asked. "After all, as a military couple, you're physically separated all the time. Do you want to move out? Do you want to date other women? Do you want to hire a lawyer to draw up the paperwork for a legal separation?"

My brain was on the verge of exploding as Owen escorted us to the door with no answers to those questions, no resolutions, no goals, no checklists. The session was basically two people sitting on the far ends of a couch as a third person analyzed them, probably contemplating why they were bothering with counseling at all.

Tristan couldn't make the next session, so I gladly went alone. Owen calmed me, gently peeling away my defense mechanisms. I savored our one-on-ones and the freedom to confide in a professional without worrying about Tristan's reactions.

I told Owen I wasn't sure if I loved Tristan, and I doubted his love for me. I told him I was relieved Tristan was out of the country, that life was smoother when he was gone. But my most significant admission was probably the most compelling reason to end my marriage.

"I think the only reason I'm still in the marriage is because I'm scared of life after divorce."

There. I said it. The words were real. They were on record. I could no longer ignore them.

"Tell me how you envision a life after divorce," Owen prompted.

"I can't imagine how I'll get by as a single mom," I said. "Where will I live? How will I afford it? What will I do for health insurance? What will this mean for my kids?"

The list could have continued, but as my panic grew, Owen held up his hand to pause my anxiety.

"Yes, a divorce would change just about everything in your life," he said. "But you could handle it. You have the means to figure it out. What's most important here is that you can't stay in a marriage simply because you're scared of those changes. You can't stay in a marriage where love is absent."

On that note, my hour was up. Tristan would share the couch with me at our next appointment. I had a lot to think about.

***

Despite an irregular publishing schedule, I continued blogging, and Jane, my friend who worked with Blue Star Families, joined me for a road trip to our third-annual conference for military writers in Washington, DC. I vowed not to carry my marriage troubles with me, submerging myself in the writing community whose camaraderie I'd grown to rely on.

As Jane drove us home and we recapped the weekend, I repeated a conversation I'd had with Andrea, another military spouse blogger, over chicken lettuce wraps at P.F. Chang's. After revealing to a select few blogging friends that I'd written two *New York Times* essays under my maiden name—the second one about marriage counseling published when I thought Linda was actually helping us—I shared what was going on behind my closed doors.

"We've talked about divorce a few times, but only after big fights," I told Andrea as we sipped wine.

"Wait a minute," Andrea said. "You guys talk about divorce? You've actually said the word 'divorce'?"

"Well, yeah," I said. "Don't most couples throw that word around every now and then?"

Andrea turned to face me. "No," she said. "They don't."

"Really?"

"Really," she said. "My ex-husband and I said the D word. And we got divorced. My husband now? We would never bring that word into our marriage. Because if it's put out there, then it becomes an option."

Andrea was right. Tristan and I had created an option where one shouldn't have existed, a way to opt out of our lifetime commitment. But the broader question was, did the creation of that option mean we would choose it?

***

Two weeks after the conference, my phone rang with a surprising opportunity. I was offered a job. As a writer. Making real money. Working from home. It was a dream come true, and without hesitation, I accepted.

The job offer renewed my confidence in not only my writing abilities, but my capabilities as an independent woman. This job was a direct result of my blog, a project I produced from nothing and sustained through freelancing, networking, and diligence, hard work squeezed into pockets of free time. What once felt like a distant dream—turning my passion into a career—became my reality.

This was more than a mere job. Although, at first, I'd be a contractor at the website that hired me, I could eventually transition to full-time employment. That meant a salary, benefits, job security. And I couldn't help but calculate how this development factored into my decision of whether to leave my marriage.

When Tristan handed me an envelope of what he claimed were divorce papers on my thirty-second birthday in Japan, I was a stay-at-home mom with no job, no money of my own, no way to support myself financially outside of whatever child support and alimony I might be awarded. This position was a game-changer.

If I admitted that the main reason I was staying in my bad marriage was because I feared the other side of divorce, then I also had to admit that this job was removing my biggest concern about life on my own. I no longer had a good reason to stay.

* * *

As I finished my second and final year teaching kindergarten, I could barely keep track of Tristan's travel schedule. I'd completely forgotten what day it was when Tristan called from Poland to wish me a happy anniversary.

But he didn't really call for our anniversary. He called to discuss his next duty station.

"I've been talking to my detailer," Tristan said.

"Okay," I said, waiting for the usual list of Navy bases.

"I was thinking about doing a tour in Italy or Portugal," he said. That seemed unrealistic, but I always let him think out loud and work out his circuitous reasoning, knowing most of his random ideas would never come to fruition.

"Okay," I repeated. "What else?"

There was a pause that made me check if we'd been disconnected.

"I'm thinking about geo-baching at Fort Bragg," Tristan finally said. "For a three-year tour."

Geographic bachelor tours, or geo-baching, mean that service members PCS to duty stations without their families. It could be because the tour is short or OCONUS, and the family decides it's not worth moving, house hunting, and pulling the kids out of school.

From my limited knowledge of geo-baching, military families didn't choose that option for a scenario like the one Tristan was suggesting. Service members didn't leave their families behind for a three-year stateside tour. A one-year tour overseas? That made sense. Three years in North Carolina when we currently lived in Virginia? On paper, that made no sense.

But it did make sense. I hung up, chuckling at the absurdity of Tristan's plan. He was using the military to manufacture the separation he wanted. And I almost called him back to say I was on board.

***

Tristan, back from Poland, showed up to our joint appointment twenty minutes late, giving me precious time alone with Owen for a follow-up to our last discussion. As I talked in circles about my indifference toward Tristan, saying that I felt neither love nor hate, I silently begged Owen to provide answers.

"Tell me what to do," I wanted to scream. "Make the decisions for me. Tell me whether I'm supposed to fight for my marriage or if I'm supposed to walk away."

But that wasn't Owen's job. He was there to shine a light on all the things I couldn't see. Or didn't want to.

"I want to look at my husband and feel love and attraction," I said. "But I don't. And I feel like I deserve more."

"Have you ever heard of the phrase 'fake it til you feel it'?" Owen asked. "Maybe you could start there."

I blinked in disbelief at what he was implying. My marriage therapist wanted me to pretend I loved my husband. He wanted me to fabricate an affection I no longer felt until I did feel it. Hadn't I been faking it long enough?

By the time Tristan arrived, I was already emotionally depleted. Tears had already come and gone. So I sat on my end of the sofa and listened to Tristan talk about his trip and how happy he was to be home. I listened to him claim that he missed me and looked forward to spending time with me. And it occurred to me that maybe he was the one faking it until he felt it.

I knew then that not only did I not want to fake my feelings toward my husband, I also didn't want him to fake his feelings toward me. I wanted to love and be loved. I wanted mutual passion and respect, friendship and partnership. I wanted all of these things to come naturally, not as a result of lies we told ourselves in the hopes that our brains and hearts would start believing them.

In other words, I wanted everything I expected marriage to be, not what my marriage actually was.

We weren't the people we once were, the naive kids in our twenties who romanticized marriage without projecting ahead to the adult consequences of our hasty decisions. Back then I'd imagined the metamorphosis from the intense infatuation of our newlywed stage into unconditional love through growth and time. Now I wondered if we never surpassed the growth stage because we evolved in divergent directions, developing into individuals so far away from each other there was no coming back together.

I was still contemplating Owen's advice two weeks later, when Tristan got back from a week-long trip to Florida, and within hours of his return we were squabbling.

The main issue of the fight, among a million other little things, was that I stopped concluding our calls with an "I love you."

Tristan and I always exchanged an "I love you" before hanging up the phone. But over the years, the repetition rendered the phrase powerless, as rote as "see you later" or "take care." The words didn't mean what they once did, and despite Owen's advice to fake it til I felt it, I chose to do the opposite. I chose to stop faking it to see if I would miss it enough to feel it again.

So, when Tristan was in Florida for a week, I never told him I loved him. He noticed. And he wasn't happy about it.

The argument lasted hours, a practice in futility since my heart wasn't in it and I just wanted to go to sleep.

"I understand you're upset that I'm not saying 'I love you,'" I said.

"I understand we need to figure out our marriage," I said.

"I understand we can't keep living like this," I said.

The argument kept circling. I was bored. We'd been fighting the same exact fight for years. All I wanted was to stop circling, even if it meant breaking everything.

No, I didn't want to fake it til I felt it. If we didn't feel it without having to fake it after twelve years of marriage, I didn't think we ever would.

CHAPTER 16

No More Camo

Along with my new job came the unearthing of an old issue: my name.

Piggybacking on the lengthy discussions Tristan and I had regarding my byline in my first *New York Times* essay, we decided I would continue using my maiden name in my bylines at my job. The only place my married name would appear was on my paycheck. Otherwise, all public mentions would be Heather Sweeney. In fact, my married name was so top-secret that most of my coworkers never knew the name they called me wasn't my legal name.

It was strange at first, seeing emails hit my inbox addressed to a person I hadn't been in over a decade. But it didn't take long before I realized it was a good kind of strange. My new old name was a way for me to compartmentalize not only my writing, but my entire persona.

Heather Maiden Name was a confident, capable associate editor and writer who navigated a wonky content management system, Photoshop, and professional and personal blogs on a daily basis, brainstorming and composing posts, participating in conference calls and editorial meetings, and traveling on business trips.

Heather Married Name was a frazzled working mom who struggled to get her kids to baseball practice and soccer games, who rarely saw the bottom of the laundry basket, who tried not to compare her thrown-together dinners and after-school snacks to those of her stay-at-home mom counterparts on social media.

Heather Married Name couldn't stop thinking about ending her marriage.

Even though I worked from home, the clear distinction between Heather Maiden Name and Heather Married Name hit me the instant I logged onto my laptop every morning and logged out every evening.

On nights when Tristan and I went to bed with barely a goodnight, him watching a show that numbed my brain with boredom, me popping in earbuds to listen to a playlist I compiled as the perfect mix of drowning out the television and invoking sleep, I wished I possessed the assertiveness of Heather Maiden Name to tell him what I was thinking. I wished Tristan could get to know Heather Maiden Name, witness her at work, see how intelligent she was, how motivated she was, how talented she was. I wished he could see that version instead of Heather Married Name, the woman he greeted when he walked in the door after work, that frazzled version with pasta overboiling in the pot and sizzling the burner, our kindergartener throwing a tantrum in the living room and our third grader attempting homework on his own at the kitchen table. I wished he saw more than the chaos. I wished he saw Heather Maiden Name version two. Because she was so similar to the original version he'd met in our early twenties that it was almost as if she were coming full circle. But better.

I was sure that in his eyes, other than some extra cash in our checking account, nothing had changed. But for me, this new job changed everything.

***

The theme of my next session with Owen was my newfound empowerment. And because Tristan wasn't there, I used the opportunity to explore how to apply that empowerment outside of work.

I talked about the freedom and independence the job allowed me. I talked about how my life no longer revolved around Tristan, how I was no longer in his shadow. I talked about my unofficial name change, how maybe it was practice for when Tristan and I got divorced and I legally made the switch back to my maiden name.

I said statements like, "Now that I'm making more money, I could probably support myself if Tristan and I got divorced" and "Now that my job is remote and portable, I could probably move to Florida to be close to my parents if Tristan and I got divorced."

As I listened to myself, I realized it sounded like I was plotting a getaway.

Maybe I was.

And it went beyond that session with Owen. A few days later Tristan was traveling again, and I pretended his temporary absence was a permanent one.

When I cooked dinner, I thought about the lopsidedness of sitting at a kitchen table where I never put out a fourth plate.

Then I thought about never again having to cook Tristan's favorite meals that I never liked.

After the kids went to bed, I settled onto the couch with my laptop and thought about the loneliness of not having a partner to decompress with at the end of the day. Then I thought about never having to share the television remote control and being able to turn the TV off altogether for hours of uninterrupted reading or writing.

When I slipped paid bills into the mailbox, I became keenly aware that soon the payments for those bills would come from an individual account and not a joint one.

When I contemplated downsizing to a smaller house, I imagined applying the expert packing skills I'd learned from the military moves. I knew how much packing paper and tape I'd need. I knew how to number boxes and list them on a legal pad so nothing got misplaced (and if a box went missing, I would know which one and its contents). I knew how to organize piles of possessions to pack first, things I wouldn't need to use until I arrived at my destination, and things to pack at the last minute. This time the move would be on my terms, not the military's.

When I went to bed at night, I thought about stretching my body across the span of the bed and drifting off to slumber in silence instead of a mashup of the History Channel and snores.

For each hardship, an upside. Counterbalances to erase my daunting apprehensions. Life after divorce no longer seemed impossible. In fact, it seemed astonishingly promising.

* * *

During my next solo session with Owen, he guided me toward another epiphany that led me to forgiveness not for Tristan and his role in the deterioration of our marriage, but for the Navy.

For years I pinned most of the blame for my marriage problems on the military, proclaiming the frequent separations caused us to drift apart. But Owen theorized the possibility that the Navy had actually kept us holding on longer than we might have if Tristan were home all the time.

Whenever the Navy sent him away, we postponed our problems. We didn't want to have serious conversations while he was gone because he had to focus on work and I was supposed to be missing him on the homefront. We didn't want to argue when he was preparing to leave because we were supposed to spend quality time with the kids and take care of logistics like packing and scheduling. We didn't want to hash things out when he returned because we were supposed to be overjoyed to see each other and make up for lost time. That didn't leave us much time in between to chase off the monsters that haunted us.

Maybe, if we hadn't spent so much of our marriage apart, we would have discovered we weren't meant to be married years earlier. Without the Navy interrupting us, we wouldn't have had the luxury of putting space between our problems, giving us a breather in between arguments, a time-out to collect ourselves and level out our emotional reactions. Without the Navy, we would have had no choice but to confront what we ignored when we weren't together. Without the Navy, we wouldn't have been able to play the out-of-sight, out-of-mind game.

I blamed the military for added stressors like moving and deployments, like Tristan's inability to attend counseling sessions and my resentment about delaying my career. But those hardships were background noise. They weren't fatal flaws. If Tristan and I had a solid foundation like other couples who survived military life, we would have overcome the scenarios the Navy threw at us. We didn't have a strong foundation. In fact, I'm not sure we ever had a foundation at all. And now, after years of stepping around the cracks, everything finally fell from under us.

I still held a grudge for all the sacrifices I had to make personally, but I couldn't blame the Navy for our failures as a couple.

I also had to forgive myself. Not for being the weak link in my marriage. Despite what I once believed, it was never solely my responsibility to hold my marriage together, and I couldn't shoulder all the blame for its demise. No, I had to let myself off the hook for all the mistakes I'd made, the imperfections I'd thought I could fix, the naive belief that a marriage must survive at all costs, regardless of how miserable the people holding it together with rubber bands and super glue are.

I forgave myself for holding on too tight to an unrealistic illusion of marriage and family, of love and partnership, for trying to force myself and Tristan to become people we weren't. Whether the military separations caused us to grow apart or we were always destined to branch off into two very different and incompatible people, it didn't matter. I couldn't change Tristan. And I didn't want him to change me. So I forgave myself for giving up a fight that would always be futile.

I forgave myself for releasing my marriage and letting it go.

* * *

Owen's final lesson for me was that marriage counseling doesn't always result in success, that not all marriages can—or should—be saved.

One day when Tristan was gone yet again, I called Owen to book our next appointment. Military OneSource allowed twelve free sessions, and we were running out of our allotment.

"You only have two free sessions left," Owen said. "And quite frankly, not only do I feel like there's no way I could possibly offer the help you need in two sessions, but I honestly don't think you and Tristan should stay married."

The phone went silent. My marriage counselor just told me I should get divorced.

"If you're not ready to walk away yet, maybe another therapist might be able to help," he continued. "But I know I'm already your second counselor."

"Yeah," I said. "I guess we're double marriage-counseling failures."

"I hope I'm wrong about you two," he said. "But I think you should seriously consider how you want to live the rest of your life."

Owen wished me luck, and I thanked him for everything he tried to do for us, hanging up with an eerie serenity. I didn't need more time to seriously consider my life. I knew what I wanted.

CHAPTER 17

Over in Nineteen Days

We took off our wedding rings. I applied for a credit card in my name only. I researched health insurance options.

Divorce was happening.

Before spending money on an attorney, I met with a JAG, a military lawyer, at Naval Station Norfolk to discuss my rights as a divorced military spouse. Consulting a JAG was free and part of service members' military benefits that extended to dependents. While they help with various kinds of legal assistance ranging from drawing up wills and powers of attorney to tax preparation and lease contract reviews, I knew a JAG couldn't represent me in a divorce. JAGs practice military law, not state law, and divorce is a state matter. But at the very least, I hoped I could learn more about my financial entitlements as well as some recommendations for attorneys who could represent me.

I shouldn't have been surprised that, by the time I arrived at my appointment, Tristan had already contacted the office, creating a conflict of interest for the JAG I consulted. In my brief ten-minute conversation, the JAG explained that I would retain none of my dependent benefits after divorce because my twelve-year marriage didn't qualify for the 20/20/20 rule. In order to have continued access to benefits like TRICARE health insurance and commissary shopping, a couple needed to be married for twenty years, the military member needed to serve for twenty years, and the marriage and the military service needed to overlap by twenty years. As far as child support and alimony calculations, he told me I'd have to discuss that with a civilian attorney licensed in the state of Virginia.

Offering no recommendations for local lawyers, the JAG sent me on my way with the sense that even if Tristan hadn't beaten me to the JAG office, I would have been treated just as poorly. Like Linda, the Navy-employed marriage counselor, the JAGs' priority was the service member, not the spouse. The military didn't care what happened to me after Tristan and I got divorced. The military only cared about Tristan and his ability to continue doing his Navy job.

The JAG may not have helped me, but I wasn't discouraged. Just the act of seeking legal counsel gave me a sense of control.

***

Christmas approached, but the holiday spirit couldn't alleviate the tension. Although Tristan and I hid it well. Or at least I told myself we did.

If Ava and Grady noticed any animosity between their parents, they didn't say anything. The three of us decorated the tree like we always did, blasting Christmas music and eating cookies while showing each other our favorite ornaments from the collection I'd been building since Tristan and I got married. It was a tradition I launched with the kids, one I looked forward to every holiday season, one Tristan rarely participated in, so his lack of involvement this year wasn't unusual.

The harder sell was the charade for my parents, who arrived on our doorstep to celebrate Christmas with us mere hours after Tristan and I had a fight so maddening that we could barely stand being in the same room. My parents knew our marriage was in trouble, but I didn't want the atmosphere in our house to ruin their visit.

Tristan and I had both consulted JAGs, but hadn't yet hired civilian attorneys, so technically we still didn't have any breakup news to share. We were still circling around the decision to make the first real move. We still seemed to need an impetus to make the jump, a push to make us finally take actionable steps toward divorce.

After too many years of arguing, there was no way to know we would never recover from this argument, that whatever triggered this one would also trigger the spiral of arguments that would ultimately be the demise of our marriage.

There was no way to know our marriage would be over in nineteen days.

***

The next day I got word of another major achievement in my writing career: a byline in the latest print edition of *Reader's Digest.*

Shrieking with joy, my mother and I visited every grocery store within a five-mile radius to buy as many copies as we could find. After collecting about a dozen *Reader's Digests* and spreading them on the kitchen table, Tristan came home from work. He was late and obviously still as angry as I was. He didn't congratulate me. He didn't hug me. He didn't look at the magazines.

I was infuriated. I'd spent our entire relationship supporting him even before we were married. I stood by him when he decided to join the military. I stabilized our life on the homefront while he was deployed and otherwise traveling. I uprooted my life multiple times, postponed my career, gave up proximity to my family and any semblance of geographic familiarity all because of him. Now, my hard work was reflected in the bylines I was adding to my writing resume, and I wanted him to celebrate my accomplishments as I had celebrated his. I didn't think some support of my endeavors was too much to ask.

My work was in a print magazine. He couldn't even muster a "good job"?

My parents witnessed the awkward scene that ended with Tristan strolling past the kitchen table that was covered with *Reader's Digests* and up the stairs to undress out of his uniform. They tried to compensate for their son-in-law's lack of reaction by gushing compliments and explaining to Ava and Grady why those magazines were so special. But it wasn't the same.

As we all watched a family movie, I physically distanced myself from Tristan and shared my news on social media, where my writing community lifted me and validated an achievement I refused to allow him to diminish. I was justified in my excitement, regardless of whether or not my husband—even if we were on the verge of divorce—chose to celebrate with me.

* * *

Unsure of how to act around us and hoping to push the tension out of the house, my parents offered their babysitting services to give us a date night the following evening. It was the last thing I wanted to do, but for some reason I thought we could talk things out over dinner.

Back and forth. Back and forth. We couldn't get off this roller coaster of our own making.

But Tristan opted to skip dinner out and go straight to a movie, where talking wasn't an option. I couldn't decide between relief or sadness that we had nothing left to say to each other.

I picked the movie *This Is 40* because it seemed like we could use some comic relief. In retrospect, I'm not sure why I thought a film about aging and marital strife at that particular point would be fun. It wasn't. Neither of us laughed a single time.

At times in the darkness of the theater I glanced over at Tristan, yearning to read his mind. This man had been my partner in life for fourteen years. After all that time, I should have had some ability to understand him, to predict his behavior. But as I watched him stare at the screen, my only thought was that I didn't know the man sitting beside me at all.

***

We argued on Christmas Eve. We argued on Christmas Day. And the day after Christmas, the day we planned to leave for the mountain house for our second Christmas with his parents, Tristan uninvited me. He told me to stay home. He didn't want me there.

From the window of our family room I watched him load up his truck and drive away with my children and our Labrador retriever Gunner, who we had added to our family several months earlier, wondering how he would explain my absence to his parents.

While I was dumbfounded he uninvited me to an annual family holiday gathering, it was exactly what I needed. Without realizing it, Tristan gifted me the time and space to finally end it all.

CHAPTER 18

The Optimism Issue

The six days Tristan stayed at the mountain house coincided with the final days of 2012. I embraced the timing, penning New Year's resolutions not just for a new year, but a new life. As I poured a glass of wine and saluted 2013 in solitude, I fortified myself for a different kind of war than the ones military life introduced me to.

My parents left the day after Tristan did. After holding an emergency family meeting at my kitchen table to brainstorm my next steps, my mother and I deconstructed Christmas, stowing the artificial tree and decorations in the attic. I couldn't look at them anymore, blaring reminders of my worst holiday ever. And what I hoped was my final Christmas with Tristan.

In a way, I wanted to beg my parents to stay so I could regress to a child-like state where they handled everything. In another way, I wanted isolation to clear my head. But after clearing my head, I needed guidance, preferably from someone emotionally objective and knowledgeable about divorce. So I hugged my parents goodbye, promising to follow through on the plan we formulated and assuring them I would be okay, and hours later I was in my therapist Julia's office.

Julia was our third marriage counselor. Shortly after Tristan and I stopped seeing Owen, a friend recommended Julia, and out of a sense of obligation to leave no stone unturned, I booked us an appointment. Not surprisingly, we only had three joint sessions, all of which were disastrous and filled with unproductive fighting. But even when Tristan stopped going, I continued scheduling appointments and talking to Julia alone, discovering how important having a personal therapist was going to be as I pursued divorce.

I vented, I cried, and I left Julia's couch with a roster of local divorce attorneys. I expected to feel as if an overbearing load had been lifted off my shoulders, but the load only grew heavier the more I processed the amount of work required to end my marriage.

This was no sprint. This was the starting line of a marathon.

***

I selected a divorce attorney whose firm specialized in military divorces, specifically the female half of the marriage, whether a female service member or a spouse. The ninety-minute consultation drained $285 from our joint bank account that was about to be divided in half.

I brought my newly compiled divorce folder, a stack of paperwork documenting our shared money, mistakenly anticipating a straightforward business meeting to learn what I was entitled to. I don't know if I could blame it on an apathetic male attorney, but I walked out of that office with a pocket full of soggy tissues and numbers swirling around my head, like the cost of a collaborative divorce that would rapidly rise if we disputed possessions, causing repeated court appearances. Somehow, the harshness of the legal side of divorce shocked me. The attorney scared the shit out of me.

Tristan and I had outlined our divorce so many times that I knew we didn't have big court battles in us. We both expressed a desire to take the easiest route, whatever that looked like, and let each other move on.

But this attorney wanted a fight. He seemed to think I wasn't fired up enough, voicing anger on my behalf, modeling how he would argue for me in court. His severe explanation of collaborative divorce—a process Tristan and I had already decided on because it involved the least amount of time and money—left me utterly confused. I was led to believe his transaction would require very little from an attorney, but this one was ready to assert himself.

My brain buzzed with uncertainties. Did I have the strength to do this? Did I have the money to do this? Was this lawyer right that there was no such thing as an amicable divorce, that Tristan would fight me on every detail that could possibly be fought over?

Did I need an attorney to help me fight or to help me walk away as peacefully as possible?

He confirmed that couples without the financial resources for one spouse to move out could do an in-home separation until they could figure out a way to fully separate households. Partners must sleep in different rooms, and an acquaintance who knew both of us had to testify in court that we lived "separate and apart" for that year.

So I conducted a mini move-out, transferring my clothes and nightstand from the master bedroom to the guest room and relocating my toiletries from our shared bathroom to the kids' bathroom. Then I inventoried everything in the house, making lists on a legal pad of marital possessions I wanted to keep, items Tristan could have, and question marks for others we'd have to negotiate.

"So little of this stuff belongs to me," I thought. The paintings, the rugs, the furniture. Tristan purchased nearly everything without my approval. The bookcases were filled with his books, while my small collection of favorites hid in random drawers. I would plead my case for the step *tansu* and the cherry blossom woodblock print from Japan, but I had no attachment to much else. The exercise made me increasingly thankful for our vastly disparate tastes.

It wasn't until I saw the *Reader's Digest* magazines my mother and I had bought piled on the desk Tristan and I shared that the frenetic energy driving me to stay in motion sputtered and stalled. I picked up a copy and scanned the cover I'd ignored in my excitement to flip to my essay. A magenta flower displayed the words "Cheer Up!" in bright yellow letters. The top right corner designated it "The Optimism Issue."

That Optimism Issue would end up being one of my most memorable and painful visions of the last days of my marriage. I couldn't decide if it was a sign of things to come or a sucker punch.

Bypassing all the articles about happiness and positivity, I landed on my own words. Page thirty-six. "A Navy Wife's Favorite Phrases." The editors butchered my original headline. In fact, they not only shortened my listicle from my original blog post they'd requested to republish, a post I'd written months earlier, but I was pretty sure they'd altered every single sentence. Their final draft, my first print byline that I was holding in my hands, felt nothing like my writing at all.

And I felt nothing like the woman who first wrote it.

I poured a second and then a third glass of wine as I continued itemizing every material object in the home I'd built with Tristan. The split wouldn't be easy. As I learned from the *Reader's Digest* Optimism Issue, from my article that revolved around my husband's career, I couldn't even be a successful writer without the intersection of my life and his.

***

"I want a divorce."

I repeated the sentence over and over again leading up to Tristan's return from his parents' mountain house. I recited it aloud to the audience of empty rooms. I listened to its reverberations as it bounced around my head. I practiced the diction, the intonation, the body language, the eye contact, and the seating arrangements during the delivery of these delicate words that held the balance of my future.

"I. Want. A. Divorce."

This wasn't a first for us. We'd each thrown and dodged this sentence for years. This time it had to stick.

"I'm pretty sure you're done with me," Tristan texted as he headed home on New Year's Day.

His intuition eased my pronouncement. When the kids were in bed, we sat in the family room as I slowly, and with practiced enunciation, spoke the words he apparently already knew I was going to say.

The scene was as calm and emotionless as our previous pronouncements were hostile and saturated with anger. We attempted to sort out details of living arrangements and custody schedules, but it was too much too soon, so I left him in his recliner to go to sleep in my new bedroom without him.

***

It took two hours and $1,100 to disassemble my twelve-and-a-half-year marriage.

We convened in a small room with an attorney Tristan hired who specialized in uncontested divorces, agreeing on some things, compromising on others, and ending up with a separation agreement that would roll into the divorce decree, a document that would be difficult to revise after the ink dried.

Like the JAG explained to me, our divorce would follow laws established by the state of Virginia. For instance, a couple with children had to be legally separated for an entire year before the divorce could be finalized. A year seemed excessive to me, a long time to live in the limbo of still being married yet living separate lives. But we had no choice. We needed to get that clock ticking as soon as possible by drawing up a separation agreement.

The document listed a range of factors from custody schedules to financial details. Tristan and I would share fifty-fifty custody of Grady and Ava, but their primary residence would be with me. We would alternate holidays, and whoever had Thanksgiving didn't get Christmas. We even had to include the exact dates of holiday pass-offs. For example, the parent who had the kids for Christmas would take custody after school let out on their last day before winter break and return them to the other parent the day after Christmas. If Tristan was traveling for work during a holiday, his parents could take the kids in his place if they chose to.

The separation agreement also included the exact amount of child support Tristan was required to pay me until the kids turned eighteen, which was a standard calculation based mostly on our salaries. Tristan would pay me a determined monthly amount of money for alimony for a specified number of years or until I was in a relationship that resulted in either cohabitation or marriage. And the kids would maintain their existing military health and dental insurance, with any medical costs not covered by insurance to be split equally between us.

Before meeting with the attorney, Tristan and I sat down at our kitchen table, the most neutral location in the house, with a template of a Virginia separation agreement and talked through all the bullet points so we would both know what to expect and be able to avoid debates while paying by the hour. We also hashed out particulars that wouldn't go into the document, such as our agreement to continue using our joint checking account to pay household bills until one of us moved out and that account was divided and dissolved.

But despite that preparation, I was still shocked by the concrete decisions we had to make, legally binding, pivotal decisions about ourselves and our children without the foresight of our future, where we'd be living, what our financial standings would be. We were a full year away from not being married anymore, yet we had to decide everything now. It was terrifying and somehow settling all at once.

He might have regretted some of those decisions years later. I would definitely regret some. But we did the best we could to avoid morphing into those people who needed a judge to make those decisions for us.

I intended to prove an amicable divorce did exist, and my hope was that we would be such successful co-parents that one day we could forget the strict calendar of the separation agreement and show enough flexibility and respect to execute whatever schedule we agreed upon during any given year to accommodate his continuing Navy career, my job, travel plans, and visits from family.

But these were all unknowns, wishful thinking. In that moment, all I could feel was defeat. How did we get to this place? How did the man I was once over-the-moon crazy about end up sitting across from me in the office of a divorce attorney? How could we have dismantled our marriage in a heartless document written by a woman who just met us, who didn't know what we'd been through, the potential we failed to tap, the goals we fell short of, the magnitude of this failure?

We walked to Tristan's Jeep with drafts of the separation agreement and the attorney's promise to email in the next week or so with the final copy that needed our notarized signatures. The divorce clock had started. There was no turning back now.

As Tristan wordlessly drove us home, I examined my left ring finger where my wedding ring had once lived. I couldn't remember the last time I'd worn it, but enough time had passed that the distinct indentation in my skin was barely visible.

We were only minutes into our legal separation, but the evidence of wedded bliss had begun fading long ago.

PART 3

The Beginning of the Rest

CHAPTER 19

All the Things We Never Did

Virginia, 2013

I jolted awake at three in the morning. Heart racing. Breath choppy. Panic rising.

Upright in bed, my inhales and exhales slowed. I pressed my feet into the cold hardwood below, willing the floor to ground me. I grasped onto the edge of the mattress, digging my fingernails in as if it could stop my sense of free-falling.

It was my first day waking up as a woman who was no longer referring to herself as a wife. The clock had started, and I was a day closer to getting my divorce. I thought I would awake surrounded by sunshine and conviction.

Instead, fear paralyzed me.

When one day went by and then another with the dread still squeezing my chest and fogging my brain, I knew I could either let it crush me in my quest to figure out how to live in the limbo of this in-house separation, or I could allow it to walk alongside me as I went about the business of living until I stumbled upon another emotion to replace it. I had two young children to parent and a job I needed for financial survival.

I chose the only option and put one foot in front of the other. This wasn't about taking it day by day. That was too big a task. I took everything minute by minute, footstep by footstep, breath by breath.

The first week we called ourselves separated slapped me with psychic shifts that caught me off guard even though I expected them. Each change, each repositioning of my life, made me question if I really did possess the strength I'd convinced myself I had.

***

Three days after the meeting with the divorce attorney, Tristan told me he was going to start dating.

We'd already discussed fidelity during the separation, one of the more cringe-worthy subjects that came up as we mapped out logistics, and I'd already told him to do what he wanted, that a year separation was a long time to be alone. What I didn't tell him was that in a way I wanted him to date, that the image of him with other women would make it easier for me to move on.

I tried to match his bravado by announcing that I too was going to start dating, but the words came out sounding as empty as they were. We both knew I was lying. But if nothing else, the acknowledgement of seeing other people opened my eyes to not only possibilities, but a somewhat exhilarating curiosity about how one learns to date again after fourteen years of being out of the dating pool.

I started noticing men. And noticing men noticing me. That night, while Tristan took Grady and Ava to a school event for dads, I went to Walmart for groceries. With fresh eyes open, I became very aware of men strolling through the aisles without a partner. I reached for the fat-free half and half, and an attractive man simultaneously reached for his own carton. I stole a glance at his ring finger. Naked. No wedding ring. I returned his smile.

But then I mentally checked myself out through the eyes of a potential suitor. I wore decade-old jeans with holes in both knees. Faded slip-on Sketchers that had stepped in one too many piles of my dog's poop. A black unisex Marmot winter jacket Tristan had bought me before one of our trips to the mountain house. A white Nike hat holding the sweat of at least a half dozen runs without a washing. No makeup. Eyes half swollen from intermittent crying.

I didn't need a mirror to see how disheveled I looked. This man had likely only smiled at me out of pity. I was a thirty-six-year-old woman with no wedding ring, whose smile was so forced and artificial that it exuded nothing but pain and sadness.

For forty-five minutes, I threw items into my cart and crossed them off my list. But in between the cracker aisle and the produce section, I looked at ring fingers. Was this what the dating scene was like?

* * *

If I was going to live on my own, some material things needed to stay in the past, things I'd never be able to cleanse of memories. That included any bed I'd shared with Tristan.

The double bed we had in the guest room, where I was now sleeping, was old and small. I didn't want the king-sized marital bed I'd relinquished to Tristan, but I didn't want this one either. I wanted my own bed that belonged only to me. And I wanted the ability to choose it.

As I anticipated the possibility that I would eventually be the one to move out, I didn't want to wait for that move to shop for a new bed. I had enough moves under my belt that I knew the focus would be on packing and unpacking, finding the energy and creativity to position belongings into their perfect spots. Moving time was busy and overwhelming. It was not the time for furniture shopping.

When I told Tristan I was heading to a nearby furniture store to buy a new bed, one that would be mine, not ours, he offered to come along with the kids. The separation was a mere five days old, new enough that we were still trying to break ourselves of the habit of family time with all four of us, the in-house arrangement still giving us the illusion we were a family.

I spotted the exact frame I'd always been drawn to, with a thick dark-wood headboard and drawers at the foot of the bed to enclose my journals and books, a style Tristan never liked so we never even considered, yet another example of his lack of consideration for my opinions. Ecstatic, I paid for the bed and scheduled the delivery, then meandered back through the store to find Tristan and the kids who had wandered off.

The store was like a maze, with huge sections designated for each room in the house. I walked back through the bedroom area, smiling at a mother scolding her young child for climbing up on a bed and jumping on it, wondering if my kids had the same urge.

I strolled through the living room section with sofas and recliners, coffee tables and TV stands, weaving around a family spending their Saturday looking for an upgraded sectional, then found my way to the office area, eavesdropping on a couple in search of a larger bookcase for their home office. Families surrounded me. As far as I could see, I was the only customer shopping alone.

I couldn't help but think back to the weeks before my wedding, the stores I visited and the gift registries I made alone without my soon-to-be husband. While I made preparations for my life with Tristan, he focused on the next phase of his life in the military. I remembered trying to subdue my disappointment, at the time having no idea how often I would be alone in my marriage, how frequently I would have to subdue my disappointment.

My heart hurting for my innocent younger self and the collection of disappointments she didn't see coming, I entered the dining room section, where the sight of a single table hit me so hard with a reality check that I almost fell to the floor.

Our current dining room wasn't big enough, but throughout our marriage I fantasized that Tristan and I would live in a house with a spacious formal dining room to host my family for holidays or dinner parties with friends.

That's why my heart fluttered at the sight of the dining room table of my dreams. I instinctively felt an urge to find Tristan, grab his arm, and exclaim, "We should buy this. This could be our family dining room table for the rest of our life."

But the rest of *our* life was over. And if we bought that table, it would be one more item to divvy up.

I slowly smoothed my hand over the wood. It was yet another thing we never did. We never bought a fancy dining room table. We never backpacked through Europe. We never renewed our vows on a milestone anniversary. We never took the kids on a Disney cruise. We never got matching tattoos. We never did so many things.

As my fingertips drifted off the edge of the table, I grieved for all the things we never did, all the things we would never do.

***

That first week of our in-house separation finally ended. And it ended with finality.

I pulled on a white cable-knit sweater and a pair of jeans, then breathed deeply. Tristan and I settled the kids in front of the television, poured cups of coffee, and sat side by side at the kitchen table to read through the fourteen-page final copy of the separation agreement the lawyer emailed us.

The document accurately reflected our statements a week earlier in her office, but it gutted me nonetheless. As I silently cried, Tristan maintained unwavering composure. He didn't flinch when reading sentences like, "Whereas, irreconcilable differences have arisen between the parties, making it impossible for them to live together as husband and wife," while merely the sight of my children's names printed on the same page as the word "divorce" pulverized me.

Tristan took Ava and Grady to a neighbor's house so we could "go to the bank." I tried to view the errand as what it was, a trip to Navy Federal Credit Union. "We're simply going to the bank," I told myself. "We're not completing the monumental mission of notarizing our separation agreement."

Don't cry, don't cry, don't cry. That mantra flashed continuously in my mind as the woman responsible for putting the official stamp on our termination carried out her job.

She watched us initial each page and scribble our signatures on the last one. Then she watched us do it again for the second copy. But when my penpoint touched paper on that twenty-eighth page for the very last signature, the very last ink mark required to make this official, my signature came out invisible.

The pen ran out of ink. It was fine for twenty-seven pages of initials. Page twenty-eight, the ink went dry.

I don't know if it was because Tristan knew my belief in signs, my belief that the universe has a peculiar way of either alerting or rewarding us, my belief that everything happens for a reason, but as soon as he saw the ink fading, he yanked the pen out of my hand and stuck another one in its place. It happened in the blink of an eye, as if he thought I might not keep signing my name if given too much time to analyze the symbolism.

I didn't want Tristan back. And I could never step backwards and return to the marriage and the life we'd had together. But despite everything I'd endured as a military spouse, I still harbored a salient fear of change, a fear of unknowns, a fear of endings. I hated goodbyes. Military life may have forced me to say a lot of them, but it didn't teach me how to make them less heartbreaking.

I finished signing my name and gently placed the second pen down, blinking as the bank employee stamped and signed, stamped and signed. Tristan asked her to make copies for us, and I turned my gaze to the floor, closed my eyes, and counted my inhales and exhales. With copies in hand, Tristan drove us home in silence.

The kids didn't want to end their playdate at the neighbor's house, and Tristan and I decided it was too soon to tell them about the divorce, so I retreated to the solace of my bed. I called my friend Jane, then my parents, then my brother Kurt. I talked about it until I physically couldn't talk anymore.

Tristan immediately left after dropping me off, claiming he was delivering the signed paperwork to the attorney's office, a task I found out he didn't do, a task I ended up doing myself. I wondered if, despite his outward stoicism, his lack of follow-through stemmed from a secret wish to postpone this last step before divorce.

Months later I found that white cable-knit sweater shoved in the back of my closet. I never wore it again. It only reminded me of the day I signed my marriage away.

* * *

When Tristan packed up to go out to sea for two weeks, I couldn't push him out the door fast enough.

Residing under the same roof as the man I was divorcing was frustrating, but I could deal with frustration. It was my inability to move forward, to move away from my old life, that made living together unbearable. I felt trapped in that house, stuck with my husband turned roommate. I was suffocating. I needed space.

By military standards it was a short trip, but a lot could happen in fourteen days and I was thankful for the opportunity to switch things up. One of those opportunities was a change of scenery.

I didn't know how badly I needed to get out of the house until I road-tripped to Maryland to see Jane, where she and her family had PCS'd from Virginia Beach. Taking advantage of a job I could do anywhere, Jane and I parked our laptops in her kitchen with our coffee mugs to work while our combined four children and two dogs played in the snow. Being in her house opened up my airways, helped me breathe freely again.

Drinking wine and laughing with a friend felt like a release; sleeping in her basement felt like a warm cocoon.

Like Tristan and I once did together, I escaped from reality. And it was exactly what I needed.

* * *

"Let's go see my psychic."

Typically, I would have declined Jane's invitation to book a psychic reading, claiming I didn't want to waste money on a service I was skeptical of. But I was still trudging through the fog to find reassurance in my ability to create a better life after divorce. Maybe a psychic could offer some.

With her flowing skirt, long gray hair, and soft-spoken voice, Faye welcomed us into her incense-infused shop. Still unsure if this woman could produce a meaningful glimpse into the future, I observed as she did Jane's reading.

When it was my turn, Faye asked me a series of questions and then performed calculations with the numbers from my birthday.

"You're having a bad year," she said, shuffling her deck of tarot cards.

"Wow," she continued, turning over the first card. "Are you having relationship issues?"

"Yes," I whispered, surprised by the wave of emotion that bubbled up.

"You're getting divorced." It was a statement, not a question. I nodded.

She flipped more cards, shaking her head and pausing in thought.

"You've been struggling with your marriage for about five years," she said. "You tried everything you could to make the marriage work. But you were the only one making an effort at communication."

"Yes," I confirmed.

Faye asked for my husband's birthday, and after more calculations she declared us completely incompatible, not a match at all.

"You knew when you married him that he wasn't the right person for you." I nodded, glancing over at Jane, who winked at me. She knew about the doubts on my wedding day. She knew that over the years I often replayed the words that rushed at me as I walked down the aisle: "We're not meant to grow old together." She knew this was the one sentence that would make me believe everything else about my reading.

Faye shared insights about my job (I would be hired full-time soon, surpassing my contractor status), my finances (I would struggle for a while but would eventually be fine), my transition through the divorce (the worst is happening right now), and even an important person that would enter my life ("I see the name 'Chris'").

"You've been lonely a long time," Faye said. "But a man is going to come into your life, and he is going to make you feel complete. You'll finally feel whole, like you're coming home. You don't need to worry about being alone. You won't be alone."

Once I started believing, I wanted more. But our session ended, and Jane and I went back to her house to discuss our readings over wine.

My first psychic reading didn't totally predict my future, but it did ignite an optimism I hadn't felt since telling Tristan I wanted a divorce. While it was all still fresh in my mind, I scribbled down a summary of everything I remembered.

I'm getting divorced.

I tried everything I could.

I knew he wasn't the right person for me.

I won't struggle financially forever.

A man is going to find me.

I won't be alone.

I'll finally feel whole.

Jane topped off my glass of wine and asked how I felt.

"I can do this," I said.

And for the first time, I believed it.

***

Leaving Jane's house after the brief visit was bittersweet. Being there allowed me temporary amnesia, offering a safe haven where the shaky status of my life wasn't in my face every waking minute. But I couldn't hide forever.

When I returned home, I felt an urgency to reduce. It was the same urgency I experienced every time Tristan and I got ready to PCS to a new duty station. Reduce clutter. Throw out that half-eaten jar of peanut butter that hadn't been touched in months. Toss the frozen foods we'd been "saving." Reduce the amount of crap the movers would have to pack and unpack again at the next destination.

The cleansing included my psyche as well. Reduce stress. Reduce anxiety. Reduce self-blame. Reduce mommy guilt. Reduce emotional baggage.

I was hoping the days would blur together in a haze of fast-moving change that kept my brain and heart distracted. But if anything, the days crept by in baby steps and stumbles.

One day I took a mental health day off from work, went running, and sobbed through multiple episodes of *Grey's Anatomy*. It was too much empty time on my hands. So the next day I did the opposite, returning to work and staying super productive, leaving me exhausted by bedtime. I couldn't find the balance.

I forced myself to do basic things. Wake up with a brighter outlook. Exercise. Talk to friends. Write a blog post. Go to therapy. Commonplace motions that were once instinctual had to be conscious choices or they wouldn't happen.

One thing I wasn't forcing myself to do was date, despite the coaxing from my married friends. I wanted to take that part of single life slowly, learn from observation like a science experiment.

I watched men around me, searching their facial expressions and demeanors for clues they might be interested in me. One day I noticed a man in my spinning class at the YMCA, and thought, "He has kind eyes." He smiled at me. I smiled back. I wanted to talk to him, let him know I was single, flirt until he asked me out to dinner.

But I froze. I didn't talk to the man with kind eyes, and he didn't talk to me. We both looked away and silently warmed up on our bikes. However, the interchange did accomplish something. It made me realize that, once I was ready to date, I wanted to go into it knowing what I was looking for. I didn't want to randomly date guys to figure out what I wanted in a man, in a relationship. I was too old for that. I didn't have that time to waste. I wanted to go into it well aware of what I wanted. And what I didn't want.

I'd been with the same man for nearly fifteen years, and I needed to pinpoint the traits he had that I didn't want to repeat in a partner. The man in my spinning class showed me I wanted someone whose face exudes kindness. After what I'd been through with Tristan, I didn't see kindness when I looked at him. I couldn't remember if I ever had. And so my mental list of character traits I found attractive began with its first entry: kind eyes.

***

As usual, Tristan was in and out, packing and unpacking, traveling to other countries for the Navy. He happened to be home for Grady's ninth birthday and suggested we all go out to dinner to celebrate as a family.

Family.

Were the four of us still considered a family? Tristan and I were still procrastinating on telling the kids about the divorce, mostly because neither Grady nor Ava approached us with questions. But we agreed to tell them in the next couple of weeks, aware that we needed to verbalize what they likely already sensed but couldn't label. We just didn't want to ruin Grady's birthday. From their perspective, as far as we knew, our family unit was intact.

Although the last thing I wanted to do was go out to dinner with Tristan, ensuring that the kids came out on the other side as unscathed as possible was my priority. So for the sake of the kids, I agreed to a family birthday dinner.

Tristan took us to Keagan's, the Irish pub where the Navy SEAL gave me his email address. I knew Tristan had been hanging out there since we separated, and I sensed he wanted me to see that he knew the bartenders and waitresses by name, that he was a regular there.

The hostess seated us, and I positioned myself as far as I could from Tristan, busying myself with settling five-year-old Ava in her chair. Tristan and Grady were deep in conversation over meal choices, while Ava scribbled on her paper menu with crayons. I sat motionless, admiring my beautiful children and wishing I could bottle up their innocence to save for the coming months.

Everything about the dinner was awkward. Tristan spilled a glass of water all down my leg. Conversation was forced and cumbersome. As we sang "Happy Birthday," Ava blew out the candle on Grady's birthday dessert. I couldn't wait to leave. Pretending to be a family was excruciating.

But the day wasn't about me. Or Tristan. And Grady didn't seem to pick up on any of our animosity. He looked happy. So I tried to match Grady's joy. Because this was the last birthday he would ever celebrate with what he saw as our family. On his next birthday he would be a child of divorce.

* * *

I maintained a regular schedule with my therapist, Julia, and per her advice, Tristan and I developed a custody schedule. Even though we lived at the same address, it was in everyone's best interest to get all four of us accustomed to Mommy Nights and Daddy Nights, to the flip-flop rhythm of designated time with each parent, to the parental pass-off.

The schedule gave us each two nights out a week. Tuesday and Saturday were Tristan's nights out, when he wouldn't come home until after the kids went to sleep. Wednesday and Friday were my nights out. The parent at home was responsible for all childcare duties from dinner to baths to bedtime stories.

Considering my tenure as a stay-at-home mother combined with all my solo parenting, my nights at home wouldn't be the challenging part of the schedule. It was the nights out. Grady and Ava weren't confused by their father's absence. They were used to that. It was my disappearance that would make them question what was going on. But we wanted to test the schedule out for a week first before telling them that this was a permanent change because their parents were breaking up. Luckily, the kids accepted our partial truth that we were trying something new.

I seriously considered spending the entire evening of my first night out hiding out in our backyard shed. I'd never eaten dinner at a restaurant by myself, never gone to a movie theater by myself. My fear of being conspicuously alone made me want to avoid public places at all costs.

But we needed to do this. I needed to do this. I needed to adjust to leaving my children with their father. I needed to adjust to doing things on my own. I needed to see what the world looked like through the eyes of a single woman.

I pulled on a pair of skinny jeans, a gray sweater, and my black knee-high leather boots, then applied makeup and twisted my hair into a clip. Slipping my laptop, cell phone, and a novel into my favorite oversized purse, I was ready to hit the town with a mix of curiosity and dread.

With a shaky plan, I kissed the kids goodnight, cheerfully told them to have fun with their dad, and drove away. I told myself this was actually a good deal. I mean, how often do moms wish they had more time alone to do whatever they wanted?

My first stop was Barnes & Noble. I found a vacant chair in a corner, opened my laptop, and composed an essay for work. "That wasn't too hard," I thought. "There are lots of people sitting in chairs by themselves doing their own thing without a partner."

My stomach grumbling, I packed up my computer and drove down the street to Chili's for dinner. Weighing my seating options in order to choose the most discreet location, I decided to sit at the nearly empty bar instead of in a booth surrounded by couples and families. After placing my order with the bartender, I opened my novel to wait for my southwest egg rolls, practically covering my face with the hardcover book when a man sat a few stools away from me. "Avoid eye contact," I thought. "Just read your book. Don't encourage this man to strike up a conversation." I was in no way ready for a stranger to attempt to pick me up at a bar.

After eating as quickly as possible and returning to the safety of my Subaru Outback, my GPS led me to a small spa, where I indulged in a sixty-minute discounted massage thanks to a Groupon I found online.

Tired, my skin and hair greasy from the massage oil, and out of ideas, I returned to Barnes & Noble, watching the minutes tick away until I could go home and go to sleep.

Although the hours seemed to drag on, my first night out wasn't nearly as scary as I'd imagined. Even dining alone, while slightly uncomfortable in its newness, wasn't a big deal. No one stared at me. No one looked at me with pity. The only person who seemed to notice my solitary meal was me. Maybe one day I would look forward to these nights out. Maybe one day I'd laugh at tonight's silly fears and realize I loved being alone with my own company. I wasn't quite there yet, but it no longer seemed like such an outlandish concept.

When I finally returned home at 10:30, Tristan was watching television in the family room. We had agreed that the time we spent apart on our nights out was "no questions asked." My whereabouts were none of his business, just as his were none of mine. And while I didn't have to ask him to know he was dating, it almost felt validating to let him believe I was dating too. So, when he mused aloud that I was probably out on a hot date, I didn't correct him.

***

After getting through a week trial period of our homemade custody schedule, Tristan and I told the kids the full truth.

The two Mommy Nights and two Daddy Nights weren't perfect. Tristan wasn't accustomed to the kids' normal routine, the timeline of dinner and kitchen cleanup, bathing and bedtime with limited screen time. But I tried not to criticize his parenting style. He had to figure out for himself how to be a single father, how to establish his own routines and timelines and household rules. It wasn't the end of the world if the kids skipped an occasional shower. It wasn't the end of the world if dirty dishes sat in the sink for a few hours. It wasn't the end of the world if bedtimes got pushed back on a weeknight to snuggle on the couch and watch a movie on rare occasions. Ultimately, when Tristan and I no longer lived together, I wouldn't be around to micromanage him with my own opinions, so as long as we were on the same page about the big parenting issues, I had to let go of my control over some of the smaller issues. As I always said about parenting, I had to choose my battles.

Tristan and I settled on a date and time for our family meeting with Ava and Grady, brainstorming a loose script and answers to possible questions we anticipated. We both felt the best way to break the news was together.

The four of us gathered in the living room, where I sat in one chair, Tristan in another, and the kids plopped down on the couch across from us.

I barely opened my mouth to speak when I choked up. I promised myself I wouldn't fall apart in front of my children. I needed to hold my tears in, keep my voice steady. Their reaction would depend on the composure (or lack thereof) of our delivery of the news, and I didn't want this to be dominated by sadness. I was relieved when Tristan kicked off the discussion.

"We're not getting along like a husband and wife should," Tristan said, using a line from the script we agreed on. "And that's why we're not sleeping in the same bed."

Blank stares.

"And we won't be spending much time together as a family anymore," Tristan continued, looking back and forth between Grady and Ava. "But you're going to get lots of time with each of us."

Blank stares.

Tristan and I looked at each other, and I was sure his thoughts mimicked mine: "Why aren't they reacting? At all?"

Going into this talk, I imagined Grady calmly peppering us with logistical questions, like living arrangements and the possibility of school transfers. I envisioned Ava having a dramatic meltdown, complete with body-shaking sobs and Mommy leg-clinging. I clasped, unclasped, and reclasped my fingers fidgeting in my lap.

"You're going to get Daddy time and Mommy time just like we did this week," I said, finally finding my voice.

Blank stares.

"But even though things are going to change, the one thing that won't change is that we both love you very much," I said, filling the silence. "And if you ever have questions or don't understand something, you can ask us."

That was our big speech. Tristan and I made eye contact and shrugged. We aimed to keep it age-appropriate and simple, but this seemed too simple.

"Do you have any questions right now?" Tristan asked, leaning in closer to where the kids were sitting on the couch.

"Daddy, how old are you?" Ava asked, tapping her chin as if stoically contemplating the meaning of life.

"If we have Mommy time and Daddy time, will we also get Gunner time?" Grady asked, petting the dog.

We laughed at their silliness. More serious follow-up questions would certainly come later as their young brains processed the information. We hugged them, reiterating that we loved them more than anything in the world, then adjourned the meeting, as they scampered upstairs to their rooms.

With Grady barely nine years old and Ava only five, I didn't expect a long drawn-out conversation. But I also wasn't expecting this three-minute speed chat.

Three minutes. That was all it took for us to forever alter the lives of these two little human beings.

CHAPTER 20

Finding My Red

"Have you thought about moving out of the marital house?" Julia asked in one of our counseling sessions. "It seems staying there is like living with a ghost."

I knew she was right. I couldn't live much longer in that house with my dead marriage haunting me.

By April, four months after signing the separation agreement, our in-house separation reached unbearable levels. Some days, I was disgusted by this man I shared my home with, irritated as I watched him getting dressed for dates, pissed off as he showed no signs of moving out. Some days, sorrow overwhelmed me as I glimpsed parts of my marriage I once treasured. Every wall, every cabinet, every mirror held intimate memories that I couldn't decide if I'd rather erase from my memory forever or desperately cling to as proof that our love once existed, proof that I didn't waste over a decade of my life with the wrong partner.

I didn't want to live in this house. I didn't want the old. I wanted the new. I didn't want stagnancy. I wanted forward momentum.

The only way I could move on was to move out.

When I said good morning to Tristan at the coffee pot, moved around him in the hallway, divided our mail, saw his beer in the fridge, I was constantly reminded that we weren't divorced but we weren't really married either. Some days, living in that limbo was simply a nuisance. But other days, it made me so impatient to break free that I almost got in my car with the kids and drove away, leaving all of our things behind if it meant escape.

When the Navy sent Tristan out to sea, and the kids and I had the house to ourselves, the time apart energized me. I didn't need a husband as much as his presence tricked me into believing I did. My confidence in myself and my abilities as a single mother soared when I didn't have to see him day in and day out.

It was time to get the hell out of there.

***

After calculating my budget based on my salary combined with the child support and alimony Tristan was legally obligated to pay me according to the separation agreement once one of us moved out, I faced the uphill battle of finding a place to live.

I harbored a mental block against apartments, maybe because it reminded me of Alabama, of learning how to be married while teetering on the edge of being broke. I couldn't fathom living in an apartment again, this time learning how to be unmarried. But I couldn't afford a house, especially in the better school zone I wanted to switch the kids to. After soliciting advice from friends in the area, I added the Marina Shores apartment complex to the top of my wish list.

Located about twenty minutes away, Marina Shores was situated within walking distance of the beach, a grocery store, a bank, the elementary school, and a trail to the local state park. The complex offered residents a pool, a gym, and tennis courts, and it was one of the few apartments in the city to allow large dogs. And the most important part: If I adhered to the tight budget I calculated, I could afford it.

But despite my research and enthusiasm, I waited to make any decisions, not wanting to uproot the kids until I was certain.

That came on a Saturday, Tristan's assigned day with the kids, and after spin class at the YMCA in the morning, I settled in at a Starbucks to knock out some writing for work. I'm not sure why he called me, whether he intended to pick a fight or had a question about the kids, but I hung up the phone seething with acute anger spurring me on to do something drastic, to prove myself.

This one deviated from our usual arguments. This one felt like a dare. He didn't seem to believe I would move out, didn't believe my independence stretched to finding a place to live without his help.

Fifteen minutes later I opened the door of the Marina Shores office asking for a tour.

"So why are you looking for an apartment?" the manager asked me.

I'm sure it was the standard question asked of all prospective renters, and I'm sure my bursting into tears wasn't the standard response, but when the sweet woman handed me a box of tissues without flinching, I calmed down.

"I'm getting divorced," I stuttered.

"I totally get it," she said. "I'm divorced too. I know how hard it is."

She let me collect my composure, filling the awkward pause with a description of the various units and the amenities and telling stories of people who made homes there, from newlyweds saving money for their first house to military families who would be in and out in a couple of years to freshly divorced men and women like me.

I blew my nose, and finally able to speak without hiccupping, told her I had two young children and a Labrador retriever, that I hoped to move in as soon as possible.

"I think you're going to love the unit I'm about to show you," she said with a smile that made me believe her. "Let's go take a look."

She unlocked the door and led me into the two-story, 1,300-square-foot apartment, one of their largest units. I followed her through the dining room and the kitchen, across the generic beige carpet to peek into the primary bedroom and bathroom, then through the living room to the small deck with a storage closet. We went back inside and up the stairs to open the doors hiding the washer and dryer and then into the second bedroom, through the Jack and Jill bathroom, and into the third bedroom.

It was bigger than that apartment in Alabama where the story of my marriage began. But over the years since then I'd gotten used to living larger, upgrading from that two-bedroom apartment to three-bedroom houses and ultimately the house that concluded the story of my marriage, a 2,100-square-foot, four-bedroom house with a fenced-in yard.

My throat closed up as I tried to answer the woman when we were back in the main office and she asked what I thought.

How could I explain that, while I did want to move out of my marital home, I resented being the one having to downgrade my living space? How could I put into words how much it scared me that this apartment was an example of how much I had to adjust my expectations about everything in my life going forward? How could I admit that the thought of living in this apartment as a single mother terrified me?

"It's perfect," I squeaked out instead. "How soon can I move in?"

"There's a unit with the same floor plan opening up July 29," she said after searching her computer. "In fact, it's that one right up there, overlooking the pool." She stood up and pointed out the window to the deck directly across from us.

"I'll take it," I said.

The next morning, I told Tristan that I had official plans to move out. If he was surprised, he didn't show it. We briefly talked about how great Marina Shores is and how much the kids will enjoy the apartment's pool, their new school, and living close to the beach. Then I left him at the house with Ava and Grady so I could get a money order, put down the security deposit for my apartment, and sign the lease.

I was moving in eighty-six days.

***

I'd never lived alone before. I transitioned from my parents' house to college roommates to a brief post-college roommate to moving in with Tristan. Technically, I wasn't living by myself because the kids would live with me most of the time, but I was the only adult, the only one in charge. My name was the only name on the lease. The only name on the mailbox. The only name on the utility bills. This was all mine. That level of autonomy illuminated a sense of power I didn't recall ever possessing. I couldn't wait to make the apartment my home.

After years of watching Navy-paid movers take care of all the packing, I channeled my military spouse skills now that I was the one assembling and taping boxes, wrapping delicate items in bubble wrap and keeping a running inventory.

I despised it. Not because of the physical, time-consuming labor, but because of the sentimentality of it, because I was going through everything Tristan and I owned together and dividing it all into piles of "mine" and "his." It wasn't simply the act of placing items in boxes. Packing turned into a harsh and unwelcome stroll down memory lane.

I did most of the packing while the kids played at summer camp and I could take breaks from work, mainly because I never knew how packing would twist my emotions. Some days I felt invigorated, bursting with the thrill of getting out of that house. I blasted music and wrapped items in brown paper, situating them into boxes like puzzle pieces and triumphantly taping them closed, scribbling a number on the box with a Sharpie and then adding it to my list of boxes and their contents. If the moving companies the Navy hired—especially the ones in Japan—taught me anything, it was organization and efficiency.

Other days packing felt like trudging uphill through mud. Everything I touched sparked a flashback. A tea set Tristan and I purchased in Japan. A T-shirt he bought me that I'd never wear again. Some items brought up such clear and distinct nostalgia of a better time in our marriage that I froze in that vision, sobbing on the kitchen floor as I allowed myself to feel it. As I learned the hard way throughout my marriage, stifling feelings never eliminated them. I needed to work through those grueling emotions so I could release them and leave them in that house. If I didn't address them, they might eternally smother me.

The items I didn't pack were as revealing as the items I did. When I looked at our tiny dining room table and the obnoxious oversized dresser, I became infuriated all over again thinking of when Tristan bought them without consulting me, how that lack of partnership in a financial decision was one of many little things that bothered me, but one of the many little things I didn't push back on. If he'd asked me if I liked the dining room table or the dresser, I would have said no, and we shouldn't spend money on furniture we didn't both like and want in our home for years to come. I was still mad at Tristan. And I was mad at that stupid dining room table and dresser.

"Good riddance!" I yelled at the furniture. "I never wanted you!"

It felt good to yell at something that couldn't yell back.

***

Stress pummeled me from every direction, and when I thought I had one area contained enough to put on a temporary hold, another area demanded damage control. And one stressor I always feared I was failing miserably at was explaining to my children what their parents' divorce meant for them.

One day, when I was beyond my limit with boxes and work deadlines and co-parenting logistics and budgeting question marks, hearing the kids fighting overflowed my capacity for patience.

"Separate yourselves and go to your rooms!" I scolded.

Hollering at the kids was a rare occurrence for me, so with shocked faces, Grady and Ava wordlessly marched upstairs.

I waited thirty minutes to calm down before summoning them to my room for a meeting on my bed.

"I'm sorry for yelling earlier," I said. "It's not a good excuse but I've been stressed out. But that stress isn't about you or the new apartment because I'm super excited about moving. The stress is about packing. Because packing stinks."

They nodded as I reiterated that I loved them both more than anything on this planet, a fact I'd repeated so many times recently that they practically rolled their eyes whenever I said it.

"Is Daddy going to find a new girl to marry?"

Ava caught me off guard, and I winced.

"Maybe," I said.

"Mommy, are you crying?" she asked.

I nodded and glanced at Grady, whose eyes also shimmered with tears.

"There are a lot of changes coming," I whispered. "And it's okay to be sad."

Ava threw her little arms around my neck as if consoling me, as if she hadn't asked me this monumental question in the most casual of tones. Grady, on the other hand, was quietly watching me. We locked gazes. I wished I could read his thoughts.

My acknowledgement and apology for yelling appeased them both enough for a Walmart trip before an early dinner in front of a movie. Later, when they were coloring together in my bedroom and I was downstairs attempting to write, my ears picked up the word "stepdad." Curious, I crept up the stairs and leaned against the wall, hoping that eavesdropping might offer some insight into what my kids were thinking, how they might be leaning on each other.

"We don't have a stepdad right now, right?" Ava asked her brother.

"No, not right now," Grady said. "But we will have a stepdad."

"Why do we have to have a stepdad?"

"Because Dad won't be living with us anymore."

"But Dad will come and visit us."

"No, we'll go to him. Like our friend Aiden. Sometimes Aiden is with his mom and sometimes he's with his dad."

"Why?

"Because there comes a time in life when people break up."

"When I grow up, I'm going to have boyfriends. You know who?"

"Who?"

"Justin Bieber."

"Justin Bieber sucks."

"Okay, well, then Uncle Kurt."

"Uncle Kurt is already married."

"Oh." Ava paused. "What should I draw next?"

As I heard them trading crayons, I tiptoed back down the stairs. In that moment I was so thankful my kids had each other. And I was thankful they were finding their own ways to process the divorce.

* * *

It took weeks, but I finished packing, sliding boxes to the corners of rooms until the movers I hired came to permanently remove them. In the meantime, I also made lists of household items I needed to buy because our current ones now belonged to Tristan.

Some things I bought before the move, like dishes. I'd never been so excited to purchase everyday dishware. I had picked out the plates and bowls for our wedding registry. Plain white with a thin ring of dark blue circling the edges, I chose them for their versatility, but after over a decade of eating off them, I wanted more. I wanted color.

Red was my favorite color. In my mind, red signified fierceness, sassiness, a fire to stand out and be bold. As I walked around the house that was half packed and half still in place, all I saw were shades of dark blues and browns. Not a splash of red, not a splash of me, anywhere. Why had I been living all these years in a home with no red, no fierceness, no sassiness? Now that I was facing life as a single mom, I craved my boldness that had gotten lost in the span of my marriage.

I went to Target and bought red dishes. And red towels. And red bedding. If I needed red dishes, red towels, and red bedding to jumpstart that fire, then that's where I would start.

Owning these new items also felt like a gift from me to me during a time when I was losing so much. When going through a divorce, it's hard not to feel like a failure. I had to remind myself regularly that it was my marriage that failed, not me. I hadn't failed as a person because I married a person I wasn't meant to grow old with.

That thought that mysteriously appeared on my wedding day, that I wasn't meant to grow old with this man, reappeared almost daily, nudging me to dissect its meaning now that the premonition was coming true.

It wasn't warning me that Tristan would get killed during one of his deployments to the Middle East, so what did it mean? Maybe my gut was telling me on my wedding day not to marry him to begin with. Maybe my intuition wanted me to stop walking down that aisle because he wasn't my person, because calling off a wedding while it is happening, as embarrassing as it might be at the time, is exponentially easier to move on from than marrying the wrong person and getting divorced thirteen years later after creating two other human beings.

However, that explanation seemed too black and white. I had to believe I ignored the premonition, ignored the storm brewing in our background, for reasons that would expand my world, not diminish it.

I wasn't meant to grow old with Tristan, but that didn't mean I wasn't meant to marry him. Those humans we created were pretty amazing and wouldn't exist if I hadn't finished my walk down that aisle. I wouldn't have become a military spouse, a job title I wasn't sure how to wear, a role I was never really good at, but one I grew to appreciate. I wouldn't have lived in Japan and learned about a different culture while discovering my untapped love for travel.

When I got to the root of it, I believe my gut wasn't trying to stop my wedding from happening. It wasn't warning me of my future husband's impending death. I think it was purely a heads-up that this marriage wasn't going to last forever, but it would teach me so many lessons that it would ultimately transform me into the woman I needed to become, the woman capable of going after her own happiness.

My marriage would teach me the importance of finding my red, what was hidden deep beneath someone else's hues.

***

My first holiday without the kids was the Fourth of July. It wasn't one of the major holidays included in the division of custody in our separation agreement, not a day on the calendar Tristan and I were legally obligated to alternate every year. But as I spent the day alone, I felt the significance of this final holiday in my marital home.

Tristan told me one of his coworkers invited him and the kids to a party, a day of river swimming and zip-lining. I had nothing planned other than maybe going over to a neighbor's gathering and walking across the street to the elementary school to watch the Mount Trashmore fireworks. The kids would have more fun at Tristan's party, so I agreed, telling myself to take advantage of the quiet time to decompress.

I was running a 5k race that morning and wasn't sure the kids would still be home when I returned, so I kissed them both and wished them a great day.

As I hugged Grady, he said, "Mom, aren't you coming with us?"

"I wasn't invited," I said. "Dad and I won't be going to parties like this together anymore. Do you understand?"

He nodded despite his quizzical expression. Once again, I wished I could see what he was thinking so I could offer better answers.

After the adrenaline rush of the race, I decided to hide out at home, reading, getting ahead on work, and watching Wimbledon tennis. It wasn't until darkness fell that loneliness found me and I retreated into a somber introspection urging me to get out of the house.

By the time I put Gunner on his leash and we got to the school, families had already set out lawn chairs and children ran around the parking lot giggling with made-up games. I stood on the periphery in the darkness where no one could see me.

I watched the fireworks for a few minutes, listening to my neighbors' oohs and aahs as the night sky exploded with lights, tears forming puddles on my collarbones. When I started feeling tortured by everyone else's happiness, I walked back home.

But when I reached the front of my house, I couldn't go inside. It occurred to me that I'd come full circle. I was alone for the first Fourth of July in this house, and I was alone for the last. I needed to see it to its end.

Exactly five years earlier I was doing the same thing, watching fireworks in the street in front of my house by myself while Tristan and the kids slept. At the time I was trying to see the house as a new beginning for my marriage. After Tristan had told me he wanted a divorce two months earlier in Japan, I thought we just needed a fresh environment. But standing in the street outside the house of new beginnings by myself hadn't seemed like a good start.

I almost laughed when I remembered that was also the night our air conditioner got struck by lightning. If I wanted a sign, that was probably the most blatant sign the universe could offer. And I didn't listen.

As the grand finale of fireworks popped in rapid succession, I thought of that lightning strike. I thought I'd never felt more alone that night, but in reality, I'd been alone for a very long time. I told myself to stay in the present moment, that I needed to see the completion of these fireworks from the same standpoint where I stood five years earlier praying for change.

And then it was over. It was all over.

CHAPTER 21

Teamwork

Moving day opened with promise. It closed with a police report.

My brother Kurt flew in from Colorado to help, while Tristan voluntarily went out of town, something I probably would have done too if he was the one moving out.

The night before the big day, I said my farewells to the house, walking through each room, replaying the good times instead of the bad. These walls had witnessed the deterioration of my marriage, but they also preserved happy memories. Now I wanted different walls that held only secrets of strangers. Teeming with readiness, I hardly slept, eager to wake up and take a giant leap into my new life.

Everything coming with me was packed or labeled with a sign for the movers to load into the truck. I chose to take my beloved Japanese step *tansu* that Tristan and I bought at an auction on base in Sasebo, and left behind the bulky desk we shared. I took the TV stand that didn't fit in with the rest of our furniture because I had picked it out, but left almost everything hanging on the walls because he had picked it all out. I took the kitchen table that once belonged to Tristan's grandmother but that I always liked more than he did, and left behind the small dining room table, also from Japan, that had a removable top to transform into a game table. I took my University of West Florida coffee mug, and left behind the expensive coffee pot that brewed pods that I considered wasteful.

I didn't argue with Tristan about any of the material items we accumulated together. In fact, if he had fought to keep everything but my recent purchases, I probably would have acquiesced, despite the financial burden to furnish my apartment from scratch. The furniture, the decor, the rugs were all Tristan's tastes. So little in the house held sentimental value to me. The step *tansu*, the TV stand, my new bed, sheets, dishes, and towels were the only things I really considered mine, telling evidence of how little Tristan regarded my opinions.

I stripped the kids' beds, then mine, and after dropping Grady and Ava off at summer camp, I swung by my apartment with the bedding to wait for my cable and internet hook-up appointment. Meanwhile, Kurt stayed at the house to greet the movers at 9:00 a.m.

Nine o'clock came and went. At 9:30 I called the owner of the moving company I'd handed my hundred-dollar deposit to when he'd done a walk-through of the house two weeks prior. No answer. I called and called. For hours. If this had been a military PCS, Tristan would have placed one phone call after another to the base's Personal Property office until whoever was in charge of hiring the local movers figured out where they were and how we could replace them. But I couldn't rely on the military anymore.

By early afternoon, I admitted my moving day wasn't happening.

Still at the house, Kurt found a moving company available the next morning. I was thrilled by this good fortune on such short notice, but less than thrilled by the day delay.

Before picking up the kids from camp, I drove to the address on the moving company's business card to see if I could talk to the owner face-to-face. When I pulled into the parking lot, a police car was guarding the building. The officer approached me and asked who I was there to see. When I told her, she said, "That's who I'm looking for too."

I burst into tears. Today was supposed to be my monumental new beginning, but instead of a new beginning, I got ghosted.

"Be thankful he didn't show up," the officer said. "Because if he had, he would have loaded everything you owned onto his truck and driven to another state, and you'd never have seen any of it again."

She explained he had a warrant out for his arrest and I could kiss that hundred-dollar deposit goodbye. She recommended I file a police report, so I cursed my bad luck and filled out paperwork about the man who intended to steal all of my possessions.

With no other choice, I returned to the house, bringing back all of the bedding and remaking all of our beds so we didn't have to sleep on bare mattresses. I ordered pizza, and we went to bed early to prepare to do it all over again tomorrow.

The previous night I'd paused for a few mindful moments to thank the house for sheltering me before falling asleep for what I thought would be the last time. But tonight, I was dejected. I hated the house for trapping me. It was mocking me, taunting me as if to say, "You don't think you can actually do this, do you? You can't even move out without screwing it up. You can't possibly live on your own."

But the next day, I did do it.

The movers loaded up the boxes I spent weeks packing into their truck, I whispered one more final farewell, and I locked the door and drove away without a glance in the rearview.

I wondered how Tristan would fill the spaces I left, how quickly he would get a roommate for the bedroom I vacated and if that roommate would be male or female. I wondered how he would feel when he walked into the emptiness from my absence. I wondered why I cared.

Then I remembered his feelings were no longer my concern. I needed to focus on my own feelings, my own healing, my own life, a life no longer intertwined with his.

***

It was almost dark by the time I closed the front door of my apartment and took in the full view of the mountains of boxes and my uncertain future.

Kurt had to get to the airport mid-afternoon, so I was alone with Grady and Ava when I noticed an extra mattress on top of my bed on the first floor. "That's not right," I thought. I went up to the second floor where the kids were settling into their rooms and groaned when I saw Grady's bed frame assembled but naked without a mattress.

Uncompromising in my insistence to make our first night in our new home as normal as possible for all three of us, I had to get that double-bed mattress up the stairs so my child could sleep in his own room. I was in pretty good shape. How hard could it be to get a mattress up a flight of stairs?

As it turned out, very hard.

As soon as I attempted to lift that mattress, I knew it would take herculean strength to get it upstairs. Just moving it from atop my queen-sized bed and into an upright position strained every muscle in my body.

After shimmying it with pushes and pulls to the base of the stairs, I inhaled a deep breath and, on the exhale, threw my full weight into thrusting the mattress up.

By the time I got it to the landing where the stairs changed directions, I was drenched in sweat, my arms shaking. The mattress was defeating me.

But it was no match for teamwork led by a determined single mother.

***

I collapsed in bed too drained to analyze the magnitude of it all, but echoing affirmations to fall into sleep with positivity. "I am a single woman," I thought. "I officially left my husband. I am officially out of the house of pain and heartache. I still hurt, but I can do this. It's done. Only forward movement from here."

Life as a military spouse trained me to refer to a move as a Permanent Change of Station. But even though my life as a military spouse was over, my move to the apartment was a PCS of its own variety. It permanently changed my station in life. This move may not have required military orders, but it required those lessons the military taught me about starting over. I was no longer reconfiguring everything to fit into the Navy's puzzle, but I could use those problem-solving skills to create my own puzzle and learn as I go how my pieces fit together, tossing out any that didn't belong. This move permanently changed everything, from my geographic location to my perspective.

The apartment wasn't big, but it didn't feel small. Shared walls and the elevator outside our front door meant it wasn't quiet, but the noise brought security. It wasn't a house, but I would make it a home.

It wasn't perfect. But it was mine.

***

With my migration to the other side of town came a revised custody schedule. The kids and the dog would stay with me during the week and with Tristan on weekends, with any variations, like deployments or travel for either of us, discussed with as much advance notice as possible.

We both vowed to maintain amicable communications, reasonably talking out modifications instead of taking minor issues to court.

Tristan and I legally shared fifty-fifty custody of Ava and Grady, but realistically that was impossible. Tristan had an unpredictable schedule, while my work-from-home job lent itself to getting the kids on and off the school bus in addition to being available for emergencies, days off from school, and general weekday flexibility. But even though I had the kids most of the time, I dreaded the back and forth, the here then gone, the weekly packing of overnight bags.

Fortunately, I didn't have time to overthink the first co-parenting pass-off, because it happened the day after I moved into the apartment.

My mom guilt surfaced along with relief that Tristan wanted to road-trip with the kids to the mountain house for a week and a half, but with my nerves frayed and my patience short from the chaos of the move, it was probably to everyone's benefit that I had some down time. Trips like this weren't included in the separation agreement, so Tristan and I agreed to negotiate on a case-by-case basis, and in this case, I gladly consented to his request. I looked forward to twelve child-free days to settle in and allow myself a meltdown in solitude with the added bonus that the kids would have fun with their father.

I didn't know what to expect when Tristan pulled into the parking lot outside my building. This move proved what my friends warned me about: Tristan and I had been legally separated for seven months, but we hadn't truly been separated. Now that we lived in separate dwellings, things like co-parenting schedules were no longer discussions over coffee in the kitchen before work. This was a real pass-off. And the maternal instinct to envelop my children in my arms and return them to the safety of our home crept up on me as I stood on the sidewalk with Grady and Ava and their suitcases and watched Tristan's gray Jeep drive up.

I thought I would hug the kids and wave goodbye and that would be it. I thought it would be like every other time Tristan drove away with them in his backseat. I thought it would be routine. It was none of that. It was gut-wrenching.

I stood on the sidewalk watching the Jeep disappear around the bend of the parking lot, unmoving as a woman walked past me with her dog on a leash, as a couple strolled by with grocery bags from the nearby Food Lion, as a family of four buzzed by on their bikes in the direction of the path to the park, the two young children, probably around the same ages as Ava and Grady, wearing spiked dinosaur helmets. I'd never felt more alone.

Feeling nauseous, I forced myself to move from the sidewalk and trudged up the stairs to my unit, closing the door behind me to weep on the floor.

***

During the in-house separation, when Tristan and I initially divided our nights with the kids, I left the house until the kids were asleep. On those evenings, I got used to my own company, overcoming my self-consciousness at being alone in places I'd never been alone in before.

Those beginning solo outings, those baby steps towards a single version of myself, were far outside my comfort zone, but they gave me the confidence that I could indeed thrive without a partner. I could still go out and have a life.

But that was all pseudo co-parenting. Now that Tristan and I lived in different places and the custody schedule changed, I came home not to sleeping children, not to the presence of others, but to an empty apartment. Silence. The stale air of solitude.

After the exhaustion of single parenting during the week, I thought I'd embrace the independence of weekends, feeling weightless and free while the kids were with Tristan. In actuality, I felt as if a body part had been amputated. A part of me was lost. And I struggled with phantom limb pain that couldn't be replaced with a glass of wine or a chat with a friend.

I picked up Nerf darts that hid in corners of the family room, putting them back on the table in Grady's bedroom dedicated to Legos and random toys, fighting the urge to sit there for hours assembling my own Lego creations alongside his. I folded laundry, clipping Ava's multicolored skorts to hangers, pausing to give the stuffed animals in her closet a squeeze in remembrance of why she treasured each one. I picked at their string cheese in the fridge, I watched the *Despicable Me* DVD I'd watched with the kids more times than I could count, and in the shower I washed my hair with their sweet-smelling Papa Smurf shampoo.

I sunk into the void of their absence.

As I once did when Tristan was deployed, I decided that staying busy and occupying my mind was the best way to level out my anxiety about missing my babies and to fill my open calendar.

It somehow didn't occur to me until most of my boxes were unpacked that there was an empty space where a couch should be. So one Saturday, I made it my mission of the weekend to buy a couch.

I jotted down the length, width, and height of the area I planned to position the couch and drove to an area of town with a cluster of furniture stores on one main road. My first stop was the huge warehouse I'd gone to with Tristan and the kids months earlier to buy my bed. I didn't remember it being this intimidating.

As I walked through the store for what seemed like hours, one salesperson after another asked how I was doing and if I was finding everything okay. I checked price tag after price tag, comparing couch dimensions and estimating my willingness to add this purchase to my existing credit card debt.

After I still hadn't reached the end of the sofa section within twenty minutes, I noticed my breaths were short and shallow. My chest ached like I'd eaten too much spicy food. Then dizziness, blurred vision. I sat down on one of those unaffordable couches before I fainted.

I was having a panic attack in a furniture store. Alone.

Every now and then, in those beginning days of my life without a husband, I became paralyzed by my solitary existence. I didn't fully realize how many daily decisions I'd made based on my partner's availability to go shopping with me or his opinions, input, and advice, from what kind of baseball gear Grady needed for the next season to where to book Ava's birthday party to what restaurants to try on the nights I didn't feel like cooking.

But as I tried to hide my panic attack from the chipper salespeople, I was cruelly reminded how alone being single feels.

I may not have been divorced yet, but this was what the other side looked like. I was in it. And I knew I needed to push through.

I had to push through the co-parenting pass-offs.

I had to push through the flurry of emotions when I registered Ava and Grady for their new school and for the first time, wrote separate addresses for mother and father.

I had to push through the oddness of saying "my kids' father" instead of "my husband."

I had to push through as I removed all traces of Tristan from the framed photos I hung on my blank walls.

I had to push through going to Tristan's house to pick up the kids and accept that it was *his* house, that I had to ring the doorbell at a house I co-owned, that I had to bite my tongue when one day, after I was invited inside to wait for the kids to pack their bags, I saw it was redecorated into a bachelor pad, erasing any evidence that a woman had ever crossed the threshold.

I had to push through the shift in our co-parenting relationship. We may have told ourselves that having designated Mommy Nights and Daddy Nights while living together was the same as co-parenting, but we were wrong. It wasn't even close to resembling the real co-parenting that would take years of frustrating compromises and schedule changes thanks in large part to his Navy career.

I just had to keep pushing through.

***

Part of that pushing through included the therapeutic strategies Julia taught me. Although sometimes I felt like our counseling sessions were glorified vents to a girlfriend, I knew she was giving me necessary tools to help ease my transition.

One of my continued struggles was my reactions to memories. Sometimes I'd stumble on a photo or a piece of jewelry or a restaurant or a day on the calendar, and my brain would flood with images of Tristan and our life together, my emotions inflating like a balloon about to pop. Good memories, bad memories. It didn't matter. They all triggered me.

But I couldn't delete my memory. I couldn't stop eating at restaurants I liked. I couldn't erase dates on a calendar. So Julia coached me to replace old memories with new ones, to redefine values to external triggers.

I decided to use a spontaneous road trip by myself one weekend when Grady and Ava were with Tristan to implement this approach. It was a financial splurge, but I needed a break from the day-to-day. So I asked Tristan if I could have Gunner for the weekend, booked a cheap hotel, packed a suitcase and dog food, and I headed to the Outer Banks.

The last time I'd visited the Outer Banks was two summers earlier. With the kids in the care of my in-laws, Tristan and I drove to Ocracoke for one of our reality escapes. Our marriage was always at its best on those trips. Time off from work. No children to feed. No groceries to buy. No laundry to wash. Whether we escaped to the mountain house or to the Caribbean or to the Outer Banks, the destination didn't matter. All that mattered was transporting to a place where life and love were deceptively effortless.

Those Ocracoke memories came rushing back as I drove the two hours to Kill Devil Hills, my current Outer Banks destination. Stifling giggles at Tristan trying to surf while I read a novel in a beach chair. Bringing tiny puppy Gunner to restaurants where bartenders slipped him treats. Kissing and laughing and holding hands and declaring we were fools for giving up on this marriage.

But it was easy to find a connection and the love we thought we lost when the path was temporarily cleared of obstacles. It was when the path became cluttered again and maintenance was required that our troubles returned. We could never manage the regular maintenance necessary for a successful marriage.

As memories flashed back, I reminded myself that my goal was to flip the script. I no longer wanted to associate Tristan with the Outer Banks. I wanted to attach this location to my strength, my independence, my reintroduction to myself.

So I generated new memories. I checked into my cheap hotel. I walked to the beach with Gunner. I dined at a pet-friendly sports bar. Back in my room for the night, I hunched in a moldy chair on the patio, listening to music and journaling my heart out, my tears in the shadows in stark contrast to the other guests partying boisterously at the pool.

I also unfolded the large piece of paper I kept tucked away between the pages of my journal. The white paper was covered in the handwriting of my dear friends, its jagged edges evidence of a previous girls' night out with Jane, Grace, and Rose, where we ate dinner at an Italian restaurant with paper tablecloths meant for children and crayons. Instead, they wrote down all the reasons I was divorcing Tristan surrounded by all the reasons I would be okay. I reread their words as I often did when fear tried to outweigh my persistence.

"I will be strong. I will carry on."

"I will cry, but after there are no more tears, I will realize the pain is gone."

"I will love who I can be and who I am."

"Today, I will live through this moment."

I thought about my three friends passing around a pen, their support flowing through their fingertips, then ripping the paper off the table and handing it to me, all of them urging me to never forget. Smiling, I now folded that paper back into its well-worn creases and closed it in my journal as a placeholder, as a reminder until I no longer needed reminding.

I didn't want to go back to Virginia Beach, but I couldn't fall into old patterns of skipping town to flee from my problems. I had to go back home with the mindset that my challenges were still there waiting for me, but I was in a better headspace to deal with them.

I returned to my apartment that was the same as I'd left it, but when I walked inside, I felt braver. Julia was right. It was possible to replace memories, to assign new meanings to old triggers. I knew whenever I thought of the Outer Banks, my brain wouldn't default to my trip with Tristan. Instead, I would recall my empowering solo trip. And if I could tape over the recording of those initial memories, I was certain it wouldn't take long to replace all the others attached to my soon-to-be ex-husband.

* * *

As I filled the unfamiliar holes in my weekends, I fell back on the familiar: running.

I increased my hours at the YMCA, joined a running club, and signed up for the Marine Corps Marathon to give myself a concrete goal to train for. The race also provided the motivation to accomplish a bucket list item around the time my divorce would be finalized, a way to commemorate the crossing of two kinds of finish lines.

Alan, a fellow running club member, was training for a different marathon, and since I doubted I could log the necessary miles on my own, we met up for long Sunday-morning runs and shorter hill and sprint work during the week. The pain from sore muscles felt exponentially better than the pain from divorce.

But my ruminations still plagued me.

My first panic attack during a run with Alan sprung up at Mount Trashmore, as if my body wanted to remind me of my last breakdown at that same summit. As a nurse, Alan exuded calm, sitting me down in the grass, coaching me to breathe, checking my pulse, and waiting with no judgment while I wheezed.

A week later, Alan witnessed another panic attack during a run. Tristan and I had gotten into an argument, and as I replayed the conversation with wild gesticulation and a non-stop rant, my built-up anger pushed me through two and half miles of speed work. But then a switch flipped. The rage turned on me and dissolved into debilitating anxiety. Once again, my chest constricted and I couldn't breathe.

While I appreciated Alan's listening ear, I had to stop rehashing stressful interactions. I couldn't dwell on things that were out of my control, analyzing Tristan's every word and action and Facebook post. I was running thirty to forty miles a week, but my life was stagnant, stuck in an in-between place I didn't want to be in but didn't know how to escape. I didn't know what I was trying to outrun, but I knew it wasn't working. Like training on a track, I was running in emotional circles, exerting the same energy only to repeatedly end up exactly where I started.

After my panic subsided and my breath normalized, I cut my run with Alan short and drove home to my quiet apartment. A long scalding shower settled my nerves but couldn't wash away my fears that I might never recover from this divorce. Brushing my wet hair, I stared in the mirror, hardly recognizing the woman reflected back at me. Or maybe I recognized too much of her. Maybe that was the problem. Maybe I needed to see someone else in the mirror before I could become the someone else I was searching for within myself.

***

I'd never seen Christine before, but my friend Grace highly recommended her. While she seemed hesitant to do what I asked based on the fact that I still couldn't say the word "divorce" without a shaky voice, she understood my desperation to transform my appearance.

Two hours later, six inches of my flowing hair were collected in piles on the floor and the remaining blonde locks were dyed brown.

As long as I was with Tristan, minus a brief stint as a brassy borderline redhead a few years earlier, my hair was blonde. And minus a brief period with a bob before we got married, my hair was long. If I was seeking a drastic change, I got one.

Grace snapped a photo the moment Christine chopped off my hair as tears dripped down my cheeks.

"Close your eyes," Grace whispered. "Don't look until it's over."

I did as told and focused on the music from the speakers surrounding the salon, their conversation about Grace's kids, anything but the snipping of scissors.

"Well," Christine said. "What do you think?"

When I opened my eyes and Christine handed me a half-foot-long strip of my hair, I cried harder, clutching the hair to my heart that I felt was breaking all over again.

"Leave it here," Grace said after I paid Christine. I was still holding the hair. "Leave it all behind."

As Grace and I left the salon, I looked back to see Christine sweeping my hair into a dustpan. "It's only hair," I told myself. "It'll grow back." But it was more than hair. And I struggled to leave it behind to be swept away like trash.

But as days went by, and my mirror image startled me less and less, the panic that accompanies change subsided. I liked seeing this brunette in the mirror. Even if I knew one day I'd revert back to my long blonde look, I also knew this hair spoke to the woman I was becoming right now.

Competent. Poignant. Smart. Beautiful. Strong. That's what this haircut said to me. And that's what I started to feel.

CHAPTER 22

The Finish Line

Summer's heat faded, and the divorce that once seemed far away tiptoed into sight. As I looked at the calendar, I wondered how the last nine months had disappeared, like a pregnancy that felt slow by day but in retrospect seemed to pass with the snap of a finger. Except, instead of ending up with a happy addition to my family, I was subtracting someone.

We had all just reached a comfort level with the routine when the Navy inserted itself to mix things up by giving Tristan military orders to Washington, DC, for a year. He would spend weekdays there and return to Virginia Beach on the weekends, rearranging our custody schedule yet again.

Because of his commute, Tristan asked me to bring Ava and Grady to his house on Saturday mornings and he'd take them to school on Monday mornings. It wasn't an ideal arrangement, especially considering Tristan wasn't used to getting the kids ready for school in the mornings and the distance from his house meant earlier alarms and the likelihood of rush-hour traffic jams. But I didn't argue. Flexibility was a necessity for our co-parenting relationship to remain cordial.

This development meant the kids were suddenly with me on Friday nights, a night I'd gotten used to using for rest. Yes, I loved that I could do something fun with the kids instead of always being the parent who enforced weeknight homework and bedtimes. Yes, I loved resuming our Friday-night tradition of Redbox movies and Chick-fil-A takeout we'd established years earlier when Tristan was away. Yes, I treasured these Friday nights that the kids were young enough to still treasure with me. But I was exhausted.

While Tristan's year in DC was also inconvenient in that he wasn't around if I had an emergency during the week, it opened my eyes to the bigger picture. Tristan was still in the Navy. He was still getting PCS orders. The Navy could still send him anywhere in the world. How would co-parenting work if Tristan moved out of the state? Out of the country? What if he got deployed?

I may have been divorcing this man, but as long as he stayed in the Navy, I would never be able to divorce the military.

There were many aspects of military life I would miss dearly, some of which I didn't even realize I cherished until I faced their disappearance. Obviously, I wouldn't miss sending the man I loved off on deployments while I stayed at home tempering my fears for his safety. I wouldn't miss the chaos of his last-minute travel. I wouldn't miss uprooting my life every few years.

What I would miss was the adventure, the traveling, the opportunities to see the world as I had during my three years in Japan. I'd miss the military spouse community and their camaraderie, their nods of understanding, the automatic support system. I'd miss the military uniforms in my closet, the pride that I was married to a service member, the pride that I was also playing a small role in serving my country through my support on the homefront, even if that support never came naturally to me.

All of these things, both good and bad, were about to vanish. I'd still have to deal with Tristan's career as we co-parented, but I was losing that community, that camaraderie, that understanding, that friend network, that support group. I knew many military spouses I'd remain friends with. But soon we'd no longer be able to commiserate about military-related events. I would never again PCS or attend a military ball or curse at Murphy's Law during a deployment or pin my husband at a promotion ceremony.

While I could at least claim to empathize with what my military spouse counterparts went through on a daily basis, they would never understand my struggles as a divorced military spouse. My military spouse friends would support me when I announced my divorce, but as time inched closer to the day I relinquished my military dependent ID card, I reminded myself that soon we'd no longer be members of the same club.

As much as I loved that membership, it was time for me to find another one.

* * *

Although I hated ceremonious goodbyes, my departure from the military spouse club deserved a grand gesture of recognition. I had no intention of marrying a service member again, so this was it for me. For once I didn't want to leave quietly. I wanted a goodbye to remember. I wanted closure.

Little did I know I already had one scheduled, one I'd been preparing seven months for: the Marine Corps Marathon.

When I signed up for the race, I primarily viewed it as a fitness goal and a personal achievement I could use to counterbalance whatever negative feelings might hit me when the divorce was final. What I would later realize was that completing the marathon would also act as my graceful exit from my life as a military spouse, my way of showing my gratitude toward the military community I deeply respected.

It didn't matter that the only military life I knew and understood was Navy-centered. It didn't matter that I knew nothing about the Marine Corps. The Marine Corps Marathon was known far and wide by running communities. Hardcore athletes from every branch of the military competed in it; service members and spouses mixed in with civilian runners who understood how special it was to run twenty-six miles with uniformed Marines cheering them on.

Just getting through the registration page on the marathon's website to secure a race bib within the thirty-thousand-participant limit was a feat. I figured I'd leave it up to fate if I was meant to run this race, and when my registration form was accepted after an hour and six minutes of hitting refresh on two different computers, I knew this would be my final military salute.

My months of marathon training were time-consuming and physically demanding. For all of my running experience with half marathons and countless other shorter races, I'd never logged as many miles week after week.

The intensity of the training went beyond the physical. Running saved me from succumbing to depression. It got me out of bed. It prevented me from indulging those inner voices that nagged at me to yield to the stress of divorce in unproductive ways. It kept me from drowning my loneliness in cartons of Ben & Jerry's and bottles of wine.

Even if I didn't understand it at the time, that training was my mental health boost through my anxiety.

There were days I flew through twelve-mile runs, finishing with a sense of invincibility that I could conquer anything. Other days I barely trudged through two miles, relieved to press stop on my Garmin as I collapsed on my apartment floor after an hour of being trapped inside my head. I pushed through the physical pain and the doubt until I found myself in Washington, DC, on race day, fit, lean, and with a mental toughness I couldn't wait to harness.

I tried to etch into my memory all four hours, forty-eight minutes, and fifty-nine seconds of the marathon. At the start of the race, Marines in uniform surrounded us, double-checking race bibs, collecting runners' throwaway clothes in trash bags, and offering high-fives. I absorbed the energy surrounding me—thirty-thousand runners and thousands of spectators applauding and yelling encouragement.

I ran past monuments and national landmarks. I posted photos on Facebook to share my progress and gather virtual motivation. When I needed an extra boost, I took out my earbuds and let the enthusiasm of the bystanders lift me until I fell into my groove again. I hit the proverbial wall at mile seventeen and called a friend without breaking my stride. I kept going in spite of the pain.

The sight of Marines lining the route along the final punishing hill infused me with both admiration and sorrow. I was almost done running my first marathon. I was almost done with my military life. I may not have been a service member, but the military defined me. In spite of my impending divorce, my experiences as a military spouse would always be a part of who I was.

When I crossed the finish line with a surge of adrenaline, I metaphorically closed the door on my marriage. Any doubts that remained about whether or not I could handle life after divorce were gone. I had a renewed perspective and strength.

"Bring on the divorce," I thought as I massaged my sore muscles in the backseat of my parents' car on our drive back to Virginia Beach. "I'm ready."

* * *

I may have been ready, but the court system wasn't. One delay after another, October flipping over to November. Weeks crawled by with a torturous anticipation of a court date I feared would never happen.

I wasn't sure how I felt about getting a military divorce in the month of November, otherwise known as Military Family Appreciation Month. More specifically, November 11 is Veterans Day, a day of gratitude for all service members past and present.

Normally, I'd avoid social media on an occasion that causes too much nostalgia and reflection, but because of my job, I couldn't avoid Veterans Day. The military still dictated not only how I co-parented with my soon-to-be ex-husband, but it was also the reason I was employed. I wrote articles about military discounts, and as I discovered through extended work hours and the influx of press releases, Veterans Day is the jackpot of military discounts.

For two weeks leading up to it, I worked overtime compiling a roundup of deals for what became the most viewed article I'd ever written. I added discount after discount, ecstatic at the success of something I created. But when Veterans Day arrived and the hard work was over, the true meaning of the day sunk in.

I awoke to a Facebook newsfeed overflowing with profile pictures switched to husbands in uniforms and heartfelt status updates thanking spouses for their service. From the second I logged on, social media reminded me I no longer had a spouse to thank. Because I hadn't told most people about my breakup and didn't plan to until the divorce was a done deal, I couldn't even post anything to explain why I wasn't performing the unspoken military spouse duty of expressing public appreciation for my husband's military career.

I showed my appreciation by sharing my article, this hugely successful project I'd worked so hard on, then logged off before I could see my professional triumph get lost amidst personal love fests.

I wondered if Veterans Day would always be such a contradiction of emotions.

I wondered if everything related to the military would always be such a contradiction of emotions.

***

November 22 at 10:00 a.m.

That's all the text from Tristan said. I knew what it meant. We finally got scheduled for a court hearing. After weeks of emails, phone calls, and paperwork, after Tristan's friend backed out on being our witness that we'd been living "separate and apart," after Jane agreed to drive in from Maryland to stand in, we had a divorce date.

By the beginning of November my patience was waning. "I just want this to be over," I thought. "Please let this be over. Please don't let this go into the new year."

And here it was. I'd be married for two more weeks. I read the text again, the letters and numbers blurring with a brand of tears I thought I'd already purged.

In two weeks, I would be a legally single woman. In two weeks, my husband would become my ex-husband. In two weeks, I would see the conclusion of everything I'd fought for in the last year. I thought I'd be jumping for joy, dancing around my apartment to upbeat music, calling my parents and friends to share the news we were all awaiting.

Instead, my shoulders convulsed in sobs. My hands shook. My chest tightened. My breath caught.

On one hand, I felt the lifting of a crushing weight. On the other hand, a different weight took its place, a special kind of mourning for the loss of what might have been. This was truly the end.

"See you there," I texted back.

There was too much to say, although everything had already been said. The time for words was in the past. And in two weeks, our marriage would be too.

It wasn't until Grady and Ava were on the school bus on the big day that my nerves surfaced. One thought continuously looped through my head.

"I'm getting divorced today. Today I'm getting divorced."

I'd been waiting for this day for what felt like decades, and now that it was here, I couldn't track where the time had gone. I only had a few more hours to be a married woman. And I couldn't decide if I felt emptiness or relief.

For days I obsessed over my divorce outfit. Remembering the white cable-knit sweater I wore to notarize the separation agreement that ended up in the Goodwill pile because I couldn't bring myself to wear it again, I knew whatever I wore to this hearing needed to be dispensable.

I settled on black pants that were missing a button with a flowered camisole and matching maroon sweater I vaguely recalled purchasing at Ann Taylor. As I slipped it on, I wondered what inspired me to buy the sweater set. It wasn't my style at all.

Everything I wore to the funeral of my marriage would be thrown away. Even the bra, panties, and shoes were accessories destined for the trash.

* * *

We didn't mean to be late. Jane and I left my apartment with plenty of wiggle room to get to the courthouse on time. We just didn't expect a confusing parking situation that caused us to park several blocks away or the construction that blocked our entrance to the building we needed to get into.

After leaving our phones inside a locker and scrambling through security, we jogged from Building 10B to 10A, then studied the docket to find my assigned courtroom for the day's list of uncontested divorces. Panting, we arrived at 9:58 a.m., two minutes before the start of court.

I saw Tristan standing in the hallway, surprised he was wearing a suit. "He looks nice," I thought before following him into the courtroom.

I sat between Tristan and Jane in what felt like a church pew. The judge was late, and Tristan attempted to fill the awkwardness by talking. Tuning him out, I fidgeted with my odd outfit that felt like someone else's skin on my body and fought the urge to rip my sweater off.

When the judge entered the courtroom, we all stood as the bailiff mumbled words I couldn't hear. The judge explained he was presiding over uncontested divorces and that all four couples in attendance would be divorced that day, although it would take a week or so for the paperwork to be available.

We were third in the queue. My heart raced as I watched the people involved in the first case walk to the front of the courtroom and stand before the judge. Tristan leaned toward me and whispered, "You'll be my wife for about ten more minutes."

I closed my eyes, trying to block him out. Tristan made a joke, but I didn't laugh.

The judge recited questions. The soon-to-be ex-wife, who was the plaintiff, answered. She and her husband, who wasn't present, had been separated for eleven years. Their adult daughter was their witness. There were no tears. This was a formality for them.

The second divorce was called, and the parties approached the bench.

"You'll be my wife for about five more minutes," Tristan whispered. I wished he would shut up, but maybe this twisted countdown was his way of processing and the kindest thing I could do was let him.

Tristan grabbed my right hand; Jane held my left. They both squeezed as the judge announced the last name that wouldn't be mine for much longer.

I stayed seated, as my husband, the plaintiff in our case because he was quicker than I was to hire an attorney, and my best friend, our required witness, approached the bench. I wasn't invited. In fact, my presence at my own divorce wasn't even mandatory, oddly unnecessary in the proceedings.

It was like an out-of-body experience, sitting alone in the back of a courtroom, straining to hear the judge and then Tristan and then Jane speak words that decided my fate. Jane had more of a role in the actual finalizing of my divorce than I did. It was all happening without my participation as I wordlessly observed from afar.

In minutes, it was over.

The judge announced we were divorced and, because of a little extra paperwork, my maiden name was also simultaneously restored. I stood, swaying from the heaviness of it all, the knowledge that I'd entered that courtroom as one woman and would exit as another. Jane and Tristan walked down the aisle toward me. Tears poured down my cheeks.

The doors of the courtroom hadn't even closed behind us when Tristan pulled me into an embrace so tight I thought I would suffocate. It hurt in unexpected ways. There was no instant weight lifted. This was grief. This was loss.

"This is so fucking sad," I said.

And somehow, with that outward acknowledgement, the tears stopped.

Once in the car, I pulled out of the parking lot, thankful that Jane was beside me, that I had someone to keep me company on the day my life forever changed. As I stopped at a red light waiting to turn right, Tristan pulled up in the lane beside me to take a left. The light turned green. We looked over at each other and waved. Then we turned our separate ways.

* * *

I didn't know what other people did to combine the odd celebration and mourning that divorce day warranted, but I commemorated being Heather Sweeney again by seeing my new old name on a byline. Thanks to advanced planning and a very understanding and patient editor, I announced my divorce in the *New York Times*.

I'd written the essay weeks earlier, and after explaining to the editor I'd worked with twice before about the wishy-washiness of the court system, he agreed to sit on it until I gave him the go-ahead. So as I walked from the courthouse to my car, I sent that email. About an hour later, my essay "A Military Wife No More" went live.

It was a pivotal piece for me, personally, professionally, emotionally.

I once promised Tristan I wouldn't write about our breakup publicly until it was finalized. Well, it was finalized. This piece signified a promise kept.

I secretly feared I wouldn't be successful in my career as a single woman, that my stability as a writer was dependent upon my status as a military dependent. This piece signified accomplishment on my first day as a single woman.

Moving past the anger and resentment towards Tristan about his unwillingness to let me write under my married name, I finally reached the end of the identity crisis. This piece signified an introduction to my true self, a coming-out of sorts. I was no longer pretending, writing under a name that wasn't mine.

I was Heather Sweeney in every way, shape, and form.

After I shared the essay on social media, Jane headed back to Maryland, and I enjoyed my Friday-night tradition of Chick-fil-A and a movie with Grady and Ava before putting them to bed. I poured a glass of wine and read through all the comments and private messages I'd received about the essay, words filled with shock and support and assurances that life would only improve from here. I didn't look back at wedding photos. I didn't wish I had a VCR to watch my wedding video. I didn't cry.

It was time to let go. It was time to truly move on.

***

After the series of court-date postponements, it somehow didn't occur to me that I'd be confronting Thanksgiving a mere six days after divorce.

I'd faced countless holidays without Tristan, Thanksgiving included. But this was different. My family was more than geographically challenged, as I used to say when the military separated us for birthdays or anniversaries. This Thanksgiving it wasn't the Navy splitting up our family. It was the removal of an entire member of the family from the holiday equation. The empty seat at the table held new meaning.

According to the divorce decree, Thanksgiving was my holiday that year, so as soon as school let out, I packed up the kids and the dog and drove to Jane's house in Maryland. We ate turkey and stuffing. We drank wine. We watched the kids play. I acted like this was a normal Thanksgiving, and when I could no longer keep up the act, I talked through my fears of all the abnormal things I still had to confront before they transformed into a new version of normal.

In the quiet moments I scrolled through social media, soaking in my newsfeed that was overflowing with friends' declarations of gratitude. It was the reminder I needed that there's always something to be thankful for.

I was thankful for my happy, healthy children who were dealing with this new family dynamic with grace, appropriate questions, acceptance, and the knowledge that they're loved. I was thankful for my parents and my brother who had my back and answered the phone whenever it rang. I was thankful for my dog who cuddled away bad days. I was thankful for my job that provided financial stability. I was thankful for the friends I called family and the family I called friends.

I was even thankful for the Navy as I reminisced about one of my most memorable adult Thanksgivings. It was a few years earlier, our last one in Japan, the last one I remember feeling an unbridled contentment, as if Tristan and I had done something right, both individually and as a team.

I never minded cooking a feast, but I'd always told Tristan I wouldn't pull out all the stops if we were the only adults eating it. It was too much trouble for two people. But he loved my turkey, so he'd convinced me to cook it by doling out invitations to justify the effort.

My irritation at his plan didn't last long. In fact, his enthusiasm was contagious, and I found myself extending invites as well. While he found lonely service members who had nowhere else to go, I recruited military spouses whose husbands were out to sea. Before we knew it, we lost track of how many people we'd be squeezing into our tiny house on base.

I bought the biggest turkey I could find at the commissary. I cooked for four days, preparing a feast like I'd never prepared before. I laid out munchies, chilled wine, and beer, and hoped we had enough plates and utensils. As two dozen or so people trickled in and out of our front door throughout Thanksgiving Day, some friends, some complete strangers, I aimed my gratitude at the military, for the people it brought into my life, even if only for a day.

From the geo-bachelor missing his wife's Thanksgiving spread to the Korean wife who'd never seen a Thanksgiving spread, we welcomed everyone who showed up on our doorstep. Some of those people remained dear friends, some we heard from a couple times a year, and some I never saw again. But on that Thanksgiving Day, we were all a family, bonded by our military experiences and a longing for our relatives and traditions back in the States. And it was me, it was Tristan, it was us, who created that together.

This Thanksgiving wasn't a holiday celebration like that unforgettable one in Japan, with a husband who smiled at me across a room full of guests. But this Thanksgiving, my first after divorce, uncovered a wealth of goodness that I would always be thankful for.

I vowed to remember that as I looked ahead at the next holiday hurdle: Christmas without my children.

***

I was only home a few days before that resolve slapped me in the face with Tristan's invitation to divide our Christmas decorations.

I knew this was coming since the day I moved out. I knew I'd have to go to Tristan's house, the house that was once mine but would soon belong to his girlfriend. I knew I'd have to deflect his reminiscing while taking the items I wanted and leaving behind those I didn't. What I wasn't expecting was seeing the feminine flip-flops sitting by the back door, shoes too big to be Ava's, too small to be mine, wondering if the girlfriend would come through the kitchen into the family room to introduce herself.

Similar to our division of the rest of our possessions, Tristan and I agreed on almost everything. I'd spent years adding to our collection of Christmas decorations, buying ornaments for the kids that signified something special in their lives that year. *Dora the Explorer* for Ava. Superheroes and Transformers for Grady. "Baby's First Christmas" ornaments. Homemade ornaments the kids made in school. All of those I took. While it saddened me to think of how I bought them over time with my vision of our family growing older together, I wanted them now to build upon as we evolved this new version of family.

I grabbed the stockings my grandmother hand-crafted and some other decorations Tristan didn't care about, handing over to him what remained, including a handful of "Our First Christmas" ornaments Tristan and I were gifted when our marriage was as young and hopeful as a seed freshly planted. There was nothing more to build upon in that collection.

* * *

The part of me that wanted to curl up in bed in the fetal position so I could sleep through the solitude of a Christmas alone tried to sweet-talk the rest of me into ignoring the festive decorations I'd just retrieved. I adored Christmas, and the traditions I shared with the kids were so ingrained in my maternal being that I thought it would be easier to ignore the season's existence rather than experience the heartbreak of letting my ex-husband have it.

"No one would blame you if you skipped Christmas," that part of me said. "The kids won't notice because they won't be here."

But then there was the other part of me, the part that found its voice during tough times.

"You *will* do Christmas," that voice scolded. "The kids *will* notice if you don't put up a Christmas tree. The kids *will* ask why Ernie the Elf on the Shelf isn't magically hopping from room to room and why Christmas tunes aren't playing while you cook dinner. The kids *will* ask you to read *Olive, the Other Reindeer* and let them watch *The Grinch*."

"You *will* do Christmas," the voice insisted. "If not for yourself, then for your children. Because they've had enough change and uncertainty this year."

So, despite myself, I did Christmas, with a few added twists as I promised myself this Christmas wouldn't be defined by the title of the first after divorce. Instead, I called it a Christmas of new and improved traditions.

The kids and I unpacked the ornaments and situated them on the artificial tree they'd helped me pick out while Christmas music played. We snapped pictures. We devoured cookies. We told stories about who gave us a particular ornament or why an ornament deserved to be displayed front and center. I made a conscious choice to smile at the ornaments that filled our tree instead of dwelling on those I knew were missing.

Remembering the sentiment of Thanksgiving, I focused on gratitude, especially toward that inner voice for compelling me to carry on with Christmas. I thanked that voice every morning when Ava woke up and squealed in delight after locating our Elf on the Shelf. I thanked that voice when the three of us snuggled on the couch and gazed at the lights on our tree. I thanked that voice when the kids talked about buying each other presents, something they had no interest in doing before. I even thanked that voice when Grady figured out how to find SpongeBob's Christmas album on Spotify and played it over and over and over again.

Because the pass-off to their father was several days before Christmas, I planned our holiday celebration for before they left. As resentful as I once was when the military stole Tristan when I most wanted him with me, this Christmas I included the Navy on my gratitude list. Thanks to the military, I was an expert on being flexible with dates on the calendar. I was a master at weaving explanations for the kids. I was adept at improvising and putting myself in a moment, shifting perspective so that moment felt like it matched up with the rest of the world.

I told Grady and Ava I emailed Santa about the changes in our family and updated our address, and he promised to send helper elves to our apartment early with a special delivery for them. Whether they believed me or they simply didn't care when or how their presents appeared under the tree, they accepted my tall tale without question. And as we arranged a plate of cookies for the elves and another with carrots in case Santa let the elves borrow a reindeer, it actually felt like Christmas Eve.

That improvised Christmas Eve was far from easy though. As I hid in my bedroom after the kids fell asleep, wrapped their presents, and placed them under the tree, I missed sharing this night with a partner. I missed the buzz of pouring adult beverages and coming up with outlandish explanations for what we were doing in case the kids caught us. I missed the parental speculation about how the kids would react to each gift and the stifled giggles while tiptoeing around the house playing Santa.

There were some moments when I truly missed being one half of a marriage. The long, tight hug at the end of a rough day. The unspoken language developed over time. The permanent date for parties and special events. The sounding board for decision-making. The intimacy and excitement of planning for the future.

That night was one of those moments.

But the next morning I studied the joy on my children's faces as they read the note from the elves who delivered their early presents, as they tossed wrapping paper in the air during their frenzy of excitement, as they showed each other their new stuff. I couldn't see it at the time, but this early Christmas, this improvised holiday that almost didn't happen, would become one of our most treasured traditions, one we would celebrate every other year with dates we chose together and with its own name: Fakesmas.

It was a different kind of Christmas chaos, but it felt equally as full as it always did.

And with that I felt a sense of peace.

* * *

Saying goodbye the following day twisted my insides, testing my limits of positivity. But as I hoped to do throughout all the transitions I would face as a freshly divorced mother, I acknowledged the challenge by meeting it head-on, learning from it, and carrying on.

Within a couple hours I'd completely disassembled Christmas. I removed each ornament the kids and I had meticulously placed on the tree, wrapping each one in tissue paper and dividing Ava's and Grady's into their individual shoe boxes. I unwrapped the lights and removed the star topper. I broke the tree down into its three sections and stuffed them inside the cardboard box, sitting on top of it to keep it closed while running a strip of packing tape down the center. And when all the decorations were back in their storage tubs, I dragged them out to the deck and stacked them in the catch-all closet.

The following day I was on a flight to a sunny place where I'd be blanketed in the warmth of family. My parents and I celebrated the real Christmas Eve and Christmas Day in Florida, acknowledging the odd vibes of the circumstances while taking advantage of our rare quality time together.

I knew then that my inner voice, the one that jump-started my Christmas spirit, would always show up and guide me in the right direction. I knew I could rely on that voice to help me remember on tough days that I'm stronger than I think I am.

CHAPTER 23

An Outsider Everywhere

After a year filled with ambiguity and adjustment, I was primed to make 2014 the year of embracing life, of being the version of myself I envisioned before I met Tristan. If I learned anything from the slow death of my marriage it was that I no longer found it acceptable to postpone my goals, my wants, my needs because of fear, feelings of unworthiness, and most importantly, another person.

I wanted to break free of my comfort zone, check off bucket list adventures, surround myself with a community I could relate to. But as I scribbled New Year's resolutions that intertwined with activities I'd always wanted to try, I was less scared of jumping out of an airplane than I was of figuring out where I belonged. I'd identified as a member of the military spouse community for so long I had no idea where I fit in now.

One Saturday when the kids were with Tristan, I went to a birthday party for a friend's husband. I was the only single person there. Later that night, I went out with a divorced friend from my apartment complex, Angie, who was meeting up with two other single women. In one day I flipped ends of the spectrum, first mingling with a roomful of married people talking about their children and then ordering cocktails with childless middle-aged women talking about their recent dates.

I was an outsider everywhere I went.

Most of my friends were married. Although some had ringside seats for the disintegration of my marriage, they weren't fighting in the ring with me. They didn't know exactly what I went through. Just as many military spouses say about their civilian friends who complain about their husbands going on a three-day business trip or ask why their service members don't get "normal" jobs, no one can understand unless they've lived it themselves.

Reading post-divorce self-help books and divorce-related blogs confirmed that nothing can replace a community of women who know firsthand what it feels like to pack up the kids on the weekends to ship them off to their father's house and how to deal with the prospect of both parties dating. Like a military spouse seeking solace from other military spouses as she slogs through a deployment, I felt the pull to join a circle of divorced single mothers, if for no other reason than to hear someone say, "I totally get it."

It was almost as if I was reliving the beginning days of my life as a military spouse. Back then I was clueless about how to be married to a service member, and now I was clueless about how to be a divorced single mother. I didn't know how to connect with other divorced women. I didn't know how to navigate this new station in my life.

And it wasn't solely about being divorced. I learned that the more I socialized with Angie and her group of friends, none of whom had children. Throwing kids into the mix gave me a subtitle they didn't have. They didn't have to factor in childcare when scheduling a date. They didn't have to communicate regularly with their ex-partners. They didn't have to raise two little human beings who would forever be labeled products of divorce or deal with the guilt about how their decisions would affect their children's psyches.

They didn't fully get me, and I didn't get them.

* * *

Other than the friendships, there was one other aspect of military life I missed: being a part of something bigger than myself.

I was happy for friends whose husbands returned from deployments, and I empathized with others awaiting new orders and prepping for PCS moves. But deployments and PCSs no longer held the same meaning for me. I still dealt with military-induced transitions, but only for the sake of my children as their military father's career affected their time allotted with him. I no longer celebrated homecomings. I no longer PCS'd. The gap between us seemed too wide to bridge anymore.

Their lives revolved around their husbands. Mine revolved around me.

I thought maybe I could still relate to my military spouse cohorts when it came to parenting alone. With Tristan gone a lot during our marriage, I often referred to myself as a sometimes single mom. But after my divorce I learned that being a single mother means so much more than being the lone parent physically present.

As a single mom, I was solely responsible for my financial outcomes. As a military spouse I may have parented solo sometimes, but the money still flowed into our bank account. Tristan's paycheck permitted me to be a stay-at-home mother for six years, and when he deployed, the special pays he earned boosted our savings. Any paycheck I earned when I went back to work was supplemental. As a single mom, other than my smaller-than-expected monthly child support and alimony from Tristan, I was on my own financially. And because I had a low-paying job with no benefits, money was tight.

My budget was so pinched that I couldn't afford something else I didn't have to worry about when I'd called myself a sometimes single mom: health insurance.

I knew my military health insurance, TRICARE, was inaccessible the minute I stepped out of that courtroom, but I formulated no backup plan other than crossing my fingers for a work promotion. Before the divorce was finalized, I got checkups from all my doctors, completed bloodwork, and filled as many prescriptions as the pharmacy would greenlight. When the divorce went through and TRICARE dropped me, I prayed for good health and no emergencies.

I was rationing my daily thyroid medication by taking it every other day, and then every three days, when I learned TRICARE offered a transitional health insurance program for divorced spouses. Even though I couldn't afford it, I couldn't go on much longer without healthcare. So with credit card in hand, I called TRICARE to sign up.

"I'm sorry ma'am," the TRICARE customer service representative said. "You can't apply for the transitional health insurance because your name hasn't been removed from DEERS."

The mention of DEERS, the Defense Enrollment Eligibility Reporting System, prompted flashbacks of the long, maddening phone calls I had with them over the years for various reasons like adding Grady and Ava to the database after they were born. But this situation was by far my most mind-boggling. I had to be removed from DEERS because I was no longer a military dependent. However, because I was no longer a military dependent, I didn't have the authority to remove myself from DEERS. And although my eligibility for TRICARE lapsed because I wasn't married to a service member, I couldn't apply for the transitional TRICARE because DEERS thought I was. The red tape of military procedure was still torturing me.

I may have done my fair share of complaining about Navy clinics and TRICARE as a military spouse, but in the three months I went without health insurance before getting that promotion from contractor to full-time employee with benefits, I cringed whenever I heard a military spouse doing the same complaining I once did. They had no idea that, during those precarious three months, I would have given anything to have TRICARE back.

And so the gap widened.

***

It wasn't until an encounter in the parking lot of my apartment complex that I felt hopeful I'd find other women going through the same experiences I was.

I'd seen this woman before, whether she was tossing a trash bag into the dumpster or lounging in a chair at the pool while her children swam. We'd never spoken. I didn't know her name or her circumstances. But one evening after I loaded the kids and their suitcases into Tristan's Jeep, this woman pulled up to me in her car.

"You just made my day," she said, her voice shaky. "My son was watching your kids, and he said, 'Look Mom, those kids must live in two different houses too.'"

"That's right," I answered, smiling at the little boy in the backseat. "My kids do live in two different houses. They go to their other house every weekend."

"It's hard," the woman whispered, her eyes glistening with tears. "Sometimes it's really hard."

"Yes," I thought as I nodded sympathetically. "Sometimes it's really hard."

But in that moment, I felt a little less alone.

***

Despite the establishment of routines, co-parenting remained frustrating. I'm not sure why it surprised me that even though the marriage had ended, the marital issues that had plagued us then continued to plague us now. Namely, communication.

Tristan and I had differing opinions on co-parenting interactions. He seemed to think we were friends, leaning toward a casual adherence to custody schedules and unexpected expenses, while I aimed for consistency, fairness, and an "everything in writing" policy. I learned early on the only way I could communicate effectively with him was if emotions were eliminated. Impassioned exchanges did nothing but cause arguments.

I tried to view the divorce as if we'd dissolved a business. If a topic required a conversation that wouldn't translate well via text or email, I scheduled appointments with him, organizing my bullet points in advance as if they were professional meetings. Sometimes I emailed the agenda to Tristan so he'd be prepared, my method of encouraging brevity.

Most of the time this business-like approach worked. If I pretended he was a coworker and we had a deadline, I could keep the conversation on topic, road-blocking tangents.

No, we're not going to talk about your girlfriend's job.

No, we're not going to talk about the new dog you adopted.

No, we're not going to talk about a post you saw on Facebook about a mutual friend of ours from Japan.

We're talking about the schedule revision when I have to go to San Francisco for work.

We're talking about Grady's sneakers you forgot to send back to my apartment.

We're talking about your next duty station.

I realized how effective this technique was when we met up at a local restaurant to file our taxes, the last time our financials would ever be combined. As we completed paperwork for almost four hours, the longest period of time we'd been in each other's presence since we lived in the same house, I was struck with the revelation that I didn't know this man at all anymore.

I didn't know what television shows he binged. I didn't know what he did on Friday nights. I didn't know what kind of cereal he ate for breakfast. I didn't know how much money he'd saved up. I didn't know how often he rode the motorcycle I despised. I didn't know if he still snored, if he drank the same beer, if he cooked any of the meals we used to eat together. I didn't know anything about this man I'd planned to spend the rest of my life with. And he didn't know anything about me.

This man I'd spent fifteen years of my life with was a complete stranger.

***

As it turned out, the Navy was about to put even more distance between us.

After a year of commuting back and forth to DC, Tristan got new orders. To Hawaii. For three years.

As his ex-wife I had no right to contribute my input regarding his career trajectory. All I could do was brace myself.

For the next three years, I would essentially have sole custody of Ava and Grady during the school year, upgrading my single-mom status to full-time. To compensate for that time away, he wanted the kids to stay with him in Hawaii during the summers.

Did I really have to hand over my children for entire summers?

I was so distraught at the idea of being apart from my children for such long stretches that I sought the counsel of an attorney. But no matter how many ways I spun out scenarios, apparently, I was going to have to send my kids to Hawaii for ten weeks at a time.

The attorney at the same law firm I consulted when Tristan and I first separated advised me to work out custody disputes with Tristan outside of court. If Tristan wanted summers, and I fought him to the point we went to court, I would lose. Living in a highly populated military area, judges were accustomed to dealing with military families and had a reputation for being sympathetic to service members and helping them make up for lost time with their children because of military-related separations. It was very likely a judge would grant Tristan entire summers minus two weeks for me to take the kids on a summer vacation.

The attorney detailed the extensive process I'd face if I moved forward with a court battle. Each of us would need to hire a lawyer. Then we'd probably have to pay for the court-appointed juvenile attorney, who would conduct home visits and talk to the kids' teachers during an investigation. I wanted neither the expense nor the investigation.

If things got ugly, the attorney said, I could petition for full custody. If one parent spent ninety days or less with the children, the other parent had a legal right to full custody. But at what cost? I'd drain my already hurting bank account. It would ruin any civility I currently had with Tristan. And even though the kids were young, they would absorb the strain.

There was nothing for me to do but accept it. Tristan would move to Hawaii. I would stay in Virginia Beach with the kids, and when school got out, they would spend their summers halfway across the world. And I would have to figure out how to handle it all.

***

"Do you somehow make yourself numb so you don't feel the pain you should be feeling?"

My rising stress levels landed me in a chiropractor's office, and after adjusting my neck and applying electric stimulation, he declared my muscles felt like cement.

"I'm actually surprised you're not experiencing more pain," he said.

He was referring to my neck and upper-back pain, but it could have been a statement about my entire life for the last couple of years. Maybe this physical pain was the accumulated manifestation of suppressed emotions.

While I journaled daily and vented to friends, I also became skilled at avoidance and denial. I speculated that's how I'd gotten through the separation. I avoided dealing with certain feelings, denying how sorrowful I really was that my life had unraveled and I was struggling to rebuild it.

I wondered if Tristan's departure to Hawaii was affecting me more than I allowed myself to admit. I told everyone who would listen that his PCS was the best thing that could happen. It would give me a break from the constant texting, the frequent arguing. But the thought of not seeing him for three years was a strange cocktail of feelings.

Three years is a long time. By the end of Tristan's tour, Grady would be thirteen and Ava would be approaching her tenth birthday. I'd be forty-one. I'd close out my thirties, greeting a new decade while he was gone.

Those thoughts were both reassuring and mournful.

As Tristan told me about the movers packing up his house, the house we once lived in together, the house he finally sold, and his departure date got closer, I let myself feel all those feelings. I didn't want to avoid or deny anymore. And when I reached the underlying pain and confronted it, that's where I found relief.

Yes, it meant any personal time for me would require advance planning, a babysitter, and likely mommy guilt. Yes, it meant I couldn't attend my Sunday-morning run club meetups and dating would be even more daunting. Yes, it meant I couldn't use my weekends to recharge.

But it also meant I wouldn't see my ex-husband more than a handful of times, if at all, in the next three years. No more Saturday and Monday exchanging of the kids and their belongings. No more tension-filled face-to-face conversations. No more formulating back-up plans because of his last-minute schedule changes. No more unnecessary drama. Just five thousand miles of space.

Yes, I was ready for him to leave. In fact, I needed him to leave. Maybe I could finally, fully move forward.

***

The day I said goodbye to Tristan in mid-June before he left for Hawaii was also the day we closed on the house that still had my name on it. I hadn't lived there for nearly a year. With Tristan's PCS, I would never have to see that house again.

He'd already said his goodbyes to the kids that morning before summer camp. Ava acted as if it was a normal pass-off. Grady looked like he was about to melt into a puddle. I think Ava was too young to understand, and Grady was old enough to understand too much.

I went into the meeting worried I'd get flustered signing away the last house I ever lived in with Tristan. But as I turned each page in the stack of documents, I knew I was beyond that. I could say good riddance to a house that never felt like a home to me, a house that saw too much ugliness. "Good riddance, house," I thought as I signed. I put down the pen. Another door closed.

We walked outside together, pausing before finding our cars that were parked in opposite directions.

"Good luck," I said, already turning toward my car.

"Good luck to you too," he replied.

"See ya." I closed my car door before I could hear whether or not he responded.

No hug. No handshake. No eye contact. I inhaled deeply, exhaling fully as I drove away, returning to my apartment, my home, my life, and leaving behind a house and the man I once lived there with.

CHAPTER 24

The Classiest Woman on Match

I'd been out of the dating scene since the mid-1990s, jumping straight from my college sweetheart to Tristan. The internet barely existed, let alone online dating, and I couldn't fathom this practice of meeting men that seemed too foreign for a woman approaching middle age. I preferred to meet someone organically, not in an orchestrated way. I wanted a man to naturally appear and present himself as compatible, not as a result of a matchmaking algorithm.

As soon as Tristan and I signed the separation agreement, friends nudged me to go on blind dates with single men they knew, but I routinely declined without hesitation. However, shortly before moving into my apartment, my friend Grace helped me see that the idea of dating wouldn't always be such a scary proposition.

On one of my designated nights out when the kids had a Daddy Night, Grace and I bought tickets for a local concert. As

I drove to the venue, she mentioned she wanted to set me up with someone.

"No way," I said. "I'm not ready."

Despite my gut reaction that shrieked hell no, I asked Grace for details.

"He's really nice," Grace said. "And he's cute. He works at NAS Oceana. His name is Christopher."

I almost slammed on the brakes.

"Chris?!" I said. "His name is Chris?"

"Why?" Grace asked, startled. "What's wrong with the name Chris?"

"The psychic I saw months ago said someone named Chris would become an important part of my life," I said.

The psychic never said if Chris was the person I would end up with or if Chris was a facilitator to something else or even if Chris was a man or a woman. But this was the first mention of a Chris I'd come across since my reading. It had to be a sign.

I was sipping a beer, waiting for the concert to start, when Grace pointed at a man and said, "Hey, there he is. There's Christopher."

My heart pounded like I was a teenage girl bumping into her crush. My hands broke into a sweat. Grace was right—he was cute. I couldn't help but notice with surprise that I felt excitement at the thought of going on a date with this man.

I also couldn't help but notice this man wasn't alone. Christopher was hand-in-hand with a woman, clearly not as single as Grace thought.

I'd never met this man, didn't know of his existence until an hour earlier, but his lack of availability disappointed me. This Chris may not have been a sign from the universe, but the seed of dating was planted.

"It's time," Grace said, seeing my reaction. "You're ready."

I wasn't ready that night or that week or that month. But the far-fetched concept of dating suddenly seemed realistic, feasible, and downright thrilling.

* * *

It wasn't until two weeks after the divorce was finalized that I finally revisited the possibility of dating by doing something I swore I'd never do: I signed up for Match.com.

For months, my friend Angie had tried to convince me of the joys of middle-aged dating, but the thought of joining the local bar scene and making small talk with strange men intimidated me to the point of social paralysis. So she helped me ease into online dating, offering tips for Match—the first of which was that it wasn't cool to say "Match.com"; it was just Match—and making me feel like it might actually be fun.

As I scrolled through my phone's camera roll for a remotely sexy selfie to use as a profile picture and wrote a flattering yet humble description of myself, I vowed to use Match more for research than for a serious, reliable search for the man of my dreams. It was highly unlikely my soulmate, if I even believed in soulmates, would be hidden in the depths of this app.

Angie warned me that when I initially joined Match, sorting through all the communication with the interested men would be a full-time job, that I'd be instantly bombarded with winks and likes and private messages.

"It's exciting!" Angie said. "Look at all those guys interested in you. Look at all the possibilities. Look at all the potential boyfriends and date nights!"

I was indeed instantly overwhelmed with men expressing interest. But I was underwhelmed by the options.

Within twenty-four hours my profile was viewed over a hundred times. I received winks, likes, and emails informing me that "LeavesSeatDown" favorited me and "50ShadesOf-Nice" found me intriguing. I scrolled through that first night, hovering the fine line between feeling flattered and depressed.

Angie advised me to be proactive, not to wait for someone to message me, so I picked a guy and messaged him with her dictated words. After hitting send, I stifled my anticipation at the prospect of a response, a conversation, a date.

But days passed with no reply, and I was back where I started, searching for someone else who seemed remotely engaging.

Despite Angie's advice to never go out with guys who list their status as "separated" and not "divorced" because their wounds are too fresh, I sent the same message to a separated man I found. After all, I wasn't looking for the love of my life at that point. My own divorce was fresh enough to give us a common bond. He seemed like a good person to be my inaugural post-divorce date.

He didn't respond either. Internalizing silence as rejection, I stopped being proactive.

My first online interaction was with Rick. After bypassing too many messages that read "UR hot" or "Single ready to mingle," I liked that Rick clearly read my profile and came up with relevant questions to start a dialogue. He wrote about himself with a combination of confidence and self-deprecating humor, he seemed well established in his career, and we shared similar interests.

Unfortunately, Rick was old enough to be my father.

But because it was the sincerest email I'd received on Match, I replied.

"Thank you so much for your thoughtful email," I wrote. "However, I'm looking for someone closer to my age. But I wanted to respond and tell you I appreciated the time you took to compose an introduction that reflected both your interests and mine. I encourage you to continue that practice as you go forward with your dating journey. Best of luck."

He immediately answered.

"Thank you so much for your email," he wrote. "I understand the age difference thing, and I appreciate your effort to respond. You're the classiest lady on this site. Best of luck to you too."

I was celebrating my title as "the classiest lady" on Match when he emailed again.

"By the way, I see you're a writer. Any chance you could take a look at my profile and give me some pointers?"

I was both proud and disheartened that my first online-dating exchange ended with me editing a man's profile to help him meet other women.

Soon after that, I stumbled upon Chase. He was attractive. A runner. College degree. Military, but definitely an officer so I didn't have to worry about any blurry fraternization rules about an officer's ex-wife dating an enlisted man. I clicked the wink button, and he winked back. I messaged him, and he messaged back. "This is promising," I thought.

Chase and I emailed back and forth a dozen times throughout the weekend. Angie had experience-based feedback for just about every scenario and advised me to be up front about wanting to meet up in person and not to linger in the emailing and texting phase.

"You don't want to find you really like someone after weeks of texting only to meet in person and realize you're not really a match," she explained. "The whole idea of Match is to meet someone, not form an online relationship."

Suddenly, I was the assertive woman I didn't feel like I was and suggested a meet-up. Within minutes I had a lunch date set up with Chase the following day while the kids were at school. I was terrified.

I fought nervous butterflies all that evening. I was going on a date. I was single. I was free to go out with whoever I wanted. As Angie kept reminding me, I had a second chance at love. I had a do-over. Not everyone is lucky enough to be able to start over and choose who they want to spend time with.

In the morning, I could barely eat, barely work. When 11:30 a.m. rolled around, and it was time to leave, I was a shaky mess of jitters.

No big deal. Just my first date in fifteen years.

I arrived at Carrabba's before Chase and waited outside the front door. When I saw him walk toward me, recognizing him from his photos, the nerves evaporated. We swapped smiles and "nice to meet yous" before he opened the door for me and asked the hostess for a table for two.

Mistake number one was him ordering a Scotch. At lunch. On a Monday. Didn't he have a job to go back to? I know I did.

Mistake number two was him talking nonstop about himself. I get that you're an officer in the Navy. I get that you're a pilot. I get that you make lots of money. You don't have to tell me what the monthly payment on your house is or that you have a Banana Republic credit card.

And mistake number three was bringing my ex-husband into the date. While I wasn't trying to be deceitful, I *was* trying not to mention my affiliation with the military as he talked about his. Unfortunately, it was unavoidable when he eventually turned the spotlight on me.

"How long have you lived in Virginia Beach?" he asked.

"About six years," I said.

"That's not very long," he said. "Where did you move here from?"

I paused, aware that my answer would give away the one topic I didn't want to discuss.

"Japan," I said.

Sure enough, he asked the next logical question.

"Wow, Japan! Are you military?"

"No," I said. "I used to be a military spouse."

"Oh cool," he continued. "Is your ex Navy?"

"He is," I said, not elaborating.

"What does he do?"

Knowing that question was a way to fish around for my ex-husband's rank, knowing how awkward the conversation could become when he learned my ex was a higher-ranking officer than he was, I told him I wasn't comfortable discussing the man I was no longer married to.

Then I zoned out as he used hand gestures to describe the process of flying a jet. I'm sure most women would have been impressed. It didn't impress me. I kept telling myself this guy had potential, but if a man can't hold my attention through lunch, that's probably an indication he's not my person.

But something else was bothering me, something I wasn't sure I could move past with him or any other man. His stories about deployments brought back all of the loneliness I felt during Tristan's deployments. Just hearing the word "deployment" bummed me out. And his questions about Tristan reminded me how small the military community is. I realized the chances were high that I could end up on a date with someone who knew or worked with Tristan at some point in his career, a calculation that dwindled my already small dating pool.

Turning to my dating guru, I asked Angie what to do about Chase, especially since he texted me before I even got home asking about a second date. As always, she recommended I be direct and not waste time with a guy I wasn't into.

"Hi Chase," I texted. "I wanted to thank you for lunch and tell you I enjoyed meeting you. But I'm not quite sure we're a good match."

"I figured that," he texted back. "No worries."

It wasn't the best date. But it could have been worse. More than anything, I considered it a win that I'd gotten through my first post-divorce date. Now it was time to follow Angie's last piece of dating advice: "Now that you got that out of the way, start dating."

* * *

Next up was Russell, who messaged me a few days after my date with Chase. He wrote that he was military but "almost done." Forty-one years old, two teenage daughters. He played drums in a local cover band and had kind eyes. I was optimistic, but he must not have been because our texts fizzled out, then disappeared altogether without a meet-up.

Thomas seemed promising. I enjoyed our text threads, and excitement had replaced my apprehension for our date at a local wine bar when miscommunication about which Sunday we were meeting forced a postponement. We texted back and forth a few more times, but never managed to coordinate a new date before he got military orders to Korea.

As I reflected on these men and computed their common denominator, as I scrolled through profile pictures and noted the high-and-tight haircuts, as I scrutinized usernames that incorporated references to profession, I came to a profound and definitive conclusion.

I had no desire to get involved with a man in the military.

After my divorce, people asked me all sorts of questions, ranging from "What happened?" to "Are you dating?" to "How are the kids taking it?" Another question frequently sprinkled in that I had a tougher time answering was "Would you marry another service member?"

Despite what many of those people assumed, despite what I once assumed myself, the military wasn't the cause of my divorce. The military didn't put a rift in an otherwise healthy marriage. Our marriage wasn't healthy to begin with. It was always meant to end, not because the Navy added struggles that civilian couples didn't face, but because I wasn't enduring those struggles with the right person. My marriage would have failed regardless of his career.

And I may have walked away from my title as a military spouse with fondness and appreciation, but that didn't mean I wanted to try military life again with someone else.

"You knew what you were getting into when you married someone in the military."

It's one of the most irritating statements military spouses hear from civilian counterparts, but in reality, in most cases, they don't have the slightest idea what they're getting into. Like a new mother bringing her newborn baby home from the hospital, military spouses enter their marriages blindly, unable to fully comprehend what they signed up for until they're in the thick of it.

I walked into my marriage oblivious about military life. But I didn't walk out oblivious. If I ended up in another military relationship, I knew exactly what I was getting myself into. Just a handful of interactions with service members on Match reminded me how tough military life is on families. My divorce gave me a chance to start over, and I believed that meant leaving military life behind.

I also had my children to think about. Military brats don't choose that life. They're born into a world where they're forced to be flexible while moving all over the map, continually making new friends, switching schools, and missing the military parent who isn't around. To a military family, stability is an anomaly. Ironically, once I got divorced, I actually had the opportunity to provide stability for my children.

The kids and I stayed in the same city the military last sent us, while their father continued moving around the world. We were putting down roots that would be impossible under military circumstances. If I pursued a relationship with another service member, that hard-fought stability would disintegrate. We'd probably have to prepare to move every few years again. How would that affect my kids' ability to see their father, who would also be moving every few years? How would Grady and Ava handle another father figure leaving all the time?

Maybe I was getting ahead of myself envisioning these scenes. After all, I was supposed to keep an open mind when it came to dating, and if I met an amazing man and he happened to wear a military uniform, then following my heart and accepting those challenges was the right path to take. Considering how densely populated Virginia Beach is with service members, I doubted it was possible to avoid crossing paths with military men.

But I also couldn't ignore my relief when I connected with a man online and I learned he wasn't in the military. After ignoring my gut in the past, I knew I should listen to it now.

***

I met Matthew, who was not in the military, at a popular local restaurant, feeling confident in our connection after our text chats. But this date was the perfect example of why Angie advised me to skip the men with the "separated" status.

By the end of dinner, I knew Matthew's ex-wife's name, where she lived, and where she was from. I knew she acted like she didn't need him after they had a baby, that her mother was always butting into their lives, and that he still called her on a daily basis.

He asked about my ex-husband and what went wrong in our marriage, and after I explained I was uncomfortable talking about my ex, he pivoted and asked me for parenting advice after going into detail about his daughter's bedtime behavior. When he mentioned a sporting event he was missing because of our date, I mentally checked out, thankful when we said goodnight. We never communicated again.

Despite my discouragement, I then scheduled a date with Eric. I tried not to be judgmental when he insisted on Ruby Tuesday and again when he showed his coupon to the waitress twice before we ordered. I tried to ignore the huge stain on the sleeve of his baggy sweatshirt or the fact that he spent most of the dinner plugging his caloric intake into an app. But he completely lost me when he shared that the last woman he dated accused him of being selfish. I nodded with confusion as to why he would willingly provide me with a blatant red flag before letting me figure that out on my own. I silently sent out a thank-you note to this former girlfriend.

He was leaning in for a kiss in the parking lot after an odd rambling about the compatibility of our communication skills, but I preemptively turned to my car, briskly thanking him for the dinner he was still thrilled he had a coupon for, and saying goodnight as my door closed in his face.

My disappointment in another miserable first date nagged at me to keep my guard up, to close my heart off to protect myself from giving anyone the opportunity to hurt me.

Was I asking for too much? Was I setting my expectations too high? Was I searching for an unrealistic version of happiness? Would I ever find the happiness I felt I deserved? Did that even exist?

***

When Tristan and I first separated, a large part of my fear of dating revolved around the knowledge that I wasn't the same woman I was when I married the last man I dated. My marriage changed me, and I hadn't yet figured out in what ways. How could a man get to know me when I wasn't sure who the real me was anymore? If I didn't know myself, how could I know what I was looking for in a relationship?

Now, after all this quality time spent with myself looking inward, combined with those miserable first dates, I discovered that the checklist of things I didn't want in a relationship was helping me to create a list of what I did want. Those dates turned out to be valuable experiences.

Angie was right that the best thing to do was to keep going on dates, keep thinking of each date as practice, learning experiences, and, yes, even fun. Going into dates with that perspective reduced the pressure I put on myself to examine each man as a potential life partner and stepfather to my children. With each date, I built assurance in my wisdom and intuition.

I had to find happiness on my own terms, and I was solely responsible for determining what that meant. A man could add happiness to my life, but I couldn't allow him to be the only source of my happiness. And waiting nearly a year after the separation to start dating made me realize I would much rather be alone than in an unhappy relationship.

Yet I was certain I'd meet someone special, someone worth the bad dates and weird online interactions. So I stayed on Match, and to increase my odds, I joined eHarmony. I would let my guard down, open my heart to the possibility of love. I held tight to the hope that one day I'd find myself on another first date sitting across from a man I'd fall in love with, that one day I'd have such an amazing first date that I could hardly wait for the second.

I just needed to get to a second date.

CHAPTER 25

Already Whole

I may have felt like a failure in the dating department, but I was improving at accepting my aloneness.

Since the divorce, I'd grown accustomed to doing a lot of things solo. I was often my own date to dinner, to movies, to gatherings with friends. I enjoyed my own company, shedding my paranoia that I was overtly ambling about the earth without a second half.

However, I wasn't sure I could pull off walking into a high school reunion by myself. I didn't think I could face my former classmates and their spouses and explain that I was alone not because my husband wasn't able to attend but because I no longer had a husband.

When twentieth-reunion chatter started in my alumni Facebook group, my instinct was to come up with a good excuse to decline. I couldn't get time off from work. I couldn't afford plane tickets. Both of my arms were broken and I had casts up to my shoulders. Any excuse that wasn't I just got divorced and felt like a failure.

But my second instinct, the one I acted on, was to take the time off work, book the plane tickets, buy a fabulous dress, and accept the invitation. Because I wasn't a failure. My marriage failed, but that didn't make me a failure. In fact, starting a whole new life after overcoming unhappiness was a triumph to brag about.

I'd already reconnected with old friends from high school, and thanks to social media and my blog, most of my former classmates were aware I was divorced. No one asked about my marital status. No one looked at me like I was less than. And no one, including myself, cared that I didn't have a plus-one.

The reunion weekend showed me I'd come full circle since these people had last seen me twenty years earlier. From their perspective, not much seemed to have changed. I was told I looked exactly the same, that I was as spunky as ever. Even staying at my parents' house, the same house I lived in during high school, and Grady snapping a photo of me in the same spot on the lanai by the pool where my father took my prom pictures made me feel as if nothing had changed.

But everything had changed. Since my high school graduation, I had lived in four different states and one foreign country. I had earned two college degrees. I had switched careers, landing on the one I was passionate about. I had given birth to two children. I'd had a thirteen-year marriage.

I went through a lot, and somehow, during those twenty years, I lost that spunky girl these classmates remembered. But my divorce and the personal journey I took to rediscover myself resurrected her. That's the woman who showed up at the reunion and had the time of her life. Without a plus-one. Without a second half. She didn't need another person to complete her because she was already whole.

***

As I embraced old pieces of myself resurfacing, I decided one piece of my past high school self needed to be eliminated: my broken heart tattoo.

When my marriage ended, it occurred to me that this tattoo that I'd gotten at age fourteen wasn't the testimonial of inner strength I intended it to be. I once thought that every time I looked at it I would be reminded of that first heartbreak and use that painful memory to steer clear of similar judgement errors.

In reality, it transformed into an ugly scar that told the story of the poor choices I'd made throughout a cycle of the wrong men coming into my life at the right times, from the first love who inspired the tattoo to my last love who inspired me to remove it. The tattoo had become a self-fulfilling prophecy. It was time to end the cycle.

After throwing around the idea of covering up the tattoo by adding and blending another design, then brainstorming ideas with a few experienced tattoo artists, I knew I'd never be satisfied unless it was gone. Covering it wasn't good enough. I would always know it was still there lurking beneath the surface, unhealed and taunting. I didn't want a Band-Aid on my broken heart. I wanted it erased forever.

When I walked into the laser tattoo-removal clinic and studied the photos on the wall of the progress of other people's tattoos being burned off their bodies, I knew this was one decision that wouldn't lead to regret. After scribbling my signature on documents I didn't read, attempting to process aftercare instructions, some flat jokes about my wild teenage days, five minutes of sitting on an ice pack, and less than a minute of intense pain, the laser treatment was complete. As I walked to my car afterward, slightly woozy from the sting, reassurance washed over me.

It took over a year and a dozen treatments for the tattoo to completely disappear. But I was patient.

It takes time to get rid of a broken heart.

***

Another lesson my high school reunion opened my eyes to was how much I missed living close to family.

I left my home in Florida when I was eighteen to go to college, and I never moved back. In the last twenty years, I never seriously considered returning to be near my parents.

Until now.

Single-mom life was demanding, but when Tristan PCS'd to Hawaii, everything got harder. I felt like I could never take my mom hat off, that between work and parenting, I didn't have a lot left for me.

Sometimes I summoned my military spouse superpowers, as if this was one of Tristan's deployments. I'd done this before, right? But it wasn't a deployment. He'd be gone for three years, with no guarantee he'd return to Virginia Beach when it was time for orders again.

I didn't grow up in Virginia Beach. I didn't have any ties to the area. As I thought about my future combined with the unpredictability of Tristan's career and his ability to stay geographically close to the kids, I daydreamed about ways to make my life easier.

It was the reunion that planted the seed of moving back to Florida. Between the stress of single parenting, the appeal of my children being closer to both sets of grandparents and my parents' ability to help, my work-from-home job that traveled with me, the reconnecting with old friends, and my old military spouse mentality pestering me for a change of scenery, all signs pointed south.

But my fiercely self-sufficient side viewed it as a sign of defeat. I worked really hard to forge a new life for myself. My kids didn't want to move again, and now that the Navy was no longer forcing me to move, I felt fortunate that my kids could say they'd lived in the same city for a whopping six years. Why would I uproot them again? Why would I uproot myself again?

I had days when I was ready to call a moving company and tell my parents to clear out my old bedroom. I had days when everything fell into place and I couldn't imagine leaving a city I'd grown to consider the closest thing to home since I'd left home twenty years earlier. All I knew for sure was that I was exhausted.

I had several more months on my apartment lease and couldn't move yet anyway, so in the meantime, I'd wait for the universe to send me a sign, to direct me if I should stay or if I should go.

Little did I know I only had to wait a few more months for that sign.

***

The first year after divorce will be the hardest year of your life. That's what other divorced women told me. Give yourself a year to grieve, friends advised. Don't make major life decisions for a year. Use that year for recovery, reinvention, rediscovery.

I repeated that advice in my head routinely throughout that first year after a judge declared me a single woman. But when the calendar declared that year over, I realized it was also true what others promised me. Time heals the wounds. Forgiveness is possible. Happiness is worth the struggle.

All this time I tried to give myself grace, to welcome and celebrate progress, no matter how small, no matter how gradual. From the day I decided I could no longer be married to Tristan, I tried not to buckle under the weight of a big-picture perspective that seemed too formidable, instead taking life one breath at a time, one step at a time, one hour at a time, one new experience at a time. And as I sat alone on my deck on that one-year anniversary of my divorce, swirling a glass of my favorite wine, absorbing the buzz of the apartment complex I cherished like a friend blanketing me with security, I was overcome with pride. All those breaths, those steps, those hours, those experiences had brought me to the exact spot where I belonged, this new existence, this new self.

I was no longer the scared woman of one year earlier, suffering panic attacks just contemplating the concept of starting over as a middle-aged single mother. Back then, I couldn't fathom living even a small portion of my life without a man to hold my hand, to share my world, to validate me, to give me the love I didn't yet understand that I needed to find within myself first. Back then, I deeply questioned my ability to function on my own, and that doubt held me back in so many ways.

But that year taught me that every stage of life builds upon the next, that fortitude and courage are cumulative, that I had grown incrementally stronger throughout my marriage. And when I set out on a quest to figure out who I was as a woman without this man, I discovered that the hardships of life as a military spouse—the forced independence, the frequent loneliness, the required adaptability, the fierce resilience—had trained me for life after divorce.

I sacrificed a lot for Tristan's military career. I moved when the Navy said move. I relinquished the ability to have a career on my timeline. I lost any sense of what home meant. I dropped whatever I was doing to iron uniforms, pack seabags, drive to the airport, say goodbye. All to stand behind a man who was never willing to stand behind me.

Those sacrifices ingrained in me a skill set I didn't have in my early twenties when I met Tristan. That young woman fresh out of college would never have been strong enough to start a completely new life in the way I was doing in my late thirties, to embark on a search for identity while grieving the one she left behind, to redefine what family meant while single parenting two impressionable children. That young woman would be in awe of how far I'd come. And I was finally beginning to see that I was actually my strongest in times when I felt the weakest.

I was also beginning to see that many of the unknowns I feared about life after divorce and the questions I thought the universe was ignoring had either been answered or I'd discovered the answers didn't matter anymore. When I crossed that one-year mark, I felt like I accomplished something far greater than simply living through the last 365 days. I felt like I crossed over an invisible line that, during the year, never seemed to get any closer but suddenly appeared when I wasn't searching for it. All I wanted that year was to feel like the worst of my struggles were in my rearview, for my fears that I couldn't make it on my own to be replaced with successes proving my independence. All I wanted was to move on. And on that day, that one-year milestone, I knew I finally had.

Maybe this part of the moving-on process was because Tristan no longer lived twenty minutes down the road, I no longer had to see him twice a week, and I no longer argued with him because I rarely heard from him.

Maybe it was because my kids were thriving, and I no longer worried I'd traumatized them by splitting up with their father. Shortly after moving to the apartment, I put Grady and Ava in therapy for no other reason than I thought I should. A divorce is a lot of baggage to put on a six- and nine-year-old, and even if the decision to send them to a therapist was unwarranted, I was of the opinion that nothing bad can come from letting my children talk to an objective listener, or what we called their "talking doctor." But after months of weekly and then biweekly sessions, the therapist said there was no need to keep bringing them, that they were content, well-adjusted children.

Or maybe I felt my journey was nearing its natural end because I realized I was finally making my own choices based on my own interests instead of letting someone else dictate how to spend my time, where to live, where to vacation. I wasn't allowing someone else to make me feel guilty for pursuing personal goals, for forming friendships, for being imperfect. I was no longer giving someone else the power to define my identity.

I originally created a bucket list because I needed distractions, targets, reasons to get out of bed. Little did I know this bucket list was so much more than a compilation of activities I'd always contemplated doing. The list, the brainstorming, the planning, the executing—it all combined to awaken the feisty, bold, independent, adventurous Heather that fell dormant during her marriage, the woman who got lost in the maze of unhappiness, who faded in her husband's shadow.

Because of that bucket list, I ran a marathon. I signed up for guitar lessons. I started writing a novel. I was in the process of getting a tattoo removed. And I flipped the script on my devastation about my kids spending the entire upcoming summer in Hawaii with Tristan by booking a week-long trip to Turks and Caicos while they were gone, my first-ever vacation out of the country alone. I'm not sure I would have even admitted these dreams out loud when I was married.

My divorce proved that life can change in an instant. The road we're mindlessly, complacently following can abruptly close, forcing us to pioneer a new path where none existed, not knowing if it will lead to another dead end or a trail lined with clarity and joy.

After my marriage fell apart, I battled to find direction, to veer away from dead ends. My bucket list helped me realize I was tired of waiting for something good to happen to me. I was tired of saying "some day." I was tired of being all talk and no action. I was tired of the years passing by without that some day ever coming. Sitting around wishing for something to happen wouldn't get me any closer to making it happen. I needed to be that action. I needed to be the audacious woman I once was.

And now that I found that audacious woman again, I was never letting her go.

***

After too many bad first dates in 2014 and disabling both my Match and eHarmony accounts, I kicked off 2015 with one last stab at online dating, but with an added twist.

My friend Jane scolded me repeatedly that I was doing online dating all wrong, that I shouldn't wait for men to contact me first. She knew me well, knew the prospect of finding a boyfriend sounded equal parts appealing and frightening to me. She knew my introversion and my residual fear of the unknown were contributing to my inability to peek out of my shell and take chances in the dating department. And like she did years earlier at the first blogging conference we'd attended together, she knew I might not take that plunge unless she pushed me.

"Give me your Match password," she ordered.

"You're joking," I said.

"You're not doing it right, so I'm going to do it for you."

I had to admit that borrowing her extroversion wasn't an outlandish idea. Considering that I hadn't graduated to a second date with any of the men I'd summoned up the nerve to go out with, it occurred to me that she was right; maybe I wasn't doing it right. If I couldn't make it past the first date, I clearly lacked some key element in the dating-as-a-single-mother handbook.

So with the lone rule prohibiting her from any written correspondence with men, I gave Jane my password with permission to become my Match identity.

The next day, I logged onto Match to discover that Jane had taken her mission to find me a man more seriously than I anticipated. She'd added and subtracted photos of me. She'd completed components of my profile I'd previously skipped, such as local restaurants I like (left blank because I didn't go out often enough to have preferences), athletic accomplishments (left blank because I didn't want guys to think I was obsessive about fitness), and free-time activities (left blank because every other woman probably claims to enjoy the cliché sunsets at the beach). When I saw she'd winked at fifteen guys, I picked up the phone.

"What do you think you're doing?!" I shrieked.

"What? I'm having a blast." Jane laughed.

"Because it's not you having to meet these strangers and be tortured with small talk," I whined.

"You have a couple of messages in your inbox," she said, ignoring my tantrum. "Go respond. And loosen up. This is supposed to be fun."

This was not fun.

***

Weeks passed. Apparently, winking at fifteen men wasn't so outrageous. In fact, not a single one of those fifteen men reciprocated Jane's winks. So she winked more and more until I had a date lined up.

His name was Joe, and while I knew he was a Navy officer who had the same job as Tristan, I convinced myself that this particular community was spread out enough that he wouldn't know Tristan. But when I met him for lunch at Panera where he showed up in uniform, the conversation quickly meandered toward his profession, my knowledge of military life, what my ex-husband did for a living, and ultimately my ex-husband's name. The awareness that this man knew my ex spread a heaviness over our date before we finished our sandwiches. Regardless of how nice Joe seemed or how much potential we might have had, I knew I'd never see him again.

When I got home after the date, I couldn't shake the feeling there was something significant I was supposed to take away from the meet-up. It wasn't until I scrubbed off my makeup, laced up my running shoes, and jogged onto the trail outside my apartment complex that it dawned on me.

My date with Joe was at the same Panera where Tristan and I'd had a counseling session with our dreadful first marriage counselor, Linda. I'd sat beside Tristan in his uniform, the same uniform Joe was wearing, at a table in that same restaurant, maybe even at that same booth as we attempted to repair our marriage. Joe even resembled Tristan.

As I ran toward my favorite park, I thought back to that therapy appointment, when Tristan was a half hour late, when I was uncomfortable opening myself up in such a public place to a near stranger, when I finally let go of my emotional wall and reached a point of calm, when I walked out after ninety minutes of self-discovery and for the first time wasn't angry after a session. For the first time I felt progress and an arousal of hope.

At the time I thought that feeling after the Panera counseling session meant our marriage was fixable, that Tristan and I simply needed help finding a passageway back to each other, a return to the love we once had. But after my date with Joe and the curious déjà vu, I wondered if the letting go I allowed myself during that session wasn't the surrendering of an emotional wall that was blocking progress in my marriage, but actually the surrendering of the wall that was keeping me from progress in my life. Maybe the hope wasn't for reconciling with my husband, but reconciling with my desire to leave. Maybe that was when I saw how far I'd come in my own life, my own abilities to take care of myself, my determination to push past fear to get to whatever was waiting for me. Even though I wasn't ready to act on it yet, maybe that was the moment I had hope there was still happiness yet to find.

I texted Joe to thank him for lunch. He texted back that he googled me, that I was a great writer. He didn't ask me for a second date. But instead of feeling deflated by another first date that wouldn't lead to a second, I tapped into the sensations of progress and hope that this date tugged to the surface. The progress and hope that brought me to this precise time and place, this chapter where I was a single mother not just surviving, but thriving. And the progress and hope still to come.

***

"An adorable guy with a great smile—and not in the military—winked at you," Jane texted me. "Send him a message."

I hadn't initiated a conversation on Match since Angie hovered over me reciting the perfect words, and I practically hyperventilated trying to string together my own sentences rather than responding to someone else's. But Jane was insistent.

"I have a good feeling about this one," she said. "If you don't message him by the end of the day, I will."

Scared of what Jane might write, I spent the rest of the day typing and deleting before finally hitting the send button. Then I waited. And waited. I'd nearly given up on this guy when his username popped into my inbox a few days later.

Our communications were easy. He made me laugh. He asked me meaningful questions about my job, my family, and my running, and he answered my questions in return. By the time he suggested a date, I was optimistic in a way I'd never been about a man I knew only through photos and text messages.

I learned early in the online dating process to open the door of every first date with low expectations. So when I arrived at the local brewery to meet this man with the great smile for our first date, half my mind was on him and half was imagining myself picking up a bottle of wine on my way home and crawling into sweatpants with a Netflix movie.

But then I opened the door and saw that smile waiting for me. His name wasn't Chris like the psychic once predicted, but I was instantly drawn in by his kind eyes and a smile so bright and contagious that I couldn't hide my own. I inhaled progress.

I exhaled hope. I sat down, confident and beaming, accepting and ready.

I was meeting this man as the fullest, most evolved version of myself, the self I'd worked so hard to find, the self who didn't need a man to give her love to make her feel complete because she was already complete, the self who wanted to share her life with someone but understood that a relationship didn't define her. And with that sense of self, that freedom, I sat down across the table from a man who saw me, truly, genuinely saw me in a way I hadn't felt in a very long time.

After a first date I didn't want to end, after I drove away with a raw exhilaration I didn't know I was still capable of feeling, my phone buzzed with an incoming text message.

"I'd like to see you again," he wrote.

"I'd like to see you again too," I responded.

We planned our second date.

And my heart opened with possibility.

ACKNOWLEDGMENTS

I once wrote on my military spouse blog *Riding the Roller Coaster*, "Don't let your title as a military spouse become your entire identity. It's only a piece of who you are, not everything you are. Make sure you nurture all those other pieces of you."

My divorce made me realize I didn't heed my own advice. The life of a military spouse is not an easy one. The stress put upon these women and men who support their service members, the moves around the world, the postponements and gaps in their own career paths, the time apart from the person they love. I applaud you, dear military spouses, and I hope you remember that your "dependent" status is only a piece of who you are.

To my agent Najla Mamou, I can't thank you enough for your unwavering belief in my story from the moment I pitched you, your thoughtful advice, your dedication to getting this book published, and your excited exclamation point-filled texts. You truly made me believe.

To Debby Englander, Caitlin Burdette, Casey Peta, and the entire team at Post Hill Press, thank you for bringing this book into the world, for designing a beautiful cover, and for answering all of my debut author questions with patience and kindness.

Endless gratitude to my developmental editor Jill Rothenberg. Your stellar editing skills turned my manuscript into the book I wanted it to be, and our brainstorming sessions produced the title of this book, a title I'd been grasping for but couldn't quite get to on my own.

A huge thank you to The Witches of Pitches, Aileen Weintraub and Megan Margulies. Your critique of my original query letter not only helped me write a stronger pitch, but you also gave me renewed energy for the entire project when I was wondering if it was time to take an indefinite break from it.

Thank you to Allison K Williams. Your book *Seven Drafts* guided me through the (more than seven) drafts of my manuscript, and I couldn't have written my book proposal without your bootcamp. You've taught me invaluable lessons about the publishing industry, writing communities, and the importance of literary citizenship.

A million thank yous to Kate Lewis, Rebekah Sanderlin, Tiffany Isaacson, and Marie Schiller for taking the time to beta read and offer smart and encouraging feedback.

To Tia Levings, Karie Fugett, Simone Gorrindo, Lily Burana, Estelle Erasmus, Aileen Weintraub, Ronit Plank, and Hannah Sward, I'm beyond grateful for the time and care you put into reading my memoir and writing endorsements that brought me to tears. I'm truly honored.

My military spouse friends from Japan, you enveloped me in a community I didn't believe existed, but the one I was hoping to find when I first became a military spouse. Despite the private battles I was fighting, I think of Sasebo with incredible fondness because of your friendships.

My SpouseBuzz teammates, you transformed me from a blogger into a professional writer. Jacey Eckhart, you once told me that done is better than perfect. That advice never left me, and it helped propel me to finish the first draft of this book. To Amy Bushatz, you once told me to stop writing for free. That advice wasn't about money, it was about understanding my value as a writer, and it helped give me the confidence to aim higher.

To the #5amwritersclub, thanks for always being there to keep me company in the early, dark hours when I would otherwise feel alone and unmotivated. I'm so thankful to have found you. Together we make magic happen while most people are sleeping. Sending you all some donuts.

To the #WomenWriters, it's not easy to find a group of writers you can trust fully with not just writing issues but life issues, and I'll forever be thankful to have you in my corner. To Megan Aronson and Abby Alten Schwartz for bringing us all together. To Jocelyn Jane Cox, my fellow former athlete writer who always knows the answers to every question I have and thoughtfully responds to all of my mini freak outs. To Sarah Leibov, I'll happily walk 5,000 steps during a phone call with you anytime. And to every single woman in this group, you are amazing writers and human beings, and I'm lucky to know you.

My mil spouse blogging friends, there's so much to thank you all for. Your honesty. Your insight. Your camaraderie. You taught me so much about military life. You gave me a safe place to shed my loneliness. You held me up even when you didn't know I was falling. You stood by me when I was no longer a mil spouse. And your support of my blog and my writing beyond the blog made me believe in the importance of writing this book. *Riding the Roller Coaster* changed my life, and I'm so grateful it led me to you.

To Mrs. Bytheway, thank you for teaching me how to turn my high school angst into art.

To my former in-laws, thank you for being so supportive. To my former mother-in-law, thank you for encouraging me to start a blog all those years ago when you seemed to sense I needed something more in my life.

To my parents and my brother, thank you for reading an early draft and assuring me I did indeed have a book worthy of being released into the world. Thank you for your unconditional love, guidance, understanding, wisdom, and your presence every step of the way. Mom, you taught me that everything happens for a reason, even if we don't know at the time what that reason is. Dad, you taught me that sometimes silliness is a virtue. Both of those mantras got me through the toughest times, giving me faith that everything would work out. And big brother, it was always an honor to be known as Little Sweeney with you as my role model.

To my son and my daughter, I'm so proud of the humans you've grown into and continue to become. Thank you for allowing me to tell this story, a story that belongs to you as well. And thank you for giving me the gift of motherhood.

To the man with the great smile and kind eyes, thank you for being my partner in life. Thank you for seeing me. Thank you for understanding every time I disappeared with my laptop, every time I was distracted because I was writing in my head. Thank you for consoling me at every disappointment and celebrating alongside me with every milestone. I thank the universe every day for bringing us together.

ABOUT THE AUTHOR

Heather Sweeney's work has appeared in *The New York Times*, *The Washington Post*, *HuffPost*, TODAY.com, *Newsweek*, *Business Insider*, *Good Housekeeping*, *Healthline*, and *Military.com*. She lives in Virginia. *Camouflage* is her first book.